CANYON
DREAMS

blue
rider
press

CANYON DREAMS

A BASKETBALL SEASON
ON THE NAVAJO NATION

MICHAEL POWELL

BLUE RIDER PRESS
New York

blue
rider
press

An imprint of Penguin Random House LLC
penguinrandomhouse.com

ISBN 9780525534662 (hardcover)
ISBN 9780525534679 (ebook)

Printed in Canada
10 9 8 7 6 5 4 3 2 1

Book design by Nancy Resnick

To Evelyn, who is my North Star, and Nick and Aidan, who complete my world

CANYON DREAMS

CHAPTER ONE

The sky was milk white and vaulted. A squall tugged at the creosote and sagebrush and sent dust devils spinning off the mesas. Millennia of rain and Holy Wind, the *Nítch'i Diyini* had carved the washes and gulches and canyons that folded into the skin of this land.

To survey this world in the chill of November was to feel loneliness crawl into your bones. There were few creatures and fewer souls.

A distant clanking: A school bus rounded a bend and bounced down a pockmarked old Indian route past red-ribbed buttes that reared out of the earth like primeval monsters. It crossed a creek and passed a wickered grove of cottonwoods, the silver branches delicate as veins against the sky. The road heaved up and up again, and the bus emerged from a gap in an escarpment into a parched emptiness of plain that stretched to the end of vision.

The teenage boys on the bus called to one other and craned

their necks and pointed at a red-tailed hawk riding the currents of approaching winter.

A painted black-and-gold wildcat with pronounced claws and fangs stretched the length of this bus, which carried Navajo boys and girls from Chinle to their season-opening basketball games. They were among the more talented players on the reservation, and this was the beginning of their quest for a state championship. The seating hierarchy was as formalized as that of a royal court. Raul Mendoza, a four-decade-long coaching force on the Navajo reservation, married to a Navajo woman yet not Navajo himself, respected although perhaps not beloved, commanded the front seat and stared impassively through dark sunglasses at the gray and rutted road. He had lived a dozen lives in seventy years of wandering. His black leather shoulder bag carried his whiteboard, his scouting reports, and a dog-eared black Bible into which he talked softly at night.

The girls' coach was a former rez ball star and a mother. She sat behind Mendoza. Girls' basketball games draw thousands of fans on the rez. The male assistant coaches sat behind her—Lenny, Bo, Julian, and Ned—big men with broad shoulders, all former hoop stars in an unspoken competition to take the helm when old Mendoza retired or got fired. The end can come suddenly in the high desert.

Teenage girls occupied the next block of seats, chatting and laughing and singing to Beyoncé. They knelt on seats and on the floor and braided one another's brown hair. The boys commanded the back of the bus and slouched like cats, heads and arms on each other's shoulders and backs. Some tapped out texts to buddies or girlfriends. Some listened to hip-hop on earbuds, and some stared out the window as their land, the vast Dinétah, rolled past. Two freshmen boys, awkward fawns, had made this team and they peered, eyes wide and furtive, at the seniors, at the coach, at the girls.

All were excused early from class for the three-hour drive from Chinle, their windswept town at the sandy mouth of Canyon de Chelly, to Snowflake, a Mormon outpost on the arid plains 130 miles south.

Good luck, teachers said.

Get a win, friends said.

Play hard, parents said.

All translated into an unspoken command: You better not lose.

There was no grander sport on the reservations of the Southwest than rez ball, a quicksilver, sneaker-squeaking game of run, pass, pass, cut, and shoot, of spinning layups and quick shots and running, endless running, with an athleticism that found its origin in that Native American time before horses. Navajo learned basketball in Bureau of Indian Affairs boarding schools but long ago made it their own, a game played by grandparents and parents and children, men and women alike. Play was swift and unrelenting as a monsoon-fed stream. Custom dictated that players help their opponents to their feet. They as quickly knocked them down again.

Chinle High School was the largest school on the Navajo reservation. There have been many fine Wildcats teams but never one good enough to win a state championship, and the collective hunger to claim that trophy was insistent, immutable, an ache. Four thousand people live in Chinle, and on midwinter nights five thousand crowded into the Wildcat Den for big games. On the third day of basketball tryouts in early November, Mendoza waved a milling group of tryouts over to the baseline and asked: What is your goal? To get your name in the *Navajo Times*?

He did not wait for their answer. He had bidden goodbye to his wife for five months, and he would work every morning, afternoon, and night during the season. He would review game tape until his eyes became red and his vision grew blurry and indistinct. My goal, our goal, he told the boys, is to win a state championship. He held up his right hand and the finger with his fat state-championship ring—he was the only living coach on the rez to own one—and let the boys gawk.

"I want to get a bigger ring than this."

These teenagers were perched on that precarious cliff wall between adolescence and manhood, hand- and footholds uncertain. Soon enough they would face a primal decision: Should they leave their land, the largest and grandest Indian nation in the United States and the Navajo world of sacred peaks and spirits and clans? If they departed, if they entered college in the world of *bilagáanas,* the whites, could they survive? If they thrived, could they ever truly return?

"Hey, hey, listen to this—blunt time!"

Angelo Lewis, 'Shlow, known as Big Daddy to the little kids who liked to scale his shoulders and back before games, was Chinle's big man, the center, a broad-shouldered six-foot-three junior with a perpetual half grin. He showed teammates his cell phone with a Facebook post of a black dude smoking a cigar-size blunt. Angelo was a wiseacre with a feel for the comedy of life and a sarcasm that could crack up teammates. He skipped classes, and sometimes struggled with grades, more from inattention than lack of comprehension. He should have been a senior this year, just like his friends and summer basketball buddies.

Dewayne Tom sat next to Angelo wearing a mauve sweater and dress shirt, black slacks and black dress shoes. Lean and soft-spoken, his teeth wrapped in sky-blue braces, and jittery before the season's first game, he lived in Pinon, a tough little town at the mouth of another beautiful canyon. His lack of defense confounded

Mendoza nearly as much as his academics pleased his teachers. He took Advanced Calculus and dreamed of attending college in Phoenix or Flagstaff and becoming an engineer. Teachers and mentors told him to push himself and experience the world. That prospect filled him with delight and fear—like a leap off a canyon boulder into an icy mountain lake. His aunties and cousins and uncles who loved him lobbied him to stay and attend the Navajo Diné College, to remain on the rez. He smiled easily and his words revealed few shards of what stirred inside.

Josiah Tsosie, a senior five-foot-four point guard, sat farther back in the bus. He was one of the state's best cross-country runners, with legs and will like cords of steel. Each day in the ink of predawn he pushed himself out of bed and out on running shoes and pushed open the creaking door of his mom's trailer. He loped down a rutted road between pens with sheep barely stirring and rez dogs that growled and yapped and bolted after him. He ran to a low-slung mesa, eight miles or maybe ten or twelve. Some mornings he startled sleepy antelope and crossed paths with the trickster coyotes. When he saw them, he pulled out his corn pollen pouch and dipped his index finger in and touched the dust to his head and talked softly to the Holy People, listening in the wind for their answer.

He could be warm and introspective and suspicious and removed. He desired father figures and wondered why the most primal of all deserted him.

Cooper Burbank kept on his headphones. He had been the team's second-leading scorer as a freshman and possessed an elegant jump shot that he polished in hours of practice. Now, as a sophomore, he possessed fakes and spin moves he had yet to fully unpack. He was preternaturally calm and quiet, a tall and angular child of the Navajo northlands, an achingly beautiful and desolate corner of the rez. His parents had planted a basketball hoop in the red dirt behind their trailer within a few hundred yards of a wind-carved sandstone mesa, and Cooper wore out that hoop with shot after shot after shot. He attended a postage-stamp-size elementary school where his mother taught third grade and his father, a rodeo bull rider, was the custodian. A year ago Cooper's mom sat him down and said that he needed a bigger challenge, a high school with more course offerings and tougher teachers and a path to a four-year college. You need a mentor and coach, she told him, and this man Mendoza is a legend and will fill that role.

Cooper rested inside his silence and stared at a land elemental. An autumnal sun bathed the land in a blond light, sagebrush and goldenrod and desert grasses, and a herd of Churro sheep and their guardian dogs, which cocked their heads and sniffed at the air, trying to catch a scent of coyotes.

The bus rolled past Mitten Peak and across Wide Ruin Wash and into Holbrook, a border town beyond the southern lip of the reservation. Alcohol was banned on the reservation, and too many liquor stores in too many border towns peddled too much booze to too many stumbling natives. Navajo Boulevard was lined with gas stations and giant rubber dinosaurs and Indian jewelry shops and the adobe-brown Arizona Pawnman and cheap motels advertising cheaper off-season rates, and the boys fell silent and looked out the windows impassive and missing nothing.

Mendoza had coached in this diverse little town and won a state championship in 2011. His eldest daughter still lived here in a house he and his wife owned. He briefly coached an all-star team that featured Michael Budenholzer, who came out of this high desert town to coach the Milwaukee Bucks.

Millennia ago the Anasazi built a village here and they were followed centuries later by Pueblo tribes and then the restless and roaming Navajo. Francisco Vázquez de Coronado, the Spanish conquistador, galloped through in the sixteenth century looking for the Seven Cities of Cibola. Gaunt and consumed by gold hunger, he wandered north until his fever extinguished on the endless plains of Kansas.

I drove this way a few weeks earlier in the company of an older Navajo, a ruminative medicine man with a handsome flush of white hair and a buckskin cowboy hat, and he talked of the melancholy that could grip his generation in autumn. This was the time of year that *bilagáana* operatives from the Bureau of Indian Affairs (BIA) used to fan out across the reservation in search of Navajo children to dispatch to distant boarding schools. Federal agents infiltrated every corner, driving out to Navajo shepherd cottages and camps. Parents watched the BIA car lights bounce along rutted roads for a long while before the cars arrived and agents opened their doors and asked if they had children, warning them not to lie. The federal agents walked around as if they owned the Diné, peering inside the eight-sided hogans with dirt floors that represented home and womb to Navajo.

Children came to know what the lengthening shadows of autumn presaged. When he was seven years old, the medicine man says, he spotted a BIA school bus trailing red dust like a bridal train and he took off running barefoot into a canyon until he was sheltered by its implacable walls. He took refuge the next year beneath a cliff overhang and laid his hands against the cool sandstone and listened for the heartbeat of his land. Agents found him and packed him off to school in Oklahoma.

He looked out the back window of the bus as his parents receded into the distance.

The founder of the BIA schools, an American army captain, distilled the mission in 1890: "Kill the Indian in him and save the man." That boy was a grandfather now, and he spoke fluent English as well as tonal Navajo, with its hundreds of vowel sounds, a language no easier to shed than his skin. The Indian inside did not die. It was the memories that arrived unbidden.

"The past cannot be unwoven," he said.

The boys on the bus knew these old tales of dispossession and possession and heeded them as they did the *báhádzidii,* the taboos. Chance Harvey, a senior shooting guard, had wrapped corn pollen into his basketball socks that morning. Josiah had placed a pouch of protective bitterroot in the pocket of his shorts. Most families asked medicine men to sing Protection Way songs for their boys before the season starts, the singing and chants stretching through the fire burning night until dawn cracked open the sky. Navajo oral culture was a rope that stretched through a thousand years, and another thousand, and a thousand before that, tales passing from ancestors to grandparents to a mother whispering to a baby in her womb.

Yet the broader world intruded, pushed insistently. Dewayne, Will, and Chance played Kanye and Kendrick and Lil Uzi Vert on their iPhones, and Josiah and Angelo practiced handshakes, mimicking the elaborate pregame rituals of NBA players. Grandparents and many parents could converse in Navajo, while most of the boys speak just fractured pieces of their ancient language. Dewayne knew more words than most. Sometimes he dreamt in Navajo. He dreamed recently of winter; he told me the Navajo language has fifty words for snow. These boys were migrants in time.

Old man Mendoza confused them. He pushed them to run in practice until they gasped and gagged, and they didn't always get the point of his speeches and barbed observations. They were not sure what to make of it when the coach invited them, one by one, to sit in his concrete pillbox office and talk life and hoops. They knew this, however: Mendoza had won a championship. He knew the path, and he might yet serve as their guide if they let him in.

Three hours into their trip, the Wildcats' bus accelerated down a smooth stretch of state-tended asphalt and crossed a broad, flat valley with dusty washes and tree-lined fields crowded with longhorns. The bus turned onto Snowflake's Main Street, and the boys peered through windows at a Norman Rockwell fantasy. Immaculate old brick homes with sweeping wood porches and ice-cream parlors and a grand temple of the Latter-day Saints. Blond boys rode skateboards on sidewalks burnished burnt orange by the sun. Erastus Snow, a Mormon apostle, founded this town with his partner, William Jordan Flake, who later served time in Yuma penitentiary for the crime of taking a few too many wives. A UFO abduction supposedly took place nearby; a local logger named Travis Walton got beamed up. It brought a measure of fame to Snowflake, although some residents remained skeptical that Walton truly went intergalactic.

The bus pulled into the Snowflake High School parking lot, and the players' faces went slack. Anxiety twisted like a rodent in a burrow. Mendoza adjusted his sunglasses and turned to the boys, his face betraying nothing.

"Get your bags. This is it."

Two years ago, Mendoza inherited a fractured, rebellious, undisciplined band in Chinle, an unruly pack with just four wins. He imbued that team with purpose and a championship aspiration, and the Wildcats won many more games. Navajo fans were unforgiving. The previous evening Mendoza rattled off for me the names of coaches who were tossed aside after a single losing season, sounding like a veteran recalling comrades lost to ceaseless war.

"Chinle had three coaches in the year before I was hired."

Do you worry you might be devoured?

Mendoza shrugged. He chose this path decades back and saw no point in second-guessing that now. "That's rez ball."

Go, Wildcats! Go, go, go! C'mon, Wildcats!

The boys walked into the gym, where hundreds of Navajo filled the stands, even three hours before their game. Players spotted mothers and grandparents, uncles and aunties and cousins, brothers and sisters and neighbors, folks who'd piled into old pickup trucks and vans and Chevy sedans to make that three-hour drive. There were Chinle stars who graduated last year and the year before that and the decade before that, young men who bathed still in past glory. There was Cecil Henry, a nearly sixty-year-old silversmith with a rakish mustache and an easy smile and a mighty thirst for the bottle, who crafted and sold beautiful jewelry to tourists on the floor of Canyon de Chelly. He once played high school basketball and ran like a deer and was related to a few of the Wildcats. He'd stuck out his thumb and hitchhiked here from Chinle.

Angelo, Angelo, get ready! Go, Wildcats! Come on, Cooper, wake up! Get ready, Wildcats! REEAAADY!

Mendoza sought out the Snowflake athletic director, a tall white man and a fellow veteran of many hundreds of games and bus rides over many decades. They shared a firm handshake and chatted about former players, old favorites and rogues who still made them laugh. Whatever happened to Chee and Yazzie and Smith? No point in walking over to say hello to the parents. Mendoza knew their desire: to win a championship and to see their sons play a lot. He already had heard grumbles on the latter count, and he knew he would hear more.

Mendoza found peace in obliviousness. After the game, as the team rode the bus home through hours of darkness, he leaned in and asked his assistants: Who was there? Was the crowd loud?

What were they saying? Do I even want to know? His game-time habits and ensemble were unvarying: black dress pants, a gray shirt with a black tie, and a black leather jacket. His silver hair was clipped and scalloped close to his scalp. He idolized and modeled himself after the legendary UCLA coach John Wooden of the 1960s and 1970s, another contained and fiercely competitive man who rarely revealed what roiled within.

He had mentioned the Great Wooden to these boys several times and seen their faces go blank. Wooden had retired before most of their parents were born.

"Hey, Coach. Hey, Coach, we're going to win tonight, right?"

Mendoza didn't respond and walked to the locker room, which throbbed to the Notorious B.I.G. singing "Juicy": "I never thought it could happen, this rappin' stuff / I was too used to packin' gats and stuff."

Boys bounced on their toes and nodded, heads lost in the beat.

Mendoza flicked his eyes impatiently, and a boy flipped off the music.

"Okay, listen up!"

The boys sat and watched the old man unload his bag. Coach wasted no words on pleasantries. He turned to the whiteboard and drew plays, pointing out Snowflake's offensive and defensive tendencies. He did not demand that the boys run plays in a certain order. He was not a master strategist or choreographer; he was a teacher and counselor. He believed a game was won or lost well before the bus pulled in front of the opposing gym. Think, execute, switch, play his trademark man-to-man defense, and run and cut and be creative.

Be true to each other and yourself.

Those strapping Snowflake white boys, those milk-fed Mormons, loomed like lumberjacks next to his Navajo. "They are taller," Mendoza told his boys. "They are stronger. These guys have been playing together since kindergarten."

The coach turned and looked at his troupe. Just three of his boys reached even six feet. Only Angelo weighed more than two hundred pounds, and that's because he'd eaten too many wings this summer. His backup center was five foot ten. His reserve power forward was a five-foot-ten freshman. He shrugged. Few Navajo were big enough to play at a four-year college, and most lacked explosive jumping ability. Their playing peak was here now, this moment, and speed and will sustained them. They'd graduate high school and basketball would become a horse galloping off down the road.

"You are Diné, even the half-breeds among you. Off the rez they don't take natives seriously. They underestimate us. So what? So what? This is what we came here for. Be patient and we will win."

Angelo rose and clapped his hands hard. C'mon, c'mon, c'mon. Josiah and Dewayne and Cooper and Chance bounced and chanted and smiled. The basketball season was nipping and yipping at their heels, a dog eager to run. They bounded out of the locker room, sneakers freshly burnished, running toward the court. Mendoza slipped his whiteboard into his black leather bag.

Nervous? He shook his head. "In 1982, before my first playoff game, I felt my heart pounding and I couldn't breathe and I thought I was having a heart attack. After that I said no more. I've been through a lot worse in life than a game."

A thousand Navajo hooted and stamped and cupped their hands and yelled as though into a windstorm, exhaling hope. Cooper leaned in and whispered that he had marked this day on his calendar. "I dreamed of it for months. I couldn't sleep last night."

A few of the Snowflake Lobo players waited with hands on hips watching the Wildcats run layup drills. These white kids were desert dwellers too; they have played too many tough games in too many remote native gyms to underestimate these Navajo. Mendoza gathered his kids and, as the buzzer sounded, offered a final bit of advice.

Patient does not mean slow it down.

The Wildcat boys did not slow it down. They came streaming up court like coyotes on the hunt, and the velocity of their attack pushed the Lobos on their heels. There was something shimmering and glistening and alive about rez ball, a joyous snaking pell-mell speed. Dribbles and passes flew about in riffs as if in a jazz improvisation. Running was woven into everything. The boys did not stop, ever.

Cooper hit a three-pointer from the corner. Chance, the shooting guard who raced palominos bareback down dusty canyons in summertime competitions, hit another. Angelo faked, spun, feinted again, and banked a shot over a Lobo center three inches taller and fifteen pounds heavier. Josiah remained relentless on defense, scampering after loose balls, passing on the run.

Tired? Tug on the front of your shirt, and Coach waved in a substitute to run in your place. Mendoza resembled a hockey coach replacing one line with another on the fly. Don't stop, don't stop.

Mendoza did not scream or stomp or break whiteboards like some other coaches; he could not abide that in himself. He stood at the end of the bench, arms folded, squinting, watching, calling out instructions in a voice authoritative yet short of a yell.

Defense! Cut, cut. Wake up, Cooper! Angelo, hit those boards!

The assistant coaches had warned the boys before the game to ignore the "five-dollar Navajo coaches" in the crowd—those who would yell instructions and berate them for their mistakes. Most Navajo, in fact, have a cool-eyed appreciation and feel for the game. Many nights I would sit in the stands and listen as mothers, aunties, grandfathers, and cousins wove tales of glory past. Expectation was a constant. Mendoza and his boys last season made the playoffs; the view in Chinle was that they had the talent to take a championship. The time to win was right here, right now, always.

A delicate-boned, white-haired granny rose to her feet in the bleachers and yelled, "C'mon, Wildcats! Wake up! REEE-bound. DEE-fense!" Chance stole an inbound pass; Cooper flipped a pass to Angelo, who in turn bounced a sweet pass to Cooper for a layup. The buzzer sounded, and the Wildcats ran to their locker room leading 33–25 at halftime.

Mendoza strode in and wasted no breath on compliments. At age seventy, he saw the game with a perfectionist's eye. "We took two finger rolls and missed," he said. His voice was pained, a hoop priest describing an execrable sin for boys who play below the rim. "We don't do finger rolls. If you reach the hoop, don't get fancy. Lay it off the backboard." He set to drawing on the whiteboard, diagnosing what he saw. Keep your hands up and remain in your defensive stance. He demonstrated with knees bent, bouncing on his feet.

If you're too tired to do that, you're too tired to play. Hear me?

He made a tap-the-brakes sign with his hands. There was a fine line between fast and out of control. "We're going ninety-nine miles per hour out there. We need to get back to the speed limit."

Mendoza's team remained half-formed still and lacked a sharp edge. Most of the boys played basketball all spring and summer long, in two or three informal leagues and tournaments with teenagers and adults alike playing, running, running, running. But the seniors skipped Mendoza's more rigorous practices, the drills and conditioning and counseling that would have allowed for a quick takeoff this season. Leadership remained a crown unclaimed. Raul encouraged most of his players to find contentment in being a member of the band. To me he added a whispered coda:

"Every tribe needs a chief."

Last season he had a natural leader in Nachae Nez, but that boy graduated in the spring. A creative player and an introspective kid, Nachae now lived in Albuquerque and took night classes at the community college and tried to decipher the shape of his future. That night he would leave his class early and sit alone in his apartment in that strange city and listen to this first Wildcats game on internet radio.

Damn, I miss it, Nachae would tell me the next day.

The second half opened, and the Wildcats' attention wandered. Passes went astray and point guards tumbled toward the hoop with no discernible plan. A prayer of a layup spun high off the backboard. Angelo fouled too often, became lost and confused and frustrated with his play. He walked to the bench during a time-out and slapped his chest hard and shouted plaintively, "I don't know where I am!"

In the huddle Mendoza growled, "Are we going to play rez ball, or are we going to play this game the right way?" He had a tortured relationship with rez ball. He was a Tohono Oo'dham from a tribe whose traditional lands sprawled on either side of the border with Mexico, and like near every native in the Southwest, he'd grown up playing that brand of hoop and appreciated its dervish art. Played badly though, rez ball could become a blur of impatient passes and hurried shots and too little thinking. He preferred players who settled into defensive stances and found the open man.

Whap! Whap!

Two Lobos began to vacuum rebounds, and a long-limbed

white kid started making his long jumpers. This kid had a sure touch and pranced down court triumphant even before his shot fell through the net. Snowflake tied the game.

"Ladies and gentlemen," the Snowflake announcer said into the microphone, "let's hear it for our Lobos!"

The Mormons cheered and whooped and pounded hands, and the Navajo fans felt their jaws tighten. Snowflake edged ahead by a point and then three. Mendoza's team looked ragged, a horse with a mane flecked with foaming sweat. Defense became its savior. The Navajo kids pounced on a dribble and got a steal, and their quick hands knocked the ball away and prevented an easy layup. With two seconds left, Angelo swung the ball to Dewayne, who flicked it to Cooper, who had cut to the corner and released a picture-book jumper over a defender's outstretched hand. That ball fell through the net and Chinle had a one-point victory.

Win, baby, win!

Slapping hands and smiles and whoops and louder whoops and the boom box was thumping in the locker room. The old man came into the locker room and scolded them like a Cassandra: We were not tough mentally. We got confused and lost focus. We played hero ball. You are out of shape. "Angelo and Elijah, you ate too many wings this summer."

Josiah, his jersey drenched, emerged from the locker room and shook his head: We just won; why is Coach making us feel like we lost?

Two nights passed and the Wildcats were back on the reservation, back to Navajo versus Navajo, which invariably made for a more complicated chess game. The Wildcat bus traveled up the Chinle Valley to Many Farms, a Navajo town tucked against the foot of a mesa. The basketball star at Many Farms was a joyous natural scorer and a cousin and friend to at least half the Chinle players. A night earlier, players from both teams filled Facebook pages with love and good tidings.

"Everybody is hostile about tomorrow while Native Dream is calm as'f wishing each other a great game," wrote the Many Farms star.

Good wishes gave Mendoza a headache. He was hardscrabble and detested camaraderie among rivals. He held his players on the darkened bus in Many Farms and tried to draw them out, to knit common purpose out of disparate threads. What are your dreams? Tell us about yourselves. Can you name your parents' clans?

Clans situate a Navajo in the map of his and her universe and encompass the families of all four grandparents. So a Traditional Navajo introduces himself by saying he was born into his mother's clan and of his father's clan. Tradition holds that a Navajo should marry outside his clans. Hence, the most common pickup line on the rez: What clan are you from?

The boys kept eyes fixed on the floor of the bus, monosyllabic, flustered. Some but not all knew the names of their mother's and father's clans, the Red Running into the Water People, the Mud Clan, the Turkey People, Towering Mountain, and Slow Talking Clan and so on. In an age of TV and Facebook and Instagram, traditional knowledge leaked away like water from an old jug. Minutes passed and the silence grew uncomfortable and Mendoza shrugged. He offered a bit of advice: "Try to remember they are your opponents, not your cousins."

Many Farms had a sweatbox of a gym, and the place was packed and vibrating with a jumble of fans spilling through the doors, peering over shoulders, trying to spot an empty seat. The players took practice shots as speakers blasted Jay-Z and Kanye. A Garth

Brooks song followed. A dozen men and women stood up in the bleachers and laid down two-steps. Many were decked out in full-on cowboy gear: felt and suede cowboy hats and new jeans and leather boots and ornate belt buckles for the guys, more ornate still if they'd won those buckles riding the back of a bull; and flowing skirts and turquoise necklaces and brocades holding long and lux-uriant hair for the women. Many women wore handsome cowboy boots.

It was cousin war, summer ball in December, and every player knew the other's best moves. The Wildcats had more talent than the Many Farms team, but they struggled with wayward passes and hurried shots. Perhaps too many loving family and clan cheers rang too loud in their ears. Perhaps their desire to lay down an ankle-breaking crossover or to hit a fall-away three-point shot against their friends distracted them.

With a minute left, Josiah hit a teardrop floater to tie the game. The cheers were deafening, and it sounded as though the little guard had 105 relatives in attendance.

The game came down to Curtis Begay, a Wildcat sophomore who was spindly as a puppet and possessed a butter-soft shooting touch. The kid barely missed a shot in practices the prior week, but this was only his second varsity game. Chinle trailed by a point with four seconds left, and Angelo inbounded the ball, and the sophomore tossed a splendid stutter-step fake on his defender and sprinted toward the hoop. He received a sweet pass and in a single motion flipped the ball spinning toward the rim.

The ball rolled round and round and round and out.

None of the Wildcats would make eye contact with Begay in the locker room, and the sophomore buried his face in his hands. Mendoza grew up on the Tohono O'odham reservation where life was loss piled atop loss. Determination became his sustenance and he demanded no less of his team. You were not concentrating, you were not serious. You laughed on the bus. You laughed in warm-ups. "You treated the other team as friends."

He pointed at the sophomore. "Don't blame that kid. Blame yourself. You are not serious. You all contributed to this."

A few nights later, the Wildcats lost yet another close game in overtime to their longtime rival Page High School. Angelo had fumbled the game away in the final minutes, forcing shots and missing a rebound, and left the court distraught. They'd begun the young season with a losing record. Keep this up and they could forget championship dreams. Facebook and social media over-flowed with recriminations.

F'real, this is it, Wildcats? The old man doesn't know what he's doing. Cooper Burbank should not start, period. Why don't we run faster and play the seniors?

Mendoza saw boys stunned by the stumbles. Raise your heads, he said, and look at me. "Some people say I take the game too seriously." He shook his head at that daftness. "I don't know any other way to take it. I had a hard time as a kid. I lost all those I loved, and I didn't understand a lot that happened to me."

Several of his players had lost fathers to booze. Several had seen mothers fade to the shadows and uncles and grandfathers die in auto pileups. They peered intently at Mendoza. "You have to leave that baggage at the door. To endure, to persevere, to survive, is not easy. Get serious."

These were not the encouraging words that Josiah yearned to hear. Later that night he took to Facebook and typed words that quivered with anger:

"Why does our coach gotta put us down like that! Every time he says something on a personal level to us I lose a little more respect for him!"

Mendoza slipped on his black leather jacket and pushed through the doors into the night. High-desert temperatures roll like a marble off a table on winter nights, and he exhaled clouds of vapor. At the end of the most recent game, the mother and aunt and grandmother of a Wildcat player buried deep on his bench ran onto the court and surrounded the athletic director, Shaun Martin. The women wagged fingers and poked at his chest.

"Our son is a senior! Why is he not playing? Why is Mendoza humiliating him?"

An angry family was like an irascible bear, and it could tear a team apart and endanger even a legend, Mendoza knew that. He would drive tonight into the forests of the Chuska Mountains and sit in that family's trailer and listen as they scolded and raged. Night's cold had acquired a knife-sharp edge, and the goddess Spider Woman had knit a million stars into a milky glow, and Mendoza shook his head and sort of smiled.

"Nothing about a basketball season is easy. Neither is life." He pivoted and walked alone across the parking lot toward his pickup truck.

CHAPTER TWO

I received my baptism in rez ball a quarter century ago. My wife, Evelyn, and I lived on the reservation for a few months with our two little boys in a trailer in Fort Defiance, fifty miles southeast of Chinle. One afternoon, restless, I grabbed my basketball and set off in search of a game. Insulated by New York parochialism, I expected to find country ball, slow and soft, a few too many jumpers and not enough hard drives to hoop. Maybe I'd school them. I came upon seven young Navajo shooting lazy jumpers at a hoop on a cracked-asphalt court overlooking a red canyon wash. Then came the inevitable question: Want to run full court?

"Cool," I said.

It was akin to being caught in the wrong lane with Olympic marathon runners. Up-and-down, stutter-step, now-you-saw-it-and-now-I-did-not dribbles and whiplash passes, a juking and endless vengeance of a game until this *bilagáana* put his hands on his knees gasping like an out-of-shape hiker on a Himalayan slope.

Decades later I found myself stuck inside a Phoenix hotel, mind and spirit numbed by the hype and commercialism of a Super Bowl week. Corporate idiocy had run wild; I had to get out. So I dialed a former basketball coach of the Chinle Wildcats (the club of fired basketball coaches on the rez is capacious).

"Which is the best night to catch a game on the rez?"

"Every night," he replied. "We've got no bowling alleys and no movie theaters. We only have basketball; that's our love."

A minor correction: Window Rock, the Navajo Nation capital, an hour-and-fifteen-minute drive from Chinle, has a single movie theater, which offers a single showing of a film that rotates with the seasons. I split Phoenix like a con on the lam.

That drive curled through cactus forests and raw-boned mountains and limestone escarpments. I reached Window Rock as night fell and a knife-sharp wind blew a veil of snow off the Chuskas and five thousand fans gathered at the Window Rock arena for a showdown with Chinle. I met Raul Mendoza that night. That was the season this hoop nomad had ended his retirement and was coaching the Window Rock Scouts.

I found a seat next to Albert Wagner, a fifty-six-year-old with a ponytail of thick gray hair tucked under a cowboy hat he had carefully steamed and blocked. He had a handsome shirt with rhinestone buttons and fresh-pressed jeans, a turquoise belt buckle, and leather boots that nearly glowed. Five of his fourteen grandchildren would play this night.

"A lot of people tonight, huh?"

Wagner shrugged. "This is all the time."

The grip of hoops on the Navajo psyche was plain to see. Baskets made of baling wire and garbage pails and tubs hung off the sides of trailers and hogans. North of Black Mesa, a rusty and dented hoop was drilled into a salmon-colored butte.

Hoops genealogists traced the game back through generations from parents to grandparents to basketball-playing great-grandparents without settling on anything like an Ur-game, that moment when a Navajo kid picked up a basketball and ran off dribbling. There's no real mystery though. Navajo boys and girls were packed off to those Anglo boarding schools, and basketball became a way to pass the hours, combining a millennia-long native passion for endurance running—Navajo, Hopi, and Apache cross-country teams rank high—with a cultural emphasis on group rather than individual accomplishment.

Hoops became a harmonizing force in this immense land.

Grandfathers talked Bill Walton and Dave Cowens; fathers and mothers talked Kobe and Shaq. When we lived on the Navajo reservation in the 1990s, the NBA championship rolled around—Jordan's Bulls versus Barkley's Suns. We had no television and I had a serious basketball jones. Really, I was going to miss the Finals? Navajo told me not to worry. The reservation radio station broadcasts the NBA Finals. I laid in chips and salsa at the trailer and flipped on the radio and discovered my informants had neglected to tell me that those broadcasts were in Navajo.

I recognized four words: "Charles Barkley" and "Michael Jordan."

Two years ago, the Chinle Wildcats bottomed out, near disintegrated. The coach yelled and hectored and humiliated and watched as his team galloped off into the bush like a spooked horse. The Wildcats finished 4–17 and the coach slunk away. The humiliation of that season was a stain not easily washed away.

Shaun Martin, the athletic director, and Wayne Claw, the school board president, and Quincy Natay, the superintendent—the three most powerful men in Chinle—had a power play in mind. They invited Mendoza, still coaching at Window Rock, to lunch at the Quality Inn and Restaurant. Window Rock is the capital of the

Navajo Nation, a government town, and the Quality Inn is where the power elite put on their best cowboy hats and boots and brace- lets and eat a steak or a good Navajo taco.

The three men put the arm to Mendoza over lunch. Rescue us, please. They could dangle no extra money, as a coach's salary was set by state regulation. Mendoza had coached for more than three decades and had more than seven hundred victories but he was restricted to a salary a touch under five thousand dollars per sea- son. The gentlemen from Chinle could, however, offer a pleasant apartment for a reasonable rent if his wife took a teaching job at the middle school in Chinle. More to the point, they offered the old man another chance to pursue that white whale of a state championship.

Mendoza listened and asked questions about the sort of support he could expect from the school board, and soon enough he smiled. They had a deal.

In his inaugural season, the old man coached the Wildcats to eighteen wins and the team went two playoff rounds before losing on a last-second shot. That earned him a reservoir of goodwill; what fan would be so foolish as to complain about a slow start this season?

As the season was just three games old, I ran my theory of a goodwill reservoir by Lenny Jones, the assistant coach, and he rolled his eyes. Such naivete. You lack fluency in Navajo hoop complaints, he said. Two days earlier he had shopped at Bashas' supermarket, and in aisle after aisle friends and even strangers had sidled over and offered unsolicited diagnoses. Mendoza—everyone referred to the coach by his surname—should press more. Mendoza should bench that sophomore guard. Mendoza is too old and the game had passed him by. Time for Mendoza to retire?

Lenny pursed his lips. He credited his fellow Navajo with

knowing the game, but he tired of this. Too many Navajo, he said, think they are native Steve Kerrs.

Mendoza had in truth forecast a slow start on that first day of practice in November. He planned to start two sophomores; his junior center was out of shape and rebellious, and his senior guards were new to varsity ball. He foresaw many bumps. His team, he figured, would start slowly and round into shape by January and with luck compete in February for that El Dorado of a state championship.

For now he preached fundamental hoop gospel. Think, pass, cut, shoot. And trust. If you passed the ball and cut and set a pick, you had to know your teammate would pass the ball back to you. Any hint of selfishness broke that virtuous circle.

His players many days were like cranky pensioners and resisted his prescribed cure. Sometimes they affected boredom and pursued their own notions of offense, which was to run and shoot. Mendoza's best teams featured players so ardent they tossed elbows and traded punches in practice. Not these guys; Wildcat practices were summer-camp loose and ramshackle. It was not Mendoza's way to pound his fist and yell and demand order and allegiance. Intensity must swell from inside.

They learned nothing otherwise.

"Practices should be harder than a game," he told his players before this tournament. "We won't win until you carve up a teammate."

Whatever, Coach.

I walked around a rock outcropping and descended beneath the lip of Canyon de Chelly, the grandest of the great Navajo gorges, and slipped into mists of memory.

Three crows soared along the flanks of red sandstone cliffs, their shadows mirroring ghosts. I walked a winding path and paused at a ledge eight hundred feet up and peered at the canyon floor. There was the hogan with the green roof and the fresh-turned fields sown with corn seed and the dry river wash that curled around giant stone outcroppings. There was the glade of silver cottonwoods clustered by the bank, leaves gilt-edged in autumnal death. If winter was generous and snows piled high in the mountains, this wash would turn wet by January.

Black bears foraged under the birches and Russian olives, along with wild horses and deer and bobcats. You would not see mountain lions; they would see you.

A quarter century ago we had left our New York jobs behind for a few months and let this land and people curl beneath our skin. Evelyn worked as a midwife for the Indian health service, delivering babies in a gray stone fortress of a hospital. We walked down this same trail with our little boys, skirting caves carved by wind and rain and petrified dunes as smooth as tabletops. A hundred million years ago this was an ocean floor and all was drowned.

At the bottom ran the river, and on the other side were twelfth-century cliff dwellings and pictographs of birds and bears and of children's hands. We closed our eyes and listened for the echo of long-ago laughter and felt the ages wash over our family.

I was white-haired now and found myself wandering back here again and again.

This labyrinth was the sacred heart of the Navajo, where the Holy People taught their children to understand the world and Changing Woman called down the seasons, frozen and furnace hot, scouring winds and the heavy downpours known as male rains. The canyon's antechambers and side gorges extended many miles into mysteries, and each winter and spring the Chuska Mountains sent hundreds of thousands of gallons of precious water pouring down its gullet. The town of Tsaile sat at 7,300 feet at the forested foot of those mountains; its name means "water flowing into rock."

That water acted as sculptor, carving and smoothing and re-working before it expired in the sand banks by Chinle, which means "water flowing out of rock."

A half century ago this town was a small, dusty place of trading posts and hogans and the dark-stone Our Lady of Fatima Catholic Church. The town offered modest homes to teachers and doctors and traders, and visitors drove in over pitted dirt roads that de-voured shocks and flattened tires. The impatient flew in on four-seat airplanes that rocked and bounced like kites before setting down on a washboard dirt runway.

Navajo rode to Chinle on market days in old cars with the chassis exposed and in horse-drawn carriages with women in calico dresses and their hair in the traditional bun called a *tsiiyéél*, which is wrapped in white sheep's wool. Mothers held babies swaddled tight in blankets to cradle boards. Even twenty years ago it was rare to hear a language other than Navajo.

Not much has changed, save that Chinle has grown. There's nothing picturesque or poetic about this place, a homely adminis-trative center with a jumble of fast-food restaurants, a hospital, a drug rehabilitation center and a prison, four schools, two motels, mobile homes, and a flea market with horses and bales of hay on offer.

Chinle and Canyon de Chelly sit in equipoise between the four sacred mountains of the Navajo Nation, jagged parapets that touch the lower reaches of the heavens. The Navajo Nation is by far the largest of America's native nations and sprawls across three states— a land equal in size to the Republic of Ireland. I drove from its eastern border in New Mexico to its western reaches near the

Grand Canyon along roads that snake up forested mountain passes, across wind-rocked desert plains, and into water-carved badlands.

I'd grown fond of nosing my old station wagon onto the dirt and basalt tracks that run through thickets of sagebrush and juniper, the dust off my tires drifting like smoke. I parked and walked miles, carefully marking my trail into the realm of pronghorn sheep and elk. Rumor had it that the gray wolf roamed again after an absence of many decades, although my longing to see one loping and twisting through its original land went unrequited.

The Navajo are not taken with towns. They prefer to live dispersed in distant trailers and hogans. If that means electricity and water are difficult to come by, so be it. Those who live in Chinle speak longingly of distant hogans and ancestral camps atop mesas and deep in sandstone gorges.

When night drops a dark cloak on this land distant homes invisible to the eye during the daytime come to twinkling life. Perhaps 180,000 Navajo live on the reservation, and another 140,000 inhabit cities like Flagstaff, Phoenix, Las Vegas, and Albuquerque, as well as the more distant Chicago, Los Angeles, and San Francisco. To live off the reservation is often to have an easier life with good wages and salaries and schools. And it is to accept longing for this land as a given.

Booze bewitches the Navajo Nation, and Gallup, New Mexico, has more liquor stores per capita than any place in the Southwest. The road between Window Rock and Gallup is known as the "highway of death."

I knew of no player on Mendoza's team whose family had not lost a relative to the bottle and fetal alcohol syndrome deformed some infants. Drunkenness means that this matriarchal culture suffers strikingly high levels of abuse of women. The Navajo manager at Bashas' in Chinle advised me to follow him. He showed me a locked case where he kept the hair spray. These bottles were a favorite shoplifting target for alcoholics, who mix the spray with water. The concoction is known as "ocean."

My first week in Chinle I took a walk through the town center, which resembled nothing of the sort. Wind and dust whipped and sluiced around schools and between government buildings ringed by fences and bales of barbed wire. There were two gas stations that housed coin Laundromats and a Pic-N-Run and a little jewelry store and a Church of Latter-day Saints building with a plain white steeple rising off the roof of what looked like an oversize ranch house.

There were empty lots and hand-lettered store signs and feral horses nosing aside garbage and wrappers and chewing at nubs of brown grass.

Unemployment was a virus, at 45 percent, and many families lived by the rhythms of the social service checks, which arrived on the first and the fifteenth of every month. A Navajo cop noted that the nights after the checks arrived offered a cacophony of fights and domestic-abuse calls and much sadness.

The Navajo bureaucracy did not help matters. Even the smallest of entrepreneurial ventures, such as trying to place a boutique coffee cart on an empty lot at a crossroads in Chinle, a seemingly surefire bet in a town with many hundreds of teachers, nurses, and doctors, entailed a Dickensian shuffle of feasibility studies, bureaucratic approvals, and "proof" that your business would grow and employ more people. There had been several attempts and still Chinle had no coffee carts.

If consolation was to be had, which it was not, big employers such as Walmart and Target and Starbucks pitched into no-less-fearsome snarls of red tape and with no more success. The Navajo possess considerable entrepreneurial muscles, but those are exercised in distant cities that hold many thousands of Navajo welders and high-tower construction workers and lawyers and engineers and developers, many of whom earn fine salaries. These urban exiles often leave behind fractured families.

The underground economy ran through it all as a fast-flowing river. I sought a checkup for my old station wagon, which had taken to coughing. I asked the assistant coaches to recommend a mechanic, and they told me of Tsosie, who worked on Subarus in back of his hogan in Black Rock, and Begay, who fixed Fords over near Ventana Mesa. As I drove the dusty roads, I saw signs for haircuts and nail salons, for sheep and jewelry and silver work, and for home and television repairs.

One Sunday morning I set off to hike into Sheep Dip Canyon, driving across yellow plains and working my car slowly down a road rubbed so raw that in places it became a bed of basalt. I braked in a stand of dwarf oaks and checked my map and spotted a hand-lettered sign tacked to a tree with three improbable words: FRESH ROLLED SUSHI.

On the question of this nation and its contradictions, I struck up a conversation with Shaun Martin, the athletic director and a long-striding and world-class runner of ultramarathons. His wife grew up here and was assistant principal at an elementary school, and they were profoundly committed to Navajo life and tradition and desired only to toss down a stake and build a home. To that end, they sketched architectural plans for an elegant variation on a traditional hogan.

They faced just one problem: No one had signed off on a plot of land.

To talk of home ownership was to encounter a variation on that same six-dimensional bureaucratic puzzle as for businesses. Families can own property and buy homes outright on less than 1 percent of reservation lands. More than 90 percent of the land on the reservation was held in trust, and to build on it a family must seek approval for a lease from chapter houses, little city halls that are riven by local politics, and from central government bureaucrats. More broadly, the old sheep- and cattle-ranching families and clans hold grazing leases across much of the reservation, and those leases tend to get renewed ad infinitum.

Fallow grazing lands extend into the center of Chinle. Shaun had more than once asked to build on the smallest portion of these lands, but an entire extended family of leaseholders must sign off. That gives to older generations a chafing veto over the lives of the young, as any querulous uncle could block a deal. Shaun and his wife have encountered a few of those.

The frustrations in the telling sounded endless and maddening, and I asked Shaun if he had given thought to moving three hours west off the reservation to Flagstaff, that handsome mountain city where he and his wife had earned college degrees. Education jobs paid well there, and there was a considerable Navajo presence in its schools. Shaun answered my question with a story.

A decade ago he was appointed cross-country coach at Chinle High School and built the team into a national power, with nineteen individual state champions in eight years of coaching. He became a surrogate father to those runners, feeding and counseling and consoling them in their times of pain and struggle. When college loomed for them, he labored late into night on their applications and laughed with and cemented relationships with college coaches. Forty-nine of his runners obtained college scholarships.

Success became father to his fall. Few insults on the reservation carry a scorpion sting more painful than to be accused of self-pride, unreasonable self-conceit. A murmuring fever of whispers laid Martin low. Is he so great? Who does he think he is? We Navajo produced great runners without him.

On the day Martin quit as cross-country coach, the former athletic director all but mocked him. You're just a gym teacher. What are you going to do *now*, Shaun?

Sorrow nested within, and in the summer monsoon season Shaun took a run of many miles into Canyon de Chelly. A soft female rain began to fall, and her water filled the cistern of his soul. "As I ran down the canyon, I spooked a pack of wild horses. They had been in the trees and began to run ahead in the wash."

The four adult horses cantered and closed ranks around their colts. "I was jamming, closing on 'em, and then I threw a move on the pack. I caught it." The horses let Shaun enter their circle and he and the pack moved as one, his sweaty shoulders rubbing their sweaty flanks. At the canyon mouth, the horses pulled up as if to toe an invisible line. Shaun turned to look at them.

"They were lined up shoulder to shoulder, their nostrils flaring, their ears pointed at me."

Shaun's voice caught. "I thought, 'What is the significance of this moment?' These horses were like my young runners; I had nicknamed my favorites 'the four horsemen.'"

Not long after, he founded a well-known ultramarathon that snakes through the canyon each autumn. And he doubled down on his work as a gym teacher. An innovator and mentor, he was named National Rural Teacher of the Year. Soon after, he was appointed athletic director of Chinle High School, and he remains an informal counselor, a surrogate father, to several boys on the basketball team.

He shook his head. No, he would not, he could not, move to

Flagstaff. His family's place was here with these students by the walls of this canyon.

I stood one morning in the dry riverbed in Canyon de Chelly and closed my eyes and felt zephyrs wash across my face.

Tribes have occupied this great gorge since before the flowering of ancient Egypt. Its peach and apple trees produced bountiful harvests when Caesar conquered Gaul. Its fields yielded squash and melons when Buddha walked the earth. The archaic people gave way to the Basketmaker people, who in time built multiple-story brick-and-wood-stave houses and storehouses for goods, shells and opals and turquoise, carried up ancient highways by Aztec traders from as far away as Baja and the Yucatán. Those occupants painted images of their bent-over flutist Kokopelli on the walls of this soaring labyrinth. The Hopi, another Pueblo tribe, lived in this canyon and put their imprint on this land too.

The Navajo arrived eight hundred, perhaps nine hundred or more years ago. Their ancient exodus began many thousands of years earlier amid the mountains, dark-blue forests, and deep lakes of central Asia and Siberia. They appeared by conventional theories to have crossed the Bering Strait land bridge and settled for at least fifteen thousand years in Alaska and northwestern Canada, a sojourn spent hunting woolly mammoth and deer. Their stories suggest they tamed and rode the American horse, which lived for millions of years in the New World until its mysterious extinction eight thousand years ago.

In the seventh century A.D., for reasons based more on anthropological and environmental guesswork than on definitive evidence, they resumed their migration, wending southward through monumental mountain valleys and fording treacherous silt-laden rivers. It was an achingly long journey. When these Athabascan-language-speaking travelers arrived in the what's now the Southwest they coalesced into two tribes: the Navajo and the Apache, whose languages are roughly as similar as French is to Spanish.

Conventional history places this arrival in the sixteenth century at about the same time Spanish conquistadors marched in from the south. That claim draws a roll of the eyes and a flare of anger from Navajo historians and storytellers. Their oral history and traditions speak to a far-earlier arrival and a conflict with the Anasazi of the Chaco empire, who perhaps enslaved them. Some Anglo historians and archaeologists have come to divine a rough truth in these Navajo claims.

I spoke with Steve Lekson, a University of Colorado archaeologist who has worked at Chaco Canyon, a mysterious and dark site of Anasazi ceremony and governance and culture, a place of cosmological significance and perhaps, as times grew desperate, human sacrifice and cannibalism. He became friendly with a Navajo he hired to dig there. "As we worked inside an ancient pueblo, he started telling me what happened in a particular room. He said his mother learned this from her grandmother, who learned it from her grandmother. He offered a textured and thoroughly intelligent explanation for what happened there, one very much backed up by later archaeological evidence. As I listened to him, the hair rose on my neck."

More recently, archaeologist Jack Ives of the University of Alberta explored caves near Lake Utah that have been occupied since the eleventh century. He examined moccasins found there and matched the leather and style to Athabascan moccasins discovered on ice patches in the Yukon half a millennium earlier. It was one of several pieces of newly discovered evidence that suggested the

Navajo roamed this region many hundreds of years earlier than once thought.

Historian Robert McPherson has passed a professional lifetime studying the Navajo and their cosmology and threaded the newest archaeological evidence with native oral history. One summer morning I drove several hours north from Chinle to his white-washed pueblo office overlooking a canyon in Blanding, Utah. A doughty man with a bald pate, he rose from a desk set in blue shadow amid Navajo rugs and masks and jewelry and welcomed me. He had been reluctant to schedule this meeting, as he emphasized that he knew nothing of rez ball. I persuaded him that I wanted to know of history, not basketball.

We talked ancient migrations and arrival dates and beliefs lost in the dust of centuries and the confident arrogance that led too many academics to doubt primitives and their oral histories. "The Navajo were here earlier than most realize," McPherson said. "Their oral history is a lot closer to fact than a lot want to admit."

The reach of the Navajo in the early nineteenth century was grand. Ruled by no single chieftain, the bands were knit together by history and culture and cosmology, and their lands stretched from central New Mexico to Utah to the borderlands of the Grand Canyon.

Then came the Great Dispossession.

Young Navajo warriors were unruly and did not listen to elders and too often over the course of several decades they raided neighboring tribes and the ranches of Anglo and Spanish farmers and stole sheep and cattle and women and clashed with soldiers. Miners hungered to pan for gold in the Navajo mountains and did not scruple about stealing native land. And whites itched in their gut to be rid of a primeval people.

The government gave a military commission to a wiry little frontiersman named Kit Carson with a writ to clear out the Navajo. Carson convinced the Ute Indians, who harbored a dislike for the Navajo, to supplement his regiments. Mexicans joined, too, as the Navajo had passed centuries pilfering their horses and sheep. The Navajo knew the land like their mothers' faces and withdrew to the fastness of her canyons and buttes, to places unknown to their enemies. Less than twenty Navajo would die in this war.

The American soldiers and their native allies wasted few days on elusive searches. Carson's stroke of genius was to wage war on a beloved land rather than its people. Through the fall and winter of 1863–1864 his soldiers torched thousands of hogans, tore down corrals, destroyed crops, and tossed rocks into water holes. In a cruel stroke, Carson directed soldiers to hack down thousands of acres of peach and apple trees until not a single fruit tree was left in Canyon de Chelly.

The Navajo called this "the fearing time."

Snow piled high, and bitter winds gusted, and ragged and hungry Navajo emerged from their canyon and mountain hideaways to surrender. American soldiers forced eight thousand Navajo to take a four-hundred-mile Long Walk across volcanic flats and scrubland to a desert fort in New Mexico. Many hundreds died on this march, of fatigue and disease and brutality and broken spirits. Brigadier General James Carleton, for whom this walk was a strategic masterwork, spoke of cruel progress: "They have fought us gallantly for years on years; they have defended their mountains and their stupendous canyons with a heroism which any people might be proud to emulate but . . . at length, they found it was their destiny, too, as it had been for their brethren, tribe after tribe . . . to give way to the insatiable progress of our race."

The dispossession of the Navajo was a dolorous and infuriating American crime often visited upon native Americans. An unexpected coda set this tale apart: the Navajo Repossession.

The Navajo spent four years at Bosque Redondo in New Mexico. The land was unaccepting of their seed, the grass too sparse to feed their sheep, the drinking water so salt-laden it led to dysentery and death. The low-desert summer heat took the breath away and left elders gasping. General William Tecumseh Sherman, then forty-eight, was a brilliant and brutal Civil War strategist, the architect of the doctrine of total war. He appeared to take a liking to this austere native people and offered a choice: They could move to well-timbered, loam-rich river-bottom land in what is now Oklahoma, or, he added almost as an afterthought, they could return to the arid mesas and canyons from which they had been driven at gunpoint. General Sherman assured his superiors in Washington, DC, that those desert lands were worthless.

The Navajo choice came easy: Their heart lay in the land between the four sacred peaks. Chief Barboncito was born by Sliding Rock in Canyon de Chelly to the Coyote Pass People and was a courageous warrior and clever negotiator. He slipped into his last pair of moccasins and ceremonial cloth and stood erect before Sherman at that New Mexico fort. With eyes piercing as coals and a trail-hardened body, he spoke of the tears that wet his mustache when he learned another Navajo had died in this harsh place.

"We do not want to go right or left, but straight back to our land," he told the general. "I hope to God you will not ask us to go to any country but our own. Before I am sick or older, I want to see the land where I was born."

He promised that if they were allowed to return, they would forgo their raiding ways and embrace a pastoral life.

Barboncito, known to his people as *Hashké Yich'i' Dahilwo* ("he is anxious to run at warriors") was forty-seven years old when he spoke these words. The Navajo marched back to their lands, and at the sight of the southernmost of their sacred mountains, Tsoodził, Turquoise Mountain, men and women fell to their knees and sobbed. Three years later Barboncito fell deathly ill.

He drew his last breath in his hogan by Sliding Rock in Canyon de Chelly.

I read Barboncito's speech at night in my apartment in Chinle and the next day drove out to visit seventeen-year-old Elijah Lewis. No one on the Wildcats jumped higher than he did. His shot was silken. He could run swift as the wind. If the Wildcats were to win this year, if they were to beat their tribal rivals and those big-boned white teams from Phoenix and the Valley of the Sun, Elijah had to play his best.

Elijah was laconic with hooded eyes and a manner that suggested he could as easily curl up and nap as run the court. He was one of the inscrutables who could drive Mendoza to distraction. His charm was that he recognized this in himself and respected the old coach even as he found it difficult to mend his ways.

"My father says to listen to Mendoza. He says he knows a lot more than me."

He looked sheepish and cast his eyes downward. "He's right."

I had followed a dirt road to Elijah's family trailer, which sat in a depression of salt flats and blue shale and barn-red clay that went by the improbable name of Beautiful Valley. A corral held their horses and sheep, all of which Elijah had named and which answered his call. Black tires were piled on the roof to secure it against the winds that scoured this valley; inside a woodstove glowed red, burning cedar and piñon logs that kept November's chill at bay.

Elijah's mom spent months at a time living and working in a hotel out by the rim of the Grand Canyon and made her way back here every few weeks. His father was an itinerant construction worker, and his grandfather tended to the livestock and chopped wood and crafted jewelry and cared for Elijah.

His father huddled by the woodstove in the trailer, thick with the scent of pine, and told me a common Navajo tale: He had been sent off to boarding school as a boy and passed his first years of adulthood working in Phoenix and Las Vegas and Lake Powell even as he measured his life by its distance from Canyon de Chelly. His grandmother had lived on a bluff overlooking that canyon, and each summer she herded a flock of 240 sheep down steep paths to the hogan that was her summer home. As the years passed and her grandson became familiar with those paths, she tasked him with the herding. He carried an old breechloader to scare away the coyotes and passed summer nights counting a million desert stars.

"It was remote and we could go anywhere. It was my playground."

He taught Elijah to climb those paths and to pay attention to placement of hand and foot. But the canyon was no longer a place where a Navajo could find work and make a life. Modernity had drained this beautiful canyon of a way of life.

"You are a senior," I said to Elijah. "What do you imagine doing next year?"

"I want to go to college. Maybe become a draftsman."

"Will you leave the reservation to do that?"

"I think so. I hope so." He offered a near imperceptible shrug. "Can I leave this? I don't know yet. It's my puzzle."

I took a tour of Canyon de Chelly with a Navajo guide named Ben, who'd grown up there. When not tending to his herd of cattle, he took Anglos to the places where Kit Carson's soldiers dared not go a century and a half earlier. (I have of late had flashbacks to my boyhood in Manhattan when I read and reread an adventure book about Carson and the daring frontiersmen who rousted Indians from their magical cliff dwellings. So my soul once stirred to the romance of manifest destiny and brute dispossession.)

When we lived here in the early 1990s, 150 Navajo still lived year-round in this canyon. Civilization's inducements have put an end to that. Canyon-dwellers moved to the rim, where they could find roads and cars and water and electricity. Today a single old woman remained on the canyon floor year-round. She was Ben's aunt, and we watched workmen lay solar panels on her farmhouse roof.

Her wish was no different than that of Barboncito: She intended to breathe her last here.

Mid-canyon, Ben braked the jeep and we got out as he greeted Cecil the silversmith who was setting up his table and laying out jewelry to show to tourists. These weathered men were boyhood friends and remained young still in each other's eyes.

"*Yá'át'ééh!*"

"*Yá'át'ééh,* old man!"

They chatted in Navajo and poked fun at paunches and swapped jokes. As Navajo were fond of doing, they repeated punch lines and laughed again as if for the first time.

Ben and Cecil pointed upward at what looked to my eye like

sheer cliff faces and recalled herding sheep down those dizzying and hidden trails. At night they scrambled into the ancient Anasazi ruins. The Navajo believed that the spirits of the dead resided in such places, so their trespass was taboo, but the men laughed at their long-ago naughtiness. They slapped backs and said goodbye and promised to see each other at that night's Chinle basketball game.

Ben's jeep rolled in and out of the canyon wash, cracking through the filament of ice that covered the water. We startled four palomino horses scratching their backs on Russian willows, and they snorted and trotted toward the comfort of the trees. We passed the shadowed rock formations known as Sleeping Duck and Speaking Rock and dismounted by Spider Rock, a soaring five-hundred-foot-high natural monolith that resembled a great redstone nail tossed to earth. Spider Woman sat atop it and sang as she wove the stars.

The sky was azure, and the sun had turned the sandstone walls of the canyon translucent and pale pink, as if the canyon were a church lit from within. Ben walked down the dirt track playing a lilting and haunting melody on his flute. This was where the Navajo feel Father Sky and Mother Earth and the canyon herself put her protective arms over them. Ben crossed his arms on his wide chest and closed his eyes and intoned the Beauty Way prayer:

With beauty before me I walk.
With beauty behind me I walk. With beauty below me
    I walk. With beauty above me I walk.
With beauty all around me I walk.
With beauty from my mouth I talk.
It has become beauty again. It has become beauty again.
    It has become beauty again. It has become beauty again.

There was silence, and a hawk cried and wheeled and skimmed across the treetops.

We returned along a dirt track, old when Barboncito was a boy, and watched the walls shrink in size until we emptied into the broad, sandy wash east of Chinle, the jeep fishtailing toward an asphalt shore. Ben dropped me by my car, and we hugged, and he excused himself. He had to go. Two of his clan relatives, Cooper Burbank and Angelo Lewis, were playing for Chinle tonight, and like near everyone around here, he had a game to get to.

CHAPTER THREE

Don't talk loud to me! You listen, Coach. You listen!"

A little woman with iron ingots for eyes shook her finger in Mendoza's face. Grandma Jishie spoke for her family, who had suffered enough humiliation, enough nonsense, at the hands of this man. Her brothers and her sons, cousins and nieces, had driven long hours to sit high in the stands on the eastern side of the Wildcat Den, sixteen of them in all, and watch Branen play. They had been ready to stomp their feet and cheer so loud.

Except the coach did not put Branen into the game.

"Not one minute, Coach! Not one minute!"

The grandmother, white-haired and petite and fierce, glared at the so-called legend. Branen's mother and auntie had yelled at him minutes before and dabbed at tears. The game ended three hours ago, and they had sat with the coach and argued past midnight in this old trailer—not a double-wide; who can afford that?—on a knobby road in the pine foothills near Tsaile.

A woodstove glowered in the corner.

There was an urgency, a panic almost, to their anger. "Brano," as they called their boy, was five foot nine and a little chubby. He loved music and made hip-hop beats but struggled with his grades. To make matters more difficult, he had undergone two operations. He had lost a close friend a few months earlier; his mom was divorced and raising her children alone. Now the coach had embarrassed them.

The voice of Branen's mom sounded fragile. "Everyone should play every game. Every game, Coach. No matter what!"

Coach Mendoza sat on the couch, impassive as a totem. He had spoken few words and none loudly. He had walked this path many times with many families throughout many years. He waited for their storm to abate. No point in shouting into a gale.

Julian Parrish, Mendoza's young and buoyant aide-de-camp, sat with the old man on the couch. Broad of girth and shoulders, a man of the Chuskas born and raised and a lover of Run-DMC and a student of Navajo Traditional ways, he acted as surrogate big brother and uncle to many of the players who came out of this corner of the Navajo Nation. Branen was one of those charges, and Julian had lobbied Mendoza to take him onto the varsity team. In middle school the kid had been a cocky mop-top legend dribbling through crowds of defenders, scoring fifty points in a game and setting gym records. Those operations had slowed him and caused him to miss a few seasons.

"If Branen regains his fire, Coach, you've got gold."

Branen came to the gym in the preseason heavy and sluggish. His performance in practice offered a daily flirtation with indifference. He took long jump shots and his sneakers barely left the floor. Some shots went in and some did not, and when the ball missed and bounced away, Branen shrugged and shuffled to the end of the shooting line.

He had so many scars. A few months ago, he woke up in the middle of the night and typed out a tweet on his phone: "*4:34 am thoughts: 'fuck you.'*"

Julian felt as if he had let down the coach and kept his eyes trained on the floor. Navajo players and their families were supposed to be better than this.

"Can I say a few words?" Mendoza was careful to pose his question deferentially to the grandmother, who, in turn, nodded warily.

His day began twenty hours ago. Mendoza awoke at 5:00 a.m., made tea, studied the Bible and prayed, and left with his adult daughter for the hour-and-a-half drive to Gallup. His daughter had breast cancer and her battle had gotten complicated and he drove her each morning across the barren Defiance Plateau to chemotherapy treatments. In Gallup his daughter walked through the swinging doors to the cancer ward, and Mendoza sat in the waiting room and studied the floor tiles and sipped coffee and recited silent prayers. Hours passed and the doctors pulled tubes out of his daughter's arm and she came walking back through those doors and Mendoza drove her back to the apartment in Chinle that she shared with him and his wife. Then he drove to the Den to watch video of the last game and scratch out plans and prepare for the next one.

He told the grandmother none of this. Nor did he tell her that Branen had taken to Facebook and written scalding curse-laden sentences accusing Mendoza of playing favorites with his young sophomores.

Mendoza told the grandmother that Branen had a fine shooting touch, but the rest of what had been his game eluded him. He needed to lose weight and get his legs in shape and regain his wind, to push harder in practice and relearn and rehearse moves that once felt natural and pure.

"I know it's hard, but when you play on this varsity team, you have to set the highest goal."

If he had inserted Branen into the heat of a competitive game against a tough and talented opponent, if he had let him play in front of 3,500 fans in Chinle, he would have done the boy no favors. Branen was not ready. He would have infuriated the crowd and damaged the team.

Mendoza spoke with no edge of anger or hurt; flames were banked deep within. We are building a team, and a championship is our lodestar, he told the grandmother. If Branen remained on the team and channeled his emotions, he could make a contribution. "I'm not saying anger is a bad emotion. It's just an emotion we need to control."

Mendoza held up his hand, fingers akimbo.

"A team is like my hand," he told the Jishies. "Every finger has a purpose."

"Oh, by the way." Mendoza got to his feet and zipped his black leather jacket. He turned to the grandmother and caught her eyes in his. "I tried to send Branen into the game with two minutes left, and he cursed at me and the coaches and refused to go in." It was the grandmother's turn to remain silent.

Mendoza and Julian stepped out of the trailer past midnight and cold pressed down heavy and insistent as a giant's hand on their heads and shoulders. A dome of a moon spread a milky yellow light through the trees. The men looked at each other and shrugged.

"I'm sorry, Coach, really sorry." Julian was pained, almost talking to himself. "We're three games into the season and already everyone grumbles and complains about the team. What do they think? We're going to play the last kid on the bench in a tight game? They know better."

Mendoza put up his hand. Enough. Don't worry, forget it. In past seasons with different teams, witches had cast spells at him, and warlocks had conspired, and angry relatives had loosened the lug nuts on his tires. The other night, before the girls' varsity game in Chinle, a father had stepped out of the stands and walked to the team bench and screamed at the girls' varsity coach, a female and well-regarded former star player, for keeping his daughter out of the game. Assistant coaches and security men pulled that father off the court.

This was rez ball desperation, he said. "Let's get some sleep."

Mendoza slid into the cab of his truck, and his red taillights bobbed and hopped like a desert jackrabbit as he drove a rutted dirt track through pines and juniper searching for asphalt.

The next afternoon I walked into Mendoza's windowless bunker of an office in the belly of the Wildcat Den.

"Tired?" I asked.

Mendoza, who again had arisen before dawn to make the drive with his daughter to and from Gallup, smiled and by way of an answer pulled open a file-cabinet drawer, rummaged around, and handed me a handwritten letter he'd received that morning. It was addressed to the athletic director and the Chinle school board. This time it was Dewayne Tom's mother who fired a shot at him.

> When my child comes home from practice, he tells me what
> the coach says to them. It's just nothing but negative com-
> ments. "You don't know how to play defense, you're too
> short, I took you out because you don't know how to play

defense" . . . I'm sure there are people who attend games who wonder why these students sit on the bench with no playing time.

Two weeks earlier, Mendoza made his last cuts and ran his varsity squad through its first serious practice. The players were lackadaisical, flinging up careless shots and laughing and playing no discernible defense. Although Mendoza can sound severe, he was slow to lower discipline's boom. He preferred to model behavior and to give boys a long lead in hopes they learned to ask more of themselves.

That first practice, he watched as Chance Harvey, a quick-as-wind guard, tossed down a crossover and blew by Dewayne, who barely moved. Mendoza winced. He blew hard on his whistle. His lips pressed so tight as to turn pale, he walked to the sidelines and yanked and pulled a gray garbage can onto the court. He stared at Dewayne and pointed.

"Dewayne, you couldn't cover that garbage can."

Teammates fell silent and looked at Dewayne to gauge his reaction. The kid smiled, uneasy, eyes darting around. This would be a love tap in most high school gyms, but on the reservation where group identity and face are so knit into the culture, such words could sink deep as daggers.

Mendoza had made his point to Dewayne. Now Dewayne's mother had made hers, and the coach faced another meeting with another angry family.

Mendoza inhabited a disciplined world with habits of his own making. He had twice been voted Arizona Coach of the Year, and the coaching fraternity admired his intense defensive sets. More to the point, they noted that season after season, he crawled into the psyches of his players and as often coaxed his teams into cohering and cresting at playoff time. He tossed down no rhetorical moves to pretend he was one of the boys. He relaxed by watching reruns of *The High Chaparral* and *Bonanza*. He told corny jokes and he could name no rapper, past, present, or future.

He came from nothing, the dirt, and he took pride in his boxer's ability to take a punch without a gasp for breath. He knew, too, that parental anger and stress and jealousy could crack a team open like an egg. Mendoza glanced at his watch: time for practice.

He locked his office door and walked the shadowed hall to the floor of the arena and waved to the players. Come stand underneath the basket and listen. He did not mention his late night with Branen's family and the hot cascade of anger. The boys would know soon enough, if they did not already. There were few secrets on the rez. He began with fundamentals. We're missing a lot of defensive sets; we are selfish. Do you know how to run the double screen? Do you even know what a double screen is?

He repeats the Tao of Raul: Act, react, don't think.

He talked in a low voice, and on a good day the boys leaned in, attentive and quiet, to listen to him. That hadn't happened as often this season. Among themselves the boys joked about Mendoza's old ways and tastes and cultural references, and on social media they posted photographs of old 1970s-style pickup trucks—"Mendoza-mobiles."

Some days the coach felt like a preacher at risk of losing his congregation.

Throughout his career Mendoza had held twin jobs as a coach and school guidance counselor, which gave him a window into the psyches of his players. He knew whose father drank too much and whose mother had tuberculosis and which boy was wandering lost as a lamb on a mesa. He developed an intuitive feel for the pain of teenagers and became a coach who could use that knowledge to fire the spirit.

Long ago a star player with troubles piled high—a father who drank and a mother who was drifting away—walked into his guidance office. What's wrong? The boy shook his head and cast his eyes at the floor. Mendoza closed his door and he and that boy sat in a womb of silence.

"Coach," the boy said after many minutes, "black shadows trail after me. They are telling me to commit suicide."

Suicide is a door ajar on native reservations, where its incidence is well above the national average. It is the second-leading cause of death for Navajo teenagers. "Come with me." Mendoza took that boy for many walks, and they talked and read the Bible and talked some more. Slowly the shadows faded, dissipated, and the boy enjoyed a good season. More to the point, that boy became a man and remained alive.

When Mendoza won his state championship with a predominantly Navajo squad in Holbrook, he took that victory as a sign from God. He was in his mid-sixties and it was time. He would retire and serve as an assistant pastor and counsel young parents as lost as he once was. He would get on his knees and play and laugh with his grandchildren as he had not done with his own children.

His resolve lasted a matter of months. Retirement proved an ill-fitting coat for a restless man. He wandered into gyms and noted how players moved and settled into defensive stances. He winced at sloppiness and nodded when he saw a pass he liked. In time he took another coaching job, but he could no longer work as a guidance counselor; his retirement papers were irreversible.

Some days he felt as if he and these teenage boys were walking a canyon in opposite directions. "I want to spend time with them after practice, but they have to go home. I talk to them, but it's not the same."

In the gym this day, Mendoza brought up a charged subject: the future. What do you want from your life? When you graduate, will you be content to hang out at Bashas' supermarket and go to the Navajo Fair each September and live at home and wait for Grandma's government check? Do you want more than that?

Silence. Raul called out a name. "Angelo?"

The tallest and most powerful of the Wildcats, an eighteen-year-old blessed with balletic post moves, Angelo rarely worked out the past summer and he often complained bitterly when Mendoza pulled him from games. He sleepwalked through too many practices, joking and laughing, staging a stubborn rear-guard battle against maturity.

"What do you want from life, Angelo?"

Angelo's eyes widened and his grin flickered nervously. He joked easy enough with assistant coaches he had known since he was a little boy, and he could get bawdy about girls and parties and beer. His bad-boy act made grown-ups giggle. When talk turned serious, his face muscles went slack and he looked away. What, he asked later, did the coach expect him to say? That he could draw no sure bead on the future?

The big teenager mumbled a half-joke about liking the Navajo Fair and peered at his friends among the seniors hoping for a giggle. Laughter provided underbrush in which he could hide.

Mendoza waited for Angelo to say more, and seconds passed, and the coach nodded. He would return to this subject another day. This boy was too important to the coming season, too central to the team's championship hopes. The coach could not let him float away.

He turned to the team and said flatly, "When I graduated high school, I didn't know what I wanted, but I knew it had to be more than what I had, which was nothing at all."

The boys looked surprised whenever the old man cracked open that carefully guarded door of his. "Go ahead." Mendoza waved at the boys, his voice edged with frustration. "Go run your layups."

Mendoza got desperation; he did not get lack of passion.

Mendoza harbored special affection for the lost. He recognized desperation like an old friend, in his own life and in those of his teenage charges. To take a well-adjusted kid and train and mold him was rewarding; to break through to the desperate, to give hope where there was none, was another mission entirely.

In early November, with Mendoza's roster still unformed and five dozen boys harboring the hope or delusion that they might make the squad, Zackary Crank walked into the gym. A cross-country runner, he wore an I LOVE MUTTON T-shirt and tattered red shorts and running shoes. Frisky as a colt, he tossed himself on the floor with abandon but his rhythm was off. His shots flew like knuckleballs toward the hoop.

The boy lacked polish, and you knew after watching him for ten minutes that he could not make this team. Yet Mendoza was in no rush to cut him. The boy exuded a feral scent. He blew the whistle and called Zackary over.

The boy sidled up to the coach, eyes darting, hoping he would not be so soon cut loose.

"I will give you a few more days to show your stuff."

"Thank you, thank you," Zackary said. He walked into his trailer that night and his father curled his lips and cursed and spit nasty and vile words at him and Zackary grabbed a bottle of water and pushed out the door of the trailer and began to run.

He ran through the night and curled up in a sun-warmed canyon the next morning and slept. He ran through the next night and slept in a ditch the following morning. Days passed and temperatures tumbled and an older cousin found Zackary still running and blowing on his hands alongside a road in Flagstaff, 150 miles from Chinle.

He returned to Chinle too late for basketball tryouts.

I asked around and heard that Zackary and his younger brother lived with an uncle outside Valley Store, a hamlet halfway between Chinle and Many Farms. On a cobalt winter afternoon I drove north and found trailers and hogans set amid oaks and cottonwoods. Sand blew gritty sheets of grime, and plastic bags bounced and twirled on wire fences like prayer flags.

I nosed the car across a sandy wash and spotted Zackary atop a trotting horse. He followed me into his uncle's sandy compound and slid out of the saddle and landed light, a handsome kid, slender with high cheekbones and a powder-blue bandanna tied about his neck. "This is Woody, and he is my best friend," he said, nodding to his horse. Zackary combed the stallion's mane and whispered in its ear. "A horse's eyes are the universe," he said.

He tied Woody to a wood post and we took a walk and awkward words yielded to conversation.

Zackary and his brother had been pinballs ricocheting for years. They lived awhile with their mom, in rough and dark corners of Phoenix. Whenever she disappeared into the streets or rehab or jail, they drifted into shelters and foster homes. Eventually a social service agency used DNA to identify Zackary's biological father, and a caseworker gave the boys a name, an address, and bus fare to Chinle.

Dad was not thrilled to see them.

"He had three children and a wife," Zackary said. "He told me maybe he remembered me. He said he remembered his sister gave me a bottle when I was a baby."

Zackary's little half-brother was a plug of a kid, half black and half Navajo, and he had a fierce set to his face and fought at school and got suspended a lot. Zackary embraced the solitude of pre-dawn runs, loping miles into the plains. He watched eagles wobble on the wind and coyotes silent and taut as they stalked sheep.

He knelt toward Black Mesa and rose and spread his arms wide as possible. "I yell to the morning sun. Maybe the Holy People think, 'This guy is doing something good. Please help him.'"

Five months ago, Zackary received good news: His mom had been released from prison and wanted to see them. The boys boarded a bus and rode to visit her in Flagstaff, and she jumped up and down and clapped and gave them such big hugs and kisses. She was fragile as glass. "Her voice got all squeaky," Zackary said. "I don't know what happened to her in prison."

Zackary reached into his breast pocket and pulled out a passport-size photo of his mother. He was recognizable in her, the slender face and delicate cheekbones and those distant and dreamy eyes. He and his brother stayed with her in Flagstaff until she could not stop crying, and she put the boys on a bus back to the rez. "I told her to take her time and get her head together," Zackary said.

We heard an engine rumbling and spun round to see an old silver-gray Cadillac speeding down the dirt road, and we hopped up onto the embankment. That boat of a car fishtailed around a turn in a cloud of red dust, and the driver gunned the engine, eight cylinders firing like a fighter jet as it rumbled into the desert. That was the bootlegger, Zackary said. He sold booze and pot and kept a collection of guns. When you see his car, it's important to jump into the sagebrush, because he won't stop.

Asked of his future, Zackary spoke of college in Phoenix or Albuquerque, somewhere far away, if he could get his grades up and figure out how to apply for a scholarship. If that didn't work, he would try the rodeo. I asked if he knew how to ride a bull.

"I'm learning how to fall."

He walked past his uncle's sheep pen and into the yellow grass of the high plains toward Sheep Dip Canyon, feet slip-sliding in the sand. This was just a rest stop for the boys. Their uncle was a grudging host, and Zackary and his brother kept their bags packed.

"Maybe when I apologize enough, my father will take us back."

A few days later, Zackary showed up again at practice and walked head down across the gym and sidled up to Mendoza. The boy said he sensed he could talk with this coach, that the older man understood something about him. "I'm sorry I disappeared," he said. "I know it's too late to make the team." Mendoza extended a hand to shake, and Zackary looked startled and pulled his hand away and held it aloft. He apologized for that, too, explaining that a medicine man gave him a healing spell in hopes of speeding reconciliation with his father. He could not touch hands with anyone for fear of breaking the spell. Mendoza studied this boy's eyes and nodded.

"You are not floating alone," he told Zackary. "Stay in school and hold tight to your little brother. These troubles of yours are not the sum of your life. God's children are not a tragedy, and your life is not doomed."

Zackary cocked his head and peered back at the older man,

quizzical. He felt as if the coach had intuited his life. He mumbled thanks and retreated with self-conscious half strides toward the gym door. Night was falling like a curtain, and cold winds cut as a scythe off Black Mesa. Mendoza watched until the boy disappeared through the doorway and nodded. There were tougher tasks in this world than talking to a poor family upset about a lack of playing time for their son.

"I went through a lot of hard stuff like that boy, and it was so painful. Maybe I got lucky. Maybe it made me a better man. Life can do that for you—if you survive."

CHAPTER FOUR

Again and again in conversations Mendoza returned to a dream of a childhood memory. He was a little boy and he had climbed a hill outside his tiny village in the Sonoran Desert, that hottest and most forbidding of North American deserts, and peered across mountain ridges and salt flats and cactus thickets and seen the shimmering reflection of the Gulf of California. He felt a yearning he could not explain. Then he turned and ran back down to his grandmother and they climbed into a covered wagon crowded with men with rawhide faces and women in rebozos and black muslin wraps. The driver snapped the reins, and the donkeys pulled that wagon bumping along dirt roads to the American border. There they climbed into waiting trucks and rode to the cotton plantations of southern Arizona, where they would live six months each year, grandmother and grandson, picking cotton as a dull white sun pounded on their backs like a hammer on anvil. At night they fell aching onto bed pads.

They got three meals a day and Raul made sixty cents an hour.

When the boy turned seven, his grandmother told him to board a school bus. You will be, she told him, the first in our family to read. He nodded—yes, Grandma—and climbed into that bus, which pulled into an Arizona elementary school. Raul spoke the language of his tribe, the Tohono O'odham, the Desert People. He knew some Spanish, which was the language of his grandfather. He knew not a word of English.

He was a pilgrim in a strange world and he had no intention of turning back.

The drive south from the Navajo Nation to Mexico rolled over the edge of the Mogollon Rim, thickly forested with ponderosa pines, and snaked down through the Sonoran Desert, a mountainous and impassable wilderness of mesquite and creosote bushes, Gila monsters, wild boar, and rattlers. Shoaled and parched rivers mutated into boiling torrents in monsoon season. Mile after mile of land rendered jagged and volcanic as if the earth were molting a skin.

I slid to a stop at a sleepy border crossing in Lukeville and chatted with a Mexican border officer. She offered advice: Don't stop for any motorist who claims to be in distress. They probably are not your friends. I thanked her and pulled away.

My car curled through a yaw of mountains and ridges, and thirty miles on I reached an abandoned restaurant. Hieroglyphic graffiti was sprayed across its blue and broken walls, and the door had caved in. It was the landmark I sought. I turned onto a chalky dirt road and soon enough rolled into Quitovac, passing cinderblock homes with tin roofs and a whitewashed Catholic chapel with a red statue of the Virgin Mary and twisting metal fencing. Chalk dust made my nostrils flare.

A portly man shouted and waved and offered lunch on his veranda, and children laughed. Dogs barked a cacophony.

Raul was born and raised in this hamlet of thirty-five people, a place he ran from and holds in memory still. To come of age here was to know no national border, just mountains and sand dunes and Tohono O'odham families secreted into the pleats of the land. Quitovac is renowned, if such a word can apply to a place so tenuous that it feels at risk of returning to earth and dust, for an unlikely Sonoran gift: a spring that gave birth to a life-giving oasis. Raul had drawn for me four or five maps on scraps of paper and on the back of napkins and told me to find that water. I wandered through Quitovac and into the desert beyond and reached beds of long reeds and willows that rose like a picket fence.

I found a blue lagoon.

A white hallucination of a stallion sipped at the water's edge and a great blue heron turned and stared at me and took languorous flight.

A few grand saguaros rise amid cholla and prickly pear cactus in the surrounding desert, which with their erect stature and multiple arms call to mind Shiva, the many-armed Hindu goddess. In monsoon season, when cumulus clouds piled high and the breeze came laden with dampness, the saguaros sprouted a green-and-ruby-red fruit.

Raul's smile had turned boyish at the memory, telling me how, in early summer, his grandmother would gather bright-colored cloth satchels and eighteen-foot-long rib poles and shake Raul and his little brother Roman awake. The boys would straggle after her through the glinting desert dawn to a farm, where the rancher had more saguaro than he knew what to do with. The old woman taught the boys to use the rib poles to topple the fruits off the saguaros and then they'd scamper to fill the satchels and haul them home, where she would cut those fruits open, finding inside a startling red pulp that she would make into the sweetest of jams.

The boys spread the jam on their lips and laughed aloud.

Few other days promised joy. Raul was born to illiterate migrant laborers and his parents divorced before he could remember. His father was half Tohono O'odham and half Mexican and filled with anger and a profound taste for liquor. He fought men for the pleasure of it.

"I met him only when I was fourteen at a funeral for my aunt. He was so drunk he could not stand up, and he told me he didn't have long to live."

His father died of a busted liver. Raul attended the funeral, as he figured that was what a boy was supposed to do. Besides, he said, he owed his father a debt for giving him a lesson in what not to become. His grandmother took in Raul and Roman. Her home had no electricity and no running water and the boys read by kerosene lamps and pulled up worn blankets to ward off the desert chill.

"She did not talk much," Raul said. "She just told us, 'Things will get better.' That became our motto."

They followed her to the Arizona cotton fields, where they worked as migrant laborers. When the harvest ended in December, the farmer loaded the Tohono O'odham back onto trucks like cattle and deposited them at the Mexican border. There they found the covered wagons and rode home.

Grandma died when Raul was thirteen. His little brother Roman sobbed at her funeral and Raul shied away, lacking fluency in the language of consolation. Not long after that, Raul's mother reappeared with a man in tow and tried to assert a maternal role. Too late for that. Raul had a choice. He could remain in Mexico or he could return to central Arizona to pick cotton and attend high school.

"If I remain in Quitovac, I'm done. I knew I needed a high school degree."

I asked what lodestar guided him, and Mendoza shrugged. He tried rummaging through the closet of his psyche but found few answers.

Raul was no A student in high school, but he excelled at basketball, where his doggedness and a refusal to concede so much as a step became his armor. He was a native kid with copper-colored skin, and as a senior in high school he sat with a white guidance counselor and talked of his desire and the future.

"I want to go to college."

The counselor couldn't stop chuckling at that thought.

Raul ignored that man and took a battery of tests and aced math. An older white man in the testing office helped him decipher college requirements and fill out financial-assistance applications. Raul was admitted to Eastern Arizona College with a scholarship and soon after met Marjorie, a cute Navajo student.

She came from poverty and had seen her parents lying prostrate before an altar of liquor bottles. She wasn't much more talkative than he was, but they could recognize a fellow survivor and required no explanation of each other.

Raul cared for his little brother Roman through high school, the rope of their relationship woven of shared labor and loss and sports. When Raul left for college, they talked less and less. One day he received a letter.

Dear Raul,

I am a senior on the high school baseball team and when I look into the stands, I see no one from our family. Would you like to come and watch me play?

Roman

Not for the first time in his life Raul worried that cluelessness had taken root within him. He packed a rucksack and walked the next day to the highway and stuck out his thumb.

"I began hitchhiking to Roman's games anywhere all the time, all over the state. I didn't know how to acknowledge what he meant to me, how much I loved him. At least I can say I was there."

In his junior year Raul married Marjorie. She became pregnant with the first of their three children and his grades tumbled and he dropped out of college. He found a union job at a factory on the south side of Phoenix that paid $30,000 a year—a tray piled high with gold for this desert boy. He worked alongside older men and women with mortgages and children and weddings and bankruptcies, the prosaic challenges of adulthood. They talked and he listened carefully.

"I saw what people go through in life and I got lessons that I missed growing up."

Fatherhood and marriage proved an uncertain walk, and he stumbled again. He worked hard and he was loyal but absent. He tried to pry open the door to his emotions like a man trying to ratchet open a metal safe with a crowbar. He hammered and thunked at it but could not break through.

"I had no model, no one to say, 'This is the way you live your life.' If I was my wife, I would have kicked myself out."

Roman loved Raul's children. He walked through the door and

they came running, squealing: Uncle Roman is here! He hoisted them into his lap and they chattered and laughed. He knew how to speak to Marjorie and draw her out.

"I guess you could say he was more of a father to my kids than I was."

Raul's use of the past tense was intentional. One day Roman went hunting in the desert mountains with a friend. They climbed and descended, on the track of javelina and deer. Someone tripped and a loaded rifle fell to the ground and fired. Roman took a bullet to the stomach.

The phone rang at Raul's home and he picked up the receiver and heard a voice he did not recognize. Roman was dead. He heard nothing more except a ringing in his ears. "I could not make sense of it. I thought, 'Another loss, another loss—this is just my life.'"

Raul talked often of his brother during my months on the Navajo nation. After all these decades it was as if he had begun to roll that loss over and hold it up to the light and try to make sense of it. God granted him life and lowered Roman into the grave, and he could not decipher that puzzle other than to say that His will was unknown.

We drove back from a distant game one night and a winter moon in its fullness bathed buttes and mesas in a ghost light, the silence broken only by the thump of our tires rolling over metal cattle grids.

"I took for granted that he would be there."

There was no need to ask whom Raul was talking about.

"I thought we would have time to learn to talk and understand each other."

Not long after Roman was laid into the earth, Raul returned to college. He felt a compulsion to become a counselor and help teenagers find a way through the thickets of this life. He wanted to learn to read life's clues. His factory buddies were incredulous. "You're crazy, man! You have a family. You owe it to them to stay here. You're never going to make money this good again."

Mendoza waved them off; he wanted that diploma. Now he laughed at himself.

"Sure enough, my first job at Window Rock, I made nine thousand five hundred dollars a year."

Marjorie returned to college, too, to get her teaching degree, and she taught at Chinle Middle School.

Raul wanted to accompany me to Quitovac. He had an ancient aunt he yearned to see again. He wanted to kneel at the side of that oasis and fill a cup with water and pour it over his head and feel its coolness run down his back. He wanted to climb that mountain and look for that glimmer of the world beyond.

We plotted the best route and he drew more napkin maps, but Marjorie was not taken by our travel plans. Raul possessed no passport, and years ago he misplaced his birth certificate. To get a new one he had to find a relative who was ten years older than him to vouch for his identity. As Raul was in his eighth decade, that was no easy task. He had a tribal Tohono O'odham identity card, but she feared her husband might slip across the border and find it closed behind him.

The nativist currents that sweep this world are powerful.

I wanted to believe that Marjorie was too nervous. Selfishly I wanted to read Raul's face and emotions as we rolled into his boyhood town, but in the end I traveled alone. When I returned from Quitovac, my reception at the border was not genteel.

"Pull up!"

A muscular RoboCop of a Homeland Security officer yelled at me to move two feet forward. I apparently moved two and a half feet and he yelled again, indulging an annoyance allowed to men with badges and fingers on a semiautomatic rifle trigger.

"What the hell are you doing?"

His style of questioning called to mind a lamp-lit prison interrogation. I was insulated by my American passport and the luck of my birthplace and I waited him out. In fifteen miles I reached the town of Why and another roadblock manned by another crew-cut fellow who held a rifle and sounded like the impolite twin of the first.

The road turned east and traversed the broad desolate belly of the Tohono O'odham Reservation as the sun slipped behind razor peaks. I left the reservation near Tucson and braked at a final roadblock manned by four soldiers with semiautomatic rifles. They asked yet more questions, and I felt my bile rising and grew snappish, another luxury granted by the insulation of my skin color. It was just as well that Raul did not indulge his desire to see his native village and to smell his native desert. It was better he remained on the mile-high plateau of the Navajo Nation.

CHAPTER FIVE

The season was just three games old and a great challenge rolled in like a storm off the slopes of Naatsis'áán, the sacred peak known as Earth Head. The Wildcats were playing in a tournament, four games in three days, in which time they could face perhaps two games against Fountain Hill, a top-ranked white team from the Valley of the Sun near Phoenix. If the Wildcats prevailed, they would conclude with a game against the best Apache team in the state.

Mendoza was interested in seeing how his team reacted to these challenges. His Wildcats, he said, were not ready yet. Angelo bucked and twisted like a young horse, taking shots he should not and committing fouls he should avoid. Dewayne played defense with the energy of a flickering lamp, uncertain of himself. Cooper was talented but young and quiet, and jealousies rose around him.

Fountain Hills is a Phoenix suburb, a tony place that gives the appearance of having been sculpted a few weeks ago from sun-blasted desert. It has landscaped streets and manicured *Truman Show* squares and an oversize fountain that blasts water 560 feet into the air—"110 feet higher than the Great Pyramid of Cheops," the town's website proclaims. Middle-class adobe homes sit on the valley floor, and Spanish-tile palazzos crowd the ridgelines.

The Falcons' big men stepped off their bus with cocky hops; several were linebacker thick and sculpted. Eleven of the team's thirteen players surpassed six feet in height, and all but one of them was white. They walked into the Wildcat Den, and their eyes scanned the Wildcats and saw undersized native kids, and they exchanged knowing smirks. The Falcons bounced through warm-ups, tossing down dunks with territory-claiming emphasis. The Wildcat players stole silent looks at these Valley boys.

Just as they did against that big and white team in Snowflake, the Wildcats came out in the first quarter as if this was a familiar and very old battle indeed. Chance Harvey flicked his eyes and shoulders right, his defender flinched, and he streaked left and hit a driving layup. Then he flipped a pass to Dewayne, who hit a three-pointer. Cooper faked, cut sharp to the foul line, got the ball, and put up that butter-smooth jumper of his.

"Stay up-tempo," Mendoza advised. "Pass. No hero ball."

Josiah came in. Pass and pass and steal and steal. The little man was on his game.

Angelo, outmanned and shorter than his opponents, stoutly banged and blocked shots, collecting more rebounds than any Valley boy. He was undisciplined but rarely lacked for heart in big games. The Falcons fell ten points behind and their coach, frowning, ordered his boys to put on a full-court defensive press in hopes they could rattle the Wildcats. That was foolishness. Pass led to Wildcat pass led to layup, repeated over and over again.

To make matters worse for the Valley boys, Chinle sat a mile above sea level. They suffered a deficit of oxygen. Halfway through the third quarter, they turned red as beets and placed hands on knees at each break.

Mendoza read that behavior and instructed his boys to unfurl their own defensive press. "Wherever they go, shadow them. Stay low in your crouch and move your feet. No dribble comes easy. They get nothing." That was the coup de grâce. Falcon passes went astray, dribbles were fumbled, the big white boys became dead men running. The Wildcats won by twenty points in a demolition.

December winds gusted stiff the next morning, and the cotton-woods held tight to their remaining golden leaves. The Wildcats played the Redskins, a team from Red Mesa, a tiny high school of 380 Navajo students. The game was unlikely to be competitive. Yet hours before the game, phalanx after phalanx of pickup trucks and vans filled the lot. Fans on the reservation took no game for granted.

This tournament included varsity boys and girls and junior varsity teams, too, and required a delicate balancing of schedules. So this game would be staged in the community center, a beat-up old gym with room for 1,200 fans if they squeezed hip-to-hip on creaky bleachers. Hundreds showed up early to buy tickets, the line stretching deep into the parking lot. This had been the town's only gym before the construction of the Wildcat Den, and two decades ago fans were known to swaddle themselves in blankets and camp overnight to buy tickets for big games. When full, this place became a sweat lodge. This would be one of those days.

Mendoza declined to feel confident. His players too often played to the level of their competition, down no less than up.

"Any team can beat us," he warned his players. "Don't fall asleep." They nodded and piled onto the court and fell asleep. Red Mesa had a burly center with a feathery touch and he bewitched the Wildcats. No matter the angle, none of them could hit a basket. Josiah blew a point-blank layup and tossed foolish passes. Angelo played an unmade bed of a game, bad fouls and sloppy passes and stupid fouls. Mendoza yanked him.

"Sit down."

"This is bullshit!" Angelo's voice was loud enough for every teammate and many in the crowd to hear. Older women pursed their lips and shook their heads at his tantrum. Fans would later complain about the boy's language.

"I want to play for a coach I like!"

Mendoza never looked at Angelo. Five minutes passed, then ten. The Wildcats sputtered and wheezed and stumbled and Angelo remained bench-bound. He peered down the bench and asked, "Coach, can I go in?" Mendoza gave no appearance of having heard him. A minute later the old man strolled down the bench and without looking at Angelo said, "You're not getting back in if you act like that."

Another five minutes passed. The Wildcats still trailed.

"Coach, I'm sorry . . . really."

Mendoza sent Angelo back in and he yanked a few rebounds and made a sweet pass and Chinle pulled out a desultory win.

"No showers!"

In the locker room after the Red Mesa game, the boys vowed not to wash off the scent of victory before their tournament rematch that afternoon against Fountain Hills. This return engagement was taut and physical and chippy. The Valley boys had become better acclimated to the elevation and were well coached and intent on revenge.

The lead swung back and forth. Angelo returned to his stalwart ways, and Cooper hit three-pointers and spinning drives. The Wildcat guards played quicksilver defense.

Josiah, all five feet four of him, remained glued to the big white guards. They could not dribble without his hands pecking and slapping at the ball, setting his feet quicker than they could move, drawing offensive fouls when they tried to back him down. In the third quarter, with the score tied, Josiah came sprinting off two picks—just as the coach had drawn up the play on the bench—and curled to the top of the key and caught a pass. He squared to the hoop and let fly a high-arching three over the outstretched arm of a Falcon giant. The ball fell through the net, and the Wildcats went up by four points.

A minute or two later one of those big white Falcons whacked at Josiah and sent him tumbling end over end to the floor. The ref blew a whistle—a foul. The Fountain Hills player frowned and reached out and—*thwap!*—smacked the ball out of Josiah's hands.

"Out of my way, *little boy.*"

The Falcons had been riding Josiah all game long, mocking his size, whacking, pushing, sneering. Josiah was no hothead but he squinted, stuck out his chest, and took a step toward this white boy, who was brawny and a foot taller.

"You want me?" Josiah stared, his eyes slits. "Really?" He motioned and balled his fists.

"C'mon then."

The big dude's eyes widened a touch. Who was this crazy little man?

Josiah's teammates ran in, Chance and Angelo and Cooper, and separated the players. The Wildcats stared stonily at the Falcon players, and the Navajo fans howled. The largest crowd of the season was raucous, chanting, "De-fense!"

Mendoza gathered his players on the bench and told them to

keep the ball moving. No dribbling. Pass faster than they can move! He told Angelo to set up in the high post, where his feel for the ball and his ability to thread passes to cutters was deadly. The shooters, Cooper and Chance, would rotate around picks and head to the corners to space the floor.

As for Josiah, Mendoza leaned in and growled at his little point guard, "Keep doing exactly what you're doing to those guys."

The Wildcats won by nine points. Mendoza walked into the locker room fighting a smile; he could not disguise his pleasure. They had packed off that big Valley team for a long bus ride home.

"Josiah wanted it. He gave them nothing! This kid led us."

Josiah was surprised by Mendoza's compliment and peered intently at him. Then he, too, allowed himself a smile.

The little man slipped into jeans and his STRAIGHT OUTTA CHINLE T-shirt and sneakers and walked back to the basketball floor. He stood and trained his eyes on those big Fountain Hill boys as they slowly walked out of the Wildcat Den to their bus. A few of the guys spotted him and said nothing or looked away. Josiah just stared.

So difficult to read these young men, their hurts, tiffs, braggadocio—sometimes they were open books, and other times their cover slapped shut. Two years ago Josiah played for the varsity Wildcats, and that was a disaster. The former coach was officious and yelled at and mocked the boys. Josiah was fourteen years old, his mind moving with the chaotic speed of the early teen years, and he had no idea what to make of this man.

The players rebelled. You yell at and treat us like rez dogs, they told that coach, and we're losing all the time anyway?

Josiah joined that upwelling. One day the players threatened not to ride the bus to a game, and another evening they nearly remained in their locker room. They did not want to keep putting on the black-and-yellow Chinle uniform for this man. Shaun Martin, the athletic director and a mentor to Josiah, stepped in and persuaded the boys not to humiliate themselves or the coach or Chinle. They finished the season.

That coach was fired and Mendoza the Legend arrived. He left Josiah off his team last season, making the boy play junior varsity. Was that punishment for the part Josiah had played in the mutiny, or because Josiah dribbled too much and, too often, out of control?

Even now, in his senior year, Josiah could not hide his frustration with his inability to read his coach. Late one night, he logged on to Facebook and wrote that Mendoza was playing favorites, that he was giving time to sophomores Cooper and Curtis that should be the preserve of the seniors.

Such talk can be as dangerous as a flood barreling through a canyon wash.

Mendoza knew as much of Facebook as he did of rocket ship travel to Mars. But he learned of Josiah's posting and wondered again what to make of this kid. His system and this season would rise and fall on the ability of point guards to see the court, to direct cutting and intersecting teammates. He saw Josiah as quick and intelligent, mercurial and moody.

Josiah saw Mendoza as remote and critical.

They shared only the awareness that their championship dreams could turn on their ability to decipher one another. No less than the coach, I, too, wanted to draw the measure of Josiah. So the Saturday after the Fountain Hill game, I followed the teenager's directions and drove up the Chinle Valley, my car buffeted by crosscutting winds. I arrived just north of mileage marker 130 and just south of the electrical lines. That's where his home was, sort of. "We Navajo are lousy at directions," Josiah had cautioned. I pulled onto a dirt track and then another. Finally we made cell phone contact and he guided me through a silver stockade of cottonwoods to his trailer.

He led me inside and introduced his little sister and his mom, Rosalyn, who shook my hand and read my face as carefully as her son. We sat in the living room across from a case filled with Josiah's running medals and a small Christmas tree with lights that twinkled like fireflies in the shadows.

Each morning he leapt off that top step and embarked on his run. Sometimes Rosalyn followed in the pickup truck, the lights illuminating her son's path. When the dome of the sun, Jóhonaa'éí, edged over the Chuskas and rays ignited the desert, she parked and let Josiah run on and opened her door and greeted the Holy People with a chant.

Hózhó, harmony, balance: She prayed fervently.

A lifetime ago Rosalyn and her children lived in Chinle with their father. He had a fine job with the power company and their home was a handsome double-wide filled like a Christmas stocking. The living room featured a big-screen television and video games, and the yard held trucks and cars and horses and sheep. They vacationed at the Grand Canyon, watched rodeos in Las Vegas from the expensive seats, and flew to visit cousins near Norfolk, Virginia.

"I cried if I didn't get new sneakers each season. I was the most spoiled kid around," Josiah said and frowned, as if watching his old self through a long-distance lens. Rosalyn, diminutive and with brow furrowed, listened intently. Josiah's little sister, a sickly girl, pulled a blanket over her and nuzzled Josiah. Instinctively he put his arm around her.

Dad liked a pop of beer or whiskey, and most often both. His taste for booze swelled and he started dating other women. He disappeared for a day or two or three and lied about it, and his arguments with Rosalyn were terrible to hear. They screamed and shouted recriminations and their marriage splintered. Dad moved out and Rosalyn was left alone in that double-wide surrounded by her husband's family and clan. Loyalties are primal for the Navajo, and her clan was not theirs. They told her it was time to leave.

She packed her children's bags and piled furniture into the pickup truck and moved the kids to a patch of red scrub dirt on her family's grazing lands in Valley Store. She purchased a tiny trailer for $5,000 and they lived without electricity or water for months.

Tens of thousands of Navajo, perhaps one-third of those on the reservation, live without power or running water, their daily life defined by propane generators and kerosene lamps and candles. The families pull into chapter houses in Many Farms and Chinle and pay to fill the fifty-gallon plastic water tanks that sit in their pickup trucks. They ration water for drinking, baths, dishes; per-capita water use on the reservation is a tiny fraction of what it is elsewhere in the United States. Navajo frugality is as impressive as it is maddening that so many must live this way in the United States in the twenty-first century.

Rosalyn would not put up with that for long. Her family would not tumble backward. She worked at a government office in Blue Gap, a tiny town wedged on a desolate plain between limestone escarpments. She cashed in her 401(k) fund and paid the electric company to run a line from the road to the trailer. That cost $10,000. She paid the water company to run a pipe to her trailer.

That was another $6,000. Then the IRS penalized her for tapping a retirement fund and that cost $10,000.

Debt was swift-rising and most nights she cried herself to sleep.

She got pregnant with twins, a boy and a girl, and her labor was difficult and she had an emergency caesarian. Her girl lived and the boy perished. She and her little daughter felt that loss still, the dead boy gone and perpetually present. "In our tradition, twins are forever bonded. Forever."

Rosalyn's stomach began to ache like a fist clenched, skin prickly, her windpipe constricted. Several times, an ambulance pulled up to the trailer, lights flashing off the living room wall, and they loaded her on a stretcher into the back as the children cried and held each other. After her third anxiety attack, doctors filed into her hospital room in Chinle and stood by the bed and leveled with her.

"They told me that, you know, they are going to send me off to a mental institution to get myself together."

Your children, they told her, could go to foster care until you feel better. She shook her head, rocking fiercely in bed. No, no, that was impossible; no, that could not, would not, be possible.

She sought out a *ndilniihii*, a hand trembler, who located the source of her distress, and a medicine man who performed a healing ceremony. The medicine man dabbed ash and mud on her face and placed abalone and obsidian shells around her and burned logs of cedar, and she inhaled deep the smoke of herbs picked in secret places on the slopes of holy mountains. The medicine man studied her auguries and saw disharmony. It's as if, he said, you are carrying a great sack of rocks on your back.

In time tears stopped streaming down her cheeks. She could draw a full breath again. She emerged healed enough.

"I think I know I'm happy. I just had to get myself together and be stronger."

Josiah threw himself into sports. Once a chubby little kid who cried when denied a video game, he ran and roped horses and played soccer and football. He became adept at motocross, off-road motorcycle riding, flying over dirt embankments and skidding into turns with legs flapping like bat wings. He was heedless of risk and beat teenagers five years older.

He took a bad wipeout, his body bouncing and skipping like a rock across the dirt. His mother, who was filming him, ran to him and cradled his head. She was terrified and so was he. He retired from motocross at age eleven. "I got to give it up to those who do that for a living. It's tough," Josiah said. "It's scary."

Running became his love, treks up through sage and grease-wood to mesa tops with views of so much beauty. He joined the high school team, and although his head barely reached the shoulder of his competitors, his legs churned like pistons and he became a star. He suffered from asthma, and some days it was as if a big man had knelt on his chest. He sucked on his inhaler and kept going.

Early that same morning he had woken up and stepped into the living room to sit by the warmth of the woodstove. Then he jumped rope and stretched and slipped on a small backpack and set off running to basketball practice in Chinle, eight miles down the road. At practice he ran for another two hours.

Running was about how much pain you could take.

Josiah had cousins who lived a mile marker or two to the north, and a few days earlier they had welcomed me into their blue-washed hogan. They made Navajo burgers—big patties on fry bread—and we drank freshly steeped Navajo tea and talked about callused lives, young men and women who grew up in a world with too much booze and chemicals and too few jobs. The little sister of one cousin had been murdered and the brother of another got blind drunk and fell by the side of the road and froze stiff. A poster of Tupac was taped to the wall of their hogan, and a ceremonial bundle of herbs lay in a basket on the table next to a half ounce of weed.

"Have you seen *Wind River*?" a young man asked me.

The film offered a chilly and brutal take on reservation life.

"That's us. That's our story."

Rosalyn was intent that her son's story would be different. She was intent that he leave the reservation for college and she stood fierce guard over him. Josiah's eyes were no less fixed on that goal. One night he posted on Facebook:

"What really makes me sad is that people who are so talented and probably have all the talent in the world just throw it all away with drugs and alcohol. Some are even my own family. To be honest I cry knowing what's gonna happen to them."

He was one of the state's best distance runners and his grade average was a solid B. His cousins knew he was not them. As he ran the roads of Valley Store, they waved and shooed him away in the same motion.

An uncle and the father of a close friend took him for drives and talks. When the family budget was dry and Rosalyn struggled to keep the lights on and water running, these men purchased shirts and sneakers for Josiah and his brothers and sisters. As Navajo uncles often do, they did not hesitate to place a firm hand on his shoulder and say, Listen to me, son.

Josiah's eyes carried a question mark. "Some people work out and they become like family to you," he said. Left unspoken was that some did not.

Josiah's track coach sought him out last year. He told the little runner that he had the talent to run in college and should make this high school team his own. Josiah liked that. He gathered runners in his trailer for movie parties on weekends and led everyone in stretching and taking ice baths. "I had to grow up for the sake of my teammates." Josiah loved that coach.

His relationship with Mendoza was not like that. Josiah's track season extended into November this autumn, and he missed the first weeks of basketball practice, those days when a point guard and coach might form a mind meld. Mendoza still worried that Josiah dribbled too much and attempted too many off-balance layups and did not swing the ball often enough to young Cooper, the team's best shooter and top scorer.

"Mendoza doesn't trust us. He doesn't believe we can put this together. He is so negative. Sometimes we're like, 'Really?'"

There was silence in this trailer and I asked about his father. He lives just down the road in Many Farms, Josiah replied. When did you last see him?

"Seven years ago, when I was eleven or twelve."

Josiah wrapped his arm around his little sister. "I really want my father to come back and be in my life. We need him. I need him. But only if he sobers up. He has to be a real father."

One morning not long after, Josiah woke up and typed on Facebook:

"Not once have I ever looked into the crowd or looked to the side hoping I see him cheering me on as I run or play. Just wish you could see how well I'm doing."

CHAPTER SIX

I looked for a fold in the earth, a drop into a shadowed world. My Subaru was parked miles back, as the dirt track had ruts wide enough to swallow it whole. I hiked through gray-green sagebrush and black mesquite and gnarled juniper and across basalt and granite. My map was a spider's web of lines sketched on a napkin by a Navajo friend.

I stood at a canyon's edge.

It was deep and narrow and ancient in geologic, much less human, terms. Its floor was cloaked in blue shadow, and I scratched around the rim until, as Navajo friends had said, I found a steep path, vertiginous and littered with enough slip-sliding scree and schist to cause me to question my decision to hike alone. As solitude was the point, I concentrated mind and creaky knees and in time my feet crunched on the sandy bottom. I rolled back my head and looked upward.

Six-hundred-foot-high walls of salmon-colored sandstone rose and curled and enveloped me, the canyon ridge crenellated as a castle keep. The stream running through the wash was locked in cornflower-blue ice that glimmered in the refracted light of a winter sun. I knelt and put my ear to the ice and heard a gurgle.

It was as though I had entered a long-abandoned palace.

Navajo turned to these canyons, hidden places, to take the pulse of their land, their traditions, and themselves. Their Holy People emerged from within this earth, up through three subterranean worlds—Black, Blue, and Yellow—into the fourth Glittering World. More than once I have met a basketball player walking a canyon. These were not times for talk. We nodded and smiled and moved on, seeking to fall into harmony.

A Navajo did not see himself as master of this landscape; he was part of it, in its harshness and its beauty.

A day earlier I had dropped my son Aidan at the airport after completing our cross-country drive. We hugged and I rubbed his head and I returned across high desert and through volcanic flats to Chinle. Solitude was cleansing and purifying, even as aloneness felt alive within me. Aidan was twenty-five and I was sixty-one, and who was to say how many more times I would travel and laugh in his company?

A quarter century back this achingly beautiful land and its people offered refuge to my wife and me and our boys. Evelyn, a midwife, would return from the hospital and describe families of women, grandmothers, aunties, cousins, sisters, and daughters, sitting in the waiting room while in the delivery room the expectant mother would grab a sash hanging from the ceiling and withdraw to a place within and, with little more than a low moan, push out her baby.

For months after our return to New York City, Evelyn and I resisted surrendering our loose-jawed state of grace. We balked at returning to what was. I called editors in the Southwest and inquired about the shape of a life bounded by sacred mountains and desert sands. To accept and explore a nonmaterial world seemed a fine life's journey.

Soon enough the fog of ambition and friendships and work descended and our time in Navajo became a tale to tell our children. We encountered life's permutations of loss and love. I not long ago survived an encounter with cancer, which tossed me into a more intimate dance with mortality. I looked at photos of our parents and grandparents and found myself thinking: They could not know the endpoint of their life journey. We know only that we return to mystery.

I had talked of restlessness and life choices and trying better to understand the pull and meaning of this land with Julian, Mendoza's young aide-de-camp, and other Navajo, and they offered the same advice: Time is not linear; it surrounds you. Find a fold in the earth and let your mind wander within it.

I walked west along the canyon floor and around a corner and came upon an elk. The deer had the thick coat and the gray coloration that is the gift of winter and raised its head and stared at me, our eyes locked in cross-species surprise. Then it kicked and leaped and hopped, disappearing into a stand of juniper. I walked back and forth across the ebb and flow of that ice stream and stumbled on a blackened stone. It was a fossil, a mineralized chunk of the 225-million-year-old conifer that rose hundreds of feet high when this land was a lowland forest and home to stegosaurus and T. rex and the pterodactyl that soared on tropical updrafts.

Rapid burial in river silt had let that tree escape destruction by oxygen and bugs. Volcanoes erupted and the land heaved upward. A million floods dissolved soluble ash and silica replaced living wood. I held this fossil, the rings of its long-ago life visible to my eye.

I ran my fingers along the striations of its ancient bark, touched it to my forehead and returned the wood-stone to its sediment. The Navajo say these are the fibers of the earth, as blood to the body.

The canyons twisted again and again, and as I rounded the bend I saw a black-sand embankment and climbed it, the sand so fine it stuck to the hands like cotton candy. I rolled up onto the bank and clambered to my feet. Wedged between the embankment and a cliff overhang, I found a gray-stone kiva, the rock ceiling above it blackened by the smoke of this millennium-old fireplace. On the wall of the overhang was a fan of ancient handprint pictographs, red, ochre, pink, delicate and lovely. Similar aboriginal handprints are found in southern France, in Patagonia and Mongolia and Africa and Australia. Perhaps this was our universal prehistoric script.

I extended sand-caked fingers toward those prints as if to reach across the millennia. You were here. Did you think yourself home?

I had come to know an English teacher at Chinle, tall and white haired and an expert cliff climber who loved to roam and climb and camp in these remote canyons. He harbored special affection for those gorges said by the Navajo to be haunted, places where the wind whistled through and the silver branches of the cottonwoods rattled and the blue piñon jays chattered uneasy.

He found a medicine man's joy in haunted aloneness.

Tomorrow I would drive to Albuquerque to talk with Nachae Nez, last year's star of the Chinle Wildcats. He was a thoughtful young man, introspective and probing and maybe a touch lost, and he talked often of the pull of his land, the forests and elk and these ghost canyons, these folds in the earth where you could disappear and listen to the wind sweep away your thoughts. "To live away from my land is so hard," he told me on the telephone. Climb down inside it, he advised. You will understand me better.

Perhaps that is so.

I returned along the narrow canyon floor, hopscotching the frozen stream, and climbed that path toward the cleft in the cliff walls. Evening rolled in like ocean mist, the sky lavender-blue. An eagle floated, suspended on the last updrafts of day, wobbling and arcing downward into the depths of shadow.

I turned and walked back through miles of sagebrush and pine and twilight descending to my car.

CHAPTER SEVEN

Hoop dreams burned like a desert fever. Some nights he sprinted down court, feinted left, spun right, and laid it in, the crowd casting up a wall of sound, mom and dad, cousins, aunties, and little brother in the stands. They knew his history and his ability. They loved him. They knew that he's no fake.

In his sleep he smiled.

Other nights defenders crowded him, pounced, and he fumbled the ball, watched it bounce away. He reached for it and his knee twisted, buckled, splintered, shattered. A crowd of strangers, not a face he recognized, gathered round, shaking their heads disgusted. He was a fraud.

Nachae Nez awoke in a sweat in this bed in his small apartment in this strange city. He lived in Albuquerque, a four-hour drive across the desert and ten thousand psychic miles from Tsaile in the Navajo Nation, where his father taught him to grow alfalfa and potatoes and to coolly draw back a bowstring and shoot an arrow true; where his mother taught him tribal dance steps and the chants that heat and heal the body; where his grandmother taught him to herd the sheep that nourish the soul.

He and his best friend, Jared, played on the Chinle Wildcats last season, smiling to each other as they sliced through the opposition. On weekends they rode horses through dark blue-green forests on the molted flanks of the Chuskas. They had grown their hair long and braided it into traditional ponytails. In his senior year Nachae cut off his braid and presented it to his grandfather.

His mother was unhappy with that decision. In Navajo culture, a hair braid was a connection to culture and the Holy People. She told Nachae that he should not have done this before his eighteenth birthday, that it might leave him vulnerable to the ill wind of fate.

Maybe his mom was right.

Nachae lived in the numberless Navajo diaspora, one of hundreds of thousands in exile from the land that burrowed deep into their souls. A pale-skinned young man with a shock of jet-black hair, he spotted me and grinned and stepped from behind the counter at University Pawn on Route 66 in Albuquerque. We'd last seen each other when he was a senior in Chinle, and his easy smile had not changed.

University Pawn sprawled like a brightly lit supermarket filled with the hocked detritus of distressed lives: native turquoise and jade and coral jewelry, and wrought-silver necklaces and brooches and bracelets and blankets. There were guns, too—lots of guns.

A couple of weeks ago a skinny little white dude, sweaty and with a case of the twitches, walked in straining beneath the weight of a big television. Nachae said he laid that television on the counter and the manager walked over and plugged it in and damned if the signal didn't twitch too.

The manager shrugged. Sorry, man, we can only give you twenty dollars.

The skinny white dude blinked fast and nodded: Okay, that's the way it's going to be, like that? He picked up the television, teetered to the parking lot, lifted it over his head like a barbell, and hurled it spinning like a planetoid. When that television hit the asphalt, Nachae said, it reminded him of the time he and Jared dropped a watermelon off a butte.

"This is kind of a crazy city sometimes," Nachae said as we walked to the car. "This is the first fall I did not go to cut wood, the first time I didn't wake up before dawn and feed the sheep in the cold."

Nachae peered out my car window as Albuquerque in evening rolled past, tortilla joints, Quik Marts, and a neon blur of gas stations and restaurants and fast-food joints and supermarkets. More stores with more stuff to buy in a single block than in all of Chinle. Nachae turned nineteen a few weeks back. His sister held two jobs and she had to work late that night, so he paid for take-out enchiladas and celebrated his birthday alone and prayed.

"I'm writing a paper for my English class on how the Diné are supposed to retain harmony."

Nachae was the star, the captain, and leading scorer on Mendoza's playoff team last year. He was a writer's dream, a young man willing to interrogate himself and his dreams and insecurities in far greater depth than anyone on the current team, far more than most teenagers. After graduation he got into his old car and drove to this desert city at the foot of the humpbacked Sandia Mountain. He signed up for night classes at a community college and a few fellow students, old enough to be his parents, befriended him. A blond woman with an elegant Eastern European accent helped him decipher math equations. A whiskey-voiced ex-con named Dominic gave life lessons.

"Keep your head clear, bro. Don't get sucked into no bullshit with no fools."

Nachae told them about life on the rez, and as he listened to himself it felt like he was weaving a fairy tale. He had been the senior star with the good grades, and the little kids asked for his autograph and took selfies with him, teachers called out hello, and he dated a girl who was Navajo royalty. "I guess I was sort of famous."

They nodded, uncomprehending.

He had not gone home since moving to Albuquerque. When I asked why, he slid toward vagueness. He said it was easier to be away when the bears hibernated and birds migrated and washes froze over and the Holy People turned drowsy. In Albuquerque in summer the line between scorched and cool was drawn at the edge of a shadow, while in the Chuskas the air remained delicious as a mountain stream. Maybe he'd head home then. Maybe.

We pulled into a steak house and Nachae used his arms to swing his legs out the door. He landed and winced and his knee buckled.

I asked if he was okay.

Another wince.

A month ago he played pickup hoops at the University of New Mexico gym, taking on guys bigger and older. Nachae is five feet nine and sturdy and competitive and he was on his game that night, jumper after jumper, his sweetest rhythm in months. He laid down a stutter step and spun just like he'd done a thousand times against a thousand hapless defenders . . .

Pop.

He knew before the pain galloped in. It was the anterior cruciate ligament in his knee and it had snapped like a rubber band. He'd blown the same ligament in the same knee during his sophomore year in high school. Back then he figured that was that, that he was the Navajo who couldn't play competitive basketball any longer. He was a good student and decided to pour his energies into his studies. He underwent surgery and with his mother's help transferred to Navajo Prep, a top academic school in Farmington, New Mexico, just across the border of the reservation. He trudged down to the school's weight room to lift and do balancing drills. He forced himself into the painful stretches that broke up those surgery scars.

One day his physical therapist called him over and said, You're doing really well. You could think about trying to play basketball again.

It was like being told he could fall in love again. He'd lost some of his explosiveness, but he was stronger and smarter and he had learned to slow down the game in his head and see it unfold. He led his Navajo Prep team in scoring in his junior year. For his senior year he transferred to Chinle High School so he could be closer to home. He starred as the Wildcats returned to the playoffs.

After graduation he dominated the spring tournaments and all-star games that are an obsession on the rez. Everyone wanted to know: Where you going to college, Nachae? Who are you going to play for? He answered vaguely and left for Albuquerque, waving.

Now he prepared for a second major knee surgery. He can't, he won't, go home limping on crutches. He wouldn't be able to walk around his parents' trailer with all that mud and ice; he'd have to sit inside on the couch and think about all he couldn't do. "I don't want everyone asking, 'Nachae, what happened? What about your career? Why aren't you playing ball?'"

"My Navajo name is Napi, which means 'old man' in Navajo."

I told him that meant he was wise. He shook his head and pointed to his throbbing knee: "It means I have an old body."

He felt himself becoming something that was not a basketball player, and frustration had wrapped him in a tight embrace.

The Class of Last Year at Chinle High faces precarious choices. The very best students each year go to fine four-year colleges; more than a few Chinle alumni hold Ivy League degrees and quite a few others end up with four-year college degrees. But fewer than half the graduates go to college, and fewer than half of those remain more than a year or two, and many return to Chinle to look for work. No shame came attached to that. Returnees get loving hugs from aunties and manly handshakes from uncles, and after a few months of watching the wind whip sand snakes off mesas and feeling the razor wind of winter, many wonder, Now what?

Several of Nachae's buddies, childhood friends and basketball teammates, enrolled at Diné College, the eight-sided, glass-walled office building that was modeled in the shape of a hogan and rose like a hallucination out of the pines at the foot of the Chuskas. How had that worked out? Marcus Litson, a shaggy-haired kid with a perpetually boyish aspect and the starting forward on last year's team, looked at me and shrugged.

Many mornings he worked alongside his grandfather on the family ranch that stretches off across the rolling plateau and canyon lands northwest of Tsaile, tending and chasing after their big and prosperous herd of cattle. "Riding through the woods after cattle? Heck yeah, that's the best!"

Nachae's father, Felix, was an agricultural-extension agent, and Marcus worked with him, too, hammering posts and building pens and helping to mark sheep. Marcus grew up in Nachae's house as much as in his own and this work put a few extra dollars in his pocket and a strut in his walk.

I asked again: "What about school? How good are the classes at Diné College?" Marcus was an honor roll student who'd taken college-level classes in high school. His smile turned wistful, his voice dropped an octave, his eyes shaded toward the ground.

"My classes last year in high school were tougher than my classes at Diné College. I know I can do better."

He changed direction before I could ask more questions. I often saw him behind the basket at games cheering, laughing with his dudes and all the pretty girls, a charmer, and aunties and old grannies wandered over and hugged him and tousled his hair and said they miss watching him play hoops. He walked into the locker room before games and poked fun at Angelo and joked with Josiah and Chance, and sometimes he ended up sitting in the coach's office chatting with Mendoza. They talked easily, the young guy and the old man. Marcus was the cheerful ghost of a season past.

His mom was a schoolteacher, and she pushed him to apply to a tougher college. You need to leave the reservation, she told him, you can't pretend you are in high school anymore. "I agree with her," Marcus said. "I need to get real."

Not long after, at the next Wildcat game, I ran into another boy from last year's team, Nick Begay, the lithe little guard with a gentle voice and distant eyes. He took courses at Coconino Community College in Flagstaff this autumn, and he aced those and slept on a cousin's couch until that apartment got too crowded and his cousin gave him the boot. Nick could not come up with enough cash to pay spring tuition bills, so he returned to the reservation.

Nick found friends, former teammates, working odd jobs around Chinle, cleaning cluttered family yards, chopping mesquite and piñon, herding a granny's sheep. Sometimes he and his buddies loaded pickup trucks with firewood or hauled water and people recognized them as former ballplayers. Hey, man, didn't you guys play for the Wildcats? I remember you! They would sit on the back lip of the trucks or crouch by a yard fire and chew over hoop glories. That was cool and could not sustain itself. They could talk all they wanted about old victories and ancestors and great sunsets, but they knew the reality: If a young man wandered around the reservation jobless, life could get treacherous fast.

Nick planned to drive down to Scottsdale in the Valley of the Sun in the springtime. His stepbrother had an extra room and said Nick could get work on his home-building crew while he took classes at the community college. Nick saw his future playing out somewhere far from the rez. "I want to go and find a career and just come back here and visit."

For a native to drive off the Navajo reservation, to slow cruise the shopping strips in border towns and catch too many suspicious stares, was to see and feel layers of complication, not least the wages of the Navajo's tortured relationship with the culture of the whites, the *bilagáanas*.

The border towns and cities—remote, hard-edged places that curled along I-40 like a snake around a tree, with cheap gasoline on offer and plastic teepees and industrial-size restaurants and truck chapels and Knife City outlets—have a long history of giving natives a shove and a tumble.

Shopkeepers sold rotgut to Navajo until their livers exploded or until they missed a turn in their junk-heap cars and all that was left was a crucifix and a clutch of roadside flowers. White store owners complained of drunk and belligerent and shoplifting natives and took them for a ride on prices. Look around at the trackless desert and mesas and alluvial plains and the black thunderheads forming over distant ranges. Where else are you going to shop?

Cops pushed Navajo around, whacked them, shot them when they got ornery.

Sometimes it got uglier. Farmington sits on the eastern edge of the reservation in New Mexico, and in the early 1970s the city was stacked high with racial tinder. Anglos ran the schools, the city hall, and the businesses, and their cops handled the streets. Navajo and Jicarilla Apache lived in the seams. Don't mouth off, and if you don't live here, get back across the border to the rez at night. Rolling native drunks was a favorite sport, right up there with bowling.

So it was one evening that white high school boys drove north along a dirt road, drunk hunting. They found three inebriated Navajo near white limestone Chokecherry Canyon and pushed the three men into the gorge and bludgeoned them. Then they doused the drunks with gasoline and flicked matches onto them.

Police caught the teenagers, which required no mean feat of detective work, as the boys boasted of their deed. An Anglo judge sentenced the teens to two years in a reform school. None of the boys served a day in prison.

The Navajo applied for a permit to vent their rage with a demonstration in Farmington. A judge denied the Indians and instead granted a permit to a white posse to parade through town in western regalia. The Navajo saw this for the calculated slap that it was and they gathered and shook their fists and the police fired tear gas and charged in with nightsticks and arrested thirty of them.

Red rage became a burning blaze.

———

Route 66 runs the length of downtown Gallup, which lies south of the red-stone Defiance Plateau and just over the border from the Navajo Nation. Faded matriarchal jewel hotels played host to Gregory Peck and John Wayne, the Marx brothers and Ronald Reagan. Warehouse-size native jewelry and pawnshops attracted bored travelers bound for Los Angeles. Some of that stuff was fine indeed, and some was fake, and good luck discerning one from the other. More to the point, there was one cheap liquor store after another.

Liquor had for a hundred years defined the relationship between the Navajo and many border towns, and that spider's web still traps many. Gallup by the 1970s was a liquor store Saudi Arabia. The rule of thumb for a booze peddler was not to be judgmental. Shopkeepers sold to Indians in any condition of drunkenness and despair. Some stumbled into alleys and froze and others wove across the interstate and died like stray dogs.

A letter to the *Gallup Independent* in the 1970s described the Navajo Inn, the most profitable store in New Mexico: "Two hundred yards west, an elderly man was lying on the open, damp ground in all appearances dead but accepted in that immediate environment as stone drunk."

Larry Casuse, half Navajo and half Austrian, grew up amid that carnage, a teenager with black-rimmed eyeglasses and black flowing hair, which he wrapped in a revolutionary red bandanna. He joined teenage crusades who tried to shutter the worst of the booze traps, and no one paid them any mind. If the natives were dumb enough to keep on buying, whose damn fault was that?

Larry went to the University of New Mexico and became

president of the Kiva Club as Indian activism came to militant flower. Dime Store Injun acquiescence was over; young native men held guns. Radicals with the American Indian Movement occupied Alcatraz Island from 1969 to 1971, and on February 27, 1973, militants took over the town of Wounded Knee on the Oglala Sioux reservation in South Dakota.

The world was watching.

Two days after Wounded Knee, Larry and a Navajo friend and fellow activist, Robert Nakaidinae, parked outside Gallup city hall. Larry walked inside cradling a rifle, and his friend held sticks of dynamite. They disarmed the sheriff and stuck the barrel in the back of Mayor Emmett Garcia. The mayor was a walking confluence of powerful interests, the town's most powerful pol, part owner of the Navajo Inn, and a member of the New Mexico Regents, which oversaw the university system.

They paraded the mayor down Route 66 at gunpoint.

The blocks around the liquor stores constituted a Navajo dying field, and Larry wanted to stick the mayor's nose in that manure pile. Cops surrounded and trained guns on the young natives. Larry led the mayor inside a sporting goods store and it all unraveled. The mayor bolted and hurled himself through the plate-glass window and rolled onto the sidewalk. Police officers opened fire and Larry resembled a puppet on a string, bullets piercing his chest and stomach.

Police officers stepped through the blasted window and grabbed Casuse under the armpits and deposited him on the sidewalk. Calvin Trillin, the New Yorker writer, described that scene: "Larry's body lay uncovered on the sidewalk in front of Stearn's Sporting Goods store for a while—long enough for the local paper to take a picture of it with three police standing over it like hunters who had just bagged their seasonal deer."

The mayor declared that Casuse had taken his own life, another crazy red man committing suicide. The autopsy found multiple bullet wounds.

Today Gallup, which calls itself the "Indian Capital of the World," still has thirty-five liquor licenses when by state law it should have eleven. Gallup far outpaces cities in the rest of the state in deaths from cirrhosis of the liver and in its violent crime rate. And still natives wander into interstate traffic.

Time sands sawtooth edges. Many Navajo live in border towns now and cities farther afield, and there is intermarriage and cross-racial friendship. Some merchants and hoteliers and trading post owners have gained reputations for honest dealings. Holbrook is thoroughly integrated, Anglo, Navajo, Hopi, black, and Mexican. Officials in Flagstaff and Farmington crafted protocols with the Navajo Nation for police and fire. Yet Anglos still dominated the business and political elite of most cities. Car dealers and rental centers and payday shops still siphoned off dollars from the Navajo.

And casual indignities endured.

I sat one morning chatting with Chinle superintendent Quincy Natay, a dapper middle-age man and chairman of the Navajo Nation Gaming Enterprise. He was confident and urbane and had a hand in more or less anything big and important that happened on the Navajo Nation. But when he walked into a Durango ski shop last season to buy a new pair of skis and a parka, the store manager saw not a well-heeled customer but a Navajo man of dubious intent. He instructed his clerk to follow that Indian as if he were a shoplifter with itchy hands. Natay recognized he had become prey in a tired game, and he spun on his heel and walked out. He recounted this as matter of fact, as he would recall a round of golf. Only if you watched very carefully would you have noticed his jaw tighten as he talked.

Aaron, at twenty-one, was the youngest of Mendoza's assistant coaches, and one morning over breakfast he spoke of what it was like to pass through the looking glass into the Anglo world. A Chinle High School graduate and skilled construction worker, he was muscular with a thicket of short-cut black hair. He coached during the week and often drove to Phoenix on weekends to hammer frames and staple siding on homes. Last summer he could not possibly drink enough water in the brain-boil 115-degree heat.

His every breath came desert-scorched, and some weeks he preferred to drive east to work in Oklahoma. There was humidity to deal with, but that was just about sweat, and the homebuilding firms paid better there, too—$1,000 per week. His white supervisors treated him well, this skilled and hardworking kid hammering and framing alongside Mexicans and white guys. Traveling back and forth could be another matter. He rolled into Enid, which was flat, small, and largely white, at 2:00 a.m. He had driven a dozen hours that day, across deserts and up looping river roads, and he had miles more to go when he saw police lights flash in his rearview mirror.

He heard the command: Pull over!

Four cruisers accelerated toward him and doors popped open and officers jumped out with hands on their holsters, barking, "Get out of your car. Now! Now! Put your hands up."

"What is the problem, officer?" Aaron recalled saying, concentrating so hard on keeping his voice as even as a carpenter's spirit level.

"Shut up."

The cops locked him in the back of a patrol car, and they took out flashlights and screwdrivers and dismantled his wheel cavities and car's floorboards. One cop took apart the sandwich Aaron had purchased at a Subway and another used a stick to fish around in the bottom of his cup of soda. What drugs, Aaron wondered, could survive immersion in Coca-Cola? He kept that thought to himself.

"All that is in my car," he said through the window to the cops, "is my power drill and claw hammer and nail gun and chisels. My work clothes are in that khaki duffle—"

"Did we ask you? Shut up."

Later the police talked to him of drug mules. Again and again they demanded to know where Aaron was from in Mexico.

"I'm not Mexican. I'm Navajo."

"What's a Navajo?"

As dawn tiptoed in and the eastern sky turned pink and a finger of a breeze curled through the street, the cops unlocked the cruiser door and let him out. Aaron drove oh so slowly while a police cruiser tailed his car to the city limits. I asked if the cops apologized. He looked at me and smiled.

Aaron hoped to learn every coaching trick he could from Mendoza, and after that he planned to move to Phoenix to live with his girlfriend while she completed her teaching degree at Arizona State University. Aaron hoped to get a degree in education, as he wanted to coach, and a certificate in diesel mechanics, as that was always in demand. So many Navajo lived in Phoenix that they called it "the Second Rez." Jobs were plentiful, shopping malls were big as aircraft hangars, movie theaters were everywhere, and you could even find an excellent Navajo taco.

Aaron and his girlfriend lived in Phoenix before, but they did not plan on staying. They just ended up missing family and ceremonies and mutton stew, and they loved to ride their horses into the white stone canyons of the Balakai Mesa, looking for bighorn sheep.

"I like quiet and no traffic. And no one here asks me what a Navajo is."

Nachae was what Mendoza missed this year. He had been the old man's alpha dog. When the coach needed players to lift weights and to jump rope and to run and to stretch, this senior led the way. When the team bus rolled for hours through moonlit mountain passes and across valley floors, Nachae reminded the boys of the stakes.

That squad was not as talented as this year's team. Angelo was more immature and had a tendency to fall prey to mysterious and seemingly excruciating knee injuries in big games. He would lie there on the court, pounding the floor and grabbing his knee, his season looking done for. Then the knee would mysteriously heal and he'd play the next game. But Nachae was the pack leader and that team played harder more consistently.

When the Wildcats lost a close game that year in Holbrook, the players filed into the visiting locker room. Mendoza paced, squinting, annoyed, conducting a postgame autopsy as Nachae lay on the floor and pulled his jersey up over his face. Nachae treated defeat like death and that registered with other players. Cooper Burbank, then a talented freshman, was the team's future. Nachae was its sweaty and urgent present.

How, Mendoza demanded of that team, did we lose to Holbrook? Nachae pulled his jersey off his face and raised his hand. He could chafe at Mendoza's ways, the reins pulled tight when he yearned to play a freer-flowing game and lay down his moves. But he respected the old man's knowledge and all those years poured into this game they both loved.

"We have trouble connecting with each other on that court. We don't look for each other. It's not acceptable to me."

Nachae fell in love his senior year with a girl with long hair and piercing eyes, and her intelligence made him smile. Some evenings he would pick her up and drive to a lookout over Canyon de Chelly and roll down the windows. They would talk and talk and then she would put her head on his shoulder and they'd listen for the whispers of their ancestors.

"We would fall asleep and wake up and go to school."

He lived in a trailer wedged between one grandma's trailer and that of another, and to maneuver that ice-glazed track to their home in winter required a high-suspension pickup truck. His grandma's trailer had the only working bathroom. He loved that life and felt an inchoate desire to leave it, to run away. Sometimes he could not bear to talk to his parents. "They say it's tough for a native to leave the rez; they say your favorite place is your grandma's hogan." He turned to me and asked, "These decisions are supposed to be painful, right?"

One of Nachae's aunties had graduated from Cornell University and her accomplishment became his measure of what should be possible. He had the grades to get into a four-year college, he knew that. Yet doubt gnawed like a dog at his innards.

The morning of the SAT, Nachae got dressed and drove to the test site. He sat a while in the car in the parking lot and turned the ignition back on and drove away. "I couldn't see my future off the reservation. I guess I was scared."

He needed that test to complete his application for the University of New Mexico. Without it, he became just another native kid taking night classes at the community college. "Things probably would have been really different if I'd taken that test," he said. "My life that year, it was all about my poor decisions."

Hoop love betrayed him too. No recruiters came calling. Maybe he was too small and too slow; maybe scouts shared his worries about the creaky state of his knees. A year later, living in Albuquerque, he knew he had to forget hoops. His cousin Julian told him it was time to grow up and move on, but he had trouble listening to him. He had trouble listening to himself.

"My mom used to ask me what my backup plan was. My backup plan was to work on my original plan."

Recriminations barreled through his mind like a Union Pacific freight train. What if he returned home to Tsaile? What if he had taken that damned test? His father counseled Nachae to take the test now and apply to New Mexico State University in Las Cruces and get a degree in agricultural economics. Maybe someday the Navajo Nation will cut a final deal with Arizona and Colorado and begin to draw its treaty-guaranteed share of water from the aquamarine Colorado River, and when that happened and the Navajo built aqueducts to carry that blue gold, an agricultural revival could sweep this reservation. Farms would sprout like desert coral and lupine and scorpion weed, and a man who knew water and agriculture could be king.

Nachae listened carefully; the voices of his father and mother had become a balm. "Last year I couldn't stand to talk to my parents, and now I like to talk with them. I like the sound of their voices."

He found an orthopedic surgeon and scheduled a date to cut open his knee, a surgery paid through Medicaid. He drew a regular paycheck at the pawnshop. On paydays, he walked home and slipped dollars into envelopes and put on stamps and mailed these to his parents and to family friends who helped him weather tough times as a kid, who bought him sneakers and T-shirts and dinners, and who listened and offered advice as they drove him to games.

"I owe that to a lot of people who loved me. Now I can say thank you."

He had learned to decode Albuquerque. He knew where to buy good pizza and tacos and where to find a reliable mechanic to work on his car, and he could stumble through a little Spanish with the pretty Mexican girls, the *chicas bellas* who walked into the pawn-shop. They flirted but most often cut off talk of a date when they discovered he was not a Mexican.

Many nights he would walk home and turn off the lights and lay in bed and listen to Chinle basketball games on the internet, seeing and feeling every spin to the baseline, the three-point shots, the rebounds in traffic: Come on, Angelo, wake up! Elijah, man up, play smart! Come on! His body shifted and twisted. When an ache of aloneness descended, he rose before dawn and faced east and prayed as the sun crested the raw-boned Sandia Peaks.

A few nights earlier he walked home after his pawnshop shift carrying a plastic bag with a take-out dinner. He felt a shadow at the edge of his vision. He slid his eyes to the side and noticed a car slow-rolling down the street behind him. Three men sat inside; they had him marked. He sprinted across the street, cut the wrong way up a one-way street, and knelt low behind a clump of jade bushes and organ cactus. The car circled the block twice, the men peering into the shadows, a shark cruising for prey. The car pulled away but not before he spilled his dinner across the sidewalk.

"I have to develop street radar and trust my instincts, right?" He caught himself. "I guess I could say that about a lot of things right now. No matter how much it hurts, my old life ain't coming back."

I dropped Nachae off at his whitewashed two-story apartment complex on a narrow and ill-lit street and watched as he peered about and limped to the sidewalk and passed through the security gate and shook it to make sure it was locked. I drove back through shadowed streets to I-40 and nosed my car away from the yellow luminescent glow of this city, west into the desert and the jagged El Malpais lava fields. The highway unfolded as a narrow band of lights undulating into the night. Hours later I exited at Gallup and drove north into an ink of darkness, back through the looking glass into the Navajo Nation.

CHAPTER EIGHT

Nothing this December was easily explained about this team, no win easily come by, its balance as precarious as a tightrope walker with a case of the shakes. The day after the Wildcats executed a beatdown on Fountain Hills, they met their cousins from the San Carlos Apache reservation near Phoenix in the tournament finale. The Wildcats appeared lost, faltering, stumbling across the mesas.

Josiah passed when he should have shot, and drove to the hoop when he should have pitched to an open teammate. Angelo committed a silly foul and next time down court he forced an awkward shot as defenders swarmed him. Annoyance creased Mendoza's face, and he motioned to Angelo to take a seat. Chance Harvey, the lithe shooting guard who had attacked the Fountain Hill boys like a surgeon probing for a vein, floated about, a wandering ghost.

The San Carlos Apaches played with loose-limbed abandon,

juking, whipping the ball from the corner to the top of the key to the corner, until a player launched and hit an open shot. The Apache visitors loved nothing better than to beat the Navajo, and they opened a gaping lead. Mendoza tossed down every trick he knew and came up short, a cardsharp with pockets turned inside out.

Fans grew restless, grumbling: "*What the hell? Deee-fense! Wake up, boys! Wake up!*" Nearly five thousand Navajo had showed up to watch this cousin war, and no one was amused to watch San Carlos pull away. They yelled to Mendoza to put in their favorites; they demanded he give the hook to laggards.

C'mon, son. Use your brain! Remember your brain!?

Only Cooper Burbank saved the Wildcats from humiliation. As a final move, a desperate card toss, Mendoza counseled the sophomore to forgo his disciplined and too-deferential game. *Carry us, Cooper.* Slender and tall and with a stony expression that offered no window to the fires within, Burbank hit a three-pointer. Next time up the court, he drifted to the three-point line and gave every appearance of looking for the same shot and then quickly spun by his defender and took three dribbles to the hoop and put up a floater. Next he shoveled a pass to spindly Curtis Begay, the other sophomore, who nailed a moon-shot three-pointer.

Last year as a freshman stranger, a kid from the northern buttes, Cooper lingered hours after practice in that darkened arena, honing his shot, his drives, his pivots. The only other boy in that gym was Nachae, the senior captain, who practiced at the other end of the court. They were not particularly close—too far apart in age and too different in style and temperament. They simply shared an obsession, and they had respected each other for that.

The Wildcats rallied and pulled closer, but no matter how respectable the margin, in truth the game never really was in reach.

The Apaches had opened too great a wound. Mendoza was annoyed, angry that he had been forced to resort to hero ball, an ugly concession for which his basketball gods would demand compensation. "What's the matter with you?" he asked his players. "You must treat every game as a battle. Where is your urgency?" The players looked at the old man, faces impassive as stone friezes.

Two days later the teenagers rode hours south to Holbrook, past mammoth Triassic buttes and across the plains of sagebrush and yellow grasses. This was Mendoza's former coaching haunt, the place where he claimed his state championship. While he would not acknowledge the personal and emotional importance, everyone knew he greatly preferred not to lose here. The Wildcat attack remained ragged, but the boys hustled and talent won out this night. Angelo played defense on the perimeter and blocked shots and scored inside with artful steps, ending with twenty-one points. He was raging less and leading more. Elijah, Angelo's best friend and stoic shadow, stroked jump shots. The team's record stood at 4–3. Perhaps the keel had stabilized.

The geography of the reservation schedule reared up now and then and became an implacable, painful force. The Wildcats left Holbrook after the game and arrived back in Chinle at 1:00 a.m.; thirteen hours later their bus departed for a game in Tuba City, which lay three hours away on the western edge of that reservation. Beyond Tuba was the Painted Desert and beyond that the Grand Canyon and the San Francisco Peaks, the ancient boundary lines of the known world of Navajo.

Before embarking to Tuba City, I took my morning hike into Canyon de Chelly, and as I followed that switchback trail, I heard a clatter of insistent voices. A hundred pinyon jays, their coats a brilliant hue of blue-gray, descended in a chattering, chirping cloud, like washerwomen to a canyon stream. They followed me flapping and talking and hopping from pine to juniper to cliff ledge.

Then they doubled back up the trail in search of another walker to harangue.

Near the Anasazi ruins known as the White House, I spotted a black bear rooting around in the wash, and it crashed into the underbrush without a backward glance. I waved to Cecil Henry and his niece as they laid out their silverwork and jewelry on fold-out tables beneath an overarching cottonwood. The morning was balmy and we shed our jackets and took a few minutes to chat about the topsy-turvy fortunes of that maddening Chinle basket-ball team.

All of which was grand, except for the fact that winter air should carry a talon-sharp chill, and moon frost should form on the junipers, and birds should settle in their nests, and bears should have long ago slipped into their seasonal slumbers. Navajo Nation was a land of eternal thirst, caught between dry and withered. Of late though, it had pitched into a more profound drought. Temperatures rose and rose again, and the Chuskas remained red and green when they should expect to wear a coat of powdered white.

In summertime the heat had grown more oppressive, a dry hotness that suctioned dampness from the land and that already had caused thousands of piñon pines to wither. The die-off of those trees threatened another, as my brilliant blue and talkative companions, the pinyon jays, relied on the piñon seeds for sustenance. A desert ecosystem is exquisitely fragile. The Navajo wasted little time bemoaning drought; the Holy People give what they will and to accept good and bad and plenty and want was to define living in *Hózhó*.

Yet water was life, and that, too, was truth for a desert people. The Navajo intoned those three words, "Water is life," in prayers before meals, and Navajo teenagers spray-painted the words on the windmills that pulled up water from underground aquifers. I heard it on the lips of cattlemen and in the songs of schoolchildren who showered each morning at the Chinle Aquatic Center, as their homes were among the 30 percent of reservation residences that lacked running water.

The Navajo prayers for dampness were ancient and matter-of-fact:

> *With the near darkness made of the dark cloud, of the*
> *he-rain, of the dark mist and of the she-rain, come*
> *to us.*
> *With the darkness on the earth, come to us.*

The highway to Tuba City followed an ancient dogleg of a route, crossing northwest across high desert past the towns of Rough Rock and Sumac Spring before turning south. As though blown by a giant's breath, winds rocked my car and spun red sand off the desert floor, dervishes rising to greet the cerulean sky.

This was a blood-soaked land. The Spanish conquistadors infiltrated along old burro trails trundling guns and blankets and supplies and took many thousands of native as slaves, Navajo and Utes and Hopi. The Spaniards drew few distinctions between tribes. It was estimated that by the early 1800s, more than 50 percent of Navajo families had lost a family member to slavery. The Navajo and other native peoples took slaves as well from rival tribes, although far fewer.

In the 1860s American troops galloped through to round up stray bands of Navajo and send them marching off into the New

Mexican desert to join Barboncito and the Canyon de Chelly bands. Thousands of Navajo lived in these lands, but nearly all faded into distant gorges and hid atop mesas or took up residence on ledges beneath the lips of the Grand Canyon. The baffled generals reported that they could find no Navajo. When Barboncito and his people returned, the invisibles emerged to reclaim their land.

The last long, straight stretch of road toward Tuba City skirted isolated farms and decrepit trailers, and to the east the steep flanks of the bear-paw shaped Black Mesa, Dziłíjiin, home to Navajo and Hopi. Thirty thousand Navajo lived up there alongside twelve thousand Hopi. The Hopi built the oldest of their villages on that mesa before William the Conqueror invaded England. Its forest and ravines harbored elk and mule deer and coyotes the size of small wolves. Veins of coal ran through its stone heart and gave Black Mesa its name and its dark and glistening aspect.

Lust for that coal, the greatest such deposit in the nation, led to much pain. In the 1960s Peabody Coal executives and lawyers and lobbyists descended like desert gnats, double-dealing and promising grand and often illusory profits to Hopi and Navajo leaders. And coal and energy plant jobs offered jobs. Hundreds of native families lost their homes as coal hunger and the clear-cuts that followed made refugees of them. Worst of all was the slurry line that looped miles down off the mesa. It was akin to a giant garbage disposal, as Judith Nies explored in her fine book *Unreal City*, and Peabody kept it moving by pumping a billion gallons of water each year out of the Navajo aquifer.

The Black Mesa Navajo may not recover from this aquatic pilferage. Many wells have dried up, the clanking of metal pumps dragging up not so much as a splash of water. Studies of late have found the aquifer on Black Mesa shrinking at a rate that far exceeded the "scientific estimates" of Peabody. A grand and holy landscape is left shriveled and violated.

I passed through the sparsely populated hamlet of Rare Metals—named after another of the companies that tore up and infected this land—and my car crested a rise before descending into Tuba City. To the left I noticed a brilliant aquamarine pool of water, which called to mind an outdoor aquatic center. Tuba City was home to eight thousand people, and not designated for that foghorn of a brass instrument. Rather it was named in honor of Tuuvi, a long-dead Hopi headman who converted to Mormonism. The Navajo name for this place, To'Nanees'Dizi, meant "tangled waters" and referred to the groundwater that once ran clear and clean and allowed tribes to cultivate thousands of green acres of corn and squash and cotton.

I came to Tuba City early, well ahead of the team, and walked into a Denny's to meet Rita Bilagody. She was a purely formidable woman with a prominent forehead off of which flowed a handsome tangle of graying-to-white curls. Her eyes dominated her face, keen and piercing and questioning. She was cordial without a great effusion of warmth and introduced herself by way of her mother's and father's clans: Daughter of the Bitter Water Clan and of Red Running in Water Clan. I had sought her out in hopes of a history lesson, as she had fought a lifetime of battles to preserve land and water in this scorched realm. She was in her sixties and had grown up three miles away on the desert bluffs outside Tuba City, an inquisitive little girl who never tired of asking why. She was one of ten children, and she and her siblings sang in Navajo and danced at ceremonies and prayed their parents would find a way to scrape together enough food for three meals each day.

When Rita and her siblings turned six years old, their parents packed them off to Utah to live with white families during the school year. That was not the Bureau of Indian Affairs wresting native urchins from the arms of their parents; it was a mother and father who made the heartrending decision to break a cycle of poverty and illiteracy. "My mother saw herself born of and living and dying in poverty, and she knew education was our only way out. She believed the people who said her children would live in a nice home and get clothes and go to school and that we would have enough to eat."

Rita got dipped in a well of Mormonism, baptized in that faith, living with Mormon families, attending Mormon schools. Some host families treated her well and some did not. One white mother, exhausted by her brood of twelve children, yelled incessantly at Rita, as though this little child were her breaking point. "No one spoke Navajo to me. By the time I came home each summer, I could no longer speak to my dad or my mom."

She spent summers regaining her balance in the Navajo language before returning the next autumn to live with another Mormon family. The dislocation exhausted her; her insecurities became an electrified wire. Why did last year's family not take me back? Did they not like me? Did I say something wrong? Is it because I am brown and ugly?

Through it all, she never balked at boarding the bus to Utah. She had inherited from her mother a near mystical belief in the power of education and felt an ache to read and write and do math.

She graduated near the top of her high school class in Utah and was accepted to Brigham Young University, a Navajo scholar with a tribal scholarship. She would become a lawyer and specialize in land rights. She would become a journalist and expose injustice. She met a native man and fell in love and got pregnant, and soon she was back living in Tuba City with toddlers at her feet as dreams wafted off on desert winds.

"I was young and stupid. If there is a single thing I regret most in life it's that I got married." She peered over her glasses at me. "I'm not with that man anymore, as you probably can guess."

She lived as her mother did before her, in a tarpaper shack, tacking plastic over the windows in winter and laying tires on the roof to keep it from peeling off in a gale. She worked as an optician, grinding lenses. Things fell apart. Too few customers could afford to pay, and she was reluctant to demand payment from her people, so her debts metastasized and she became depressed and began to drink. Darkness folded in. Activism, her sense of outrage at her own powerlessness and that of too many Navajo, pulled Rita out of her despondency. Too often she had seen her own government officials sweet-talk her people and push insider deals upon them. The Navajo's relationship with their government is fraught and haunted by whispers of petty corruption and double-dealing. You want land lots for your children? Get elected as a chapter house president or top official. You want to work at the casino? Get to know a Navajo council delegate and do her a favor. You want to become a school principal, a coach, an aquatic center director? Get the backing from the right politicians, the right clans.

The Navajo government, backed by powerful white gaming companies, twice put the question of tribal casinos to a vote, and twice Navajo voters rejected those proposals in the 1990s. The gambler was a feared figure in Navajo mythology, the son of the spirit of the sun who had left people starving in that time before written history. Gambling advocates persisted, and in a third vote in 2004, Navajo voters finally approved a casinos referendum. The reservation now had four casinos on its border edges. Navajo, rather than deep-pocketed white tourists, most often fill these gleaming halls, working-class and poor women and men tossing away dollar bills on dice tosses and yanks on aptly named one-armed bandits.

R. Lamar Whitmer was another sweet-talking white man, a sandy-haired developer from Scottsdale who in 2009 approached the Navajo government with a can't-miss deal. Out in the mesquite scrubland by the confluence of the Colorado and Little Colorado Rivers, where a turquoise river rolled into the Grand Canyon, he proposed to build a 420-acre resort, a Taj Mahal known as the Grand Canyon Escalade.

Whitmer's vision was grand: hotels, food pavilions, an RV park, and entertainment lawns for concerts, artist studios, and lots of boutiques. When he finished building, a tourist would think she was strolling through Fashion Square in Scottsdale. The intended genius stroke, his pièce de résistance, would be a 1.6-mile gondola tramway running from the Grand Canyon rim to floor, a drop of 3,200 feet and hundreds of millions of years of geologic strata. The tramway could deposit ten thousand tourists daily on the shores of America's most ecologically sensitive river and a holy site for native tribes. There, by the banks of the Colorado River, tourists would find an amphitheater, a restaurant, and lots of bathrooms.

Whitmer added conditions; the impolite might call these demands. He would require the Navajo Nation to guarantee $65 million to pay for a highway to his resort and for the accompanying electric and water lines. If the Navajo Nation failed to provide that money, Whitmer would find his own financing and the Navajo Nation would cover his interest payments plus 10 percent.

No Navajo businesswoman or -man would be allowed to build within fifteen miles of his project. The resort would pay no taxes to the Navajo Nation and it would draw daily on hundreds of thousands of gallons of water from the nation's aquifer.

Rita recalled the moment she read about these plans. She sat in her one-room house and stirred her coffee and read the paper and she could feel her mouth falling agape. It was that eternal and outrageous theater of the absurd in which Anglo developers talked fast and promised riches. "He's asking us to pay him sixty-five million? Are you kidding me? There are a thousand red flags flapping. He must think we were a bunch of dumb Indians."

Rita had visited that sacred confluence as a child. Her grandfather loaded Rita and her brothers and sisters into the well of a pickup truck and drove across that harsh land, with javelinas and rattlesnakes and potholes big as washbasins. Tread lightly, he told his children. This was a sacred land where the Hopi Holy People emerged into this world; the spirits of ancestral Navajo resided here. Medicine men and women came to collect their herbs for their most sacred ceremonies, and holy winds blew mysterious and powerful. Her grandfather worried that magic swirled too powerfully and dangerously, and he would not let the children stand at the precise confluence. "This was land inherent," Rita said. "To build here would be to violate everything essential to us."

Whitmer enlisted a Navajo sponsor and the president of the Navajo Nation spoke highly of his project. A promise of jobs on this hardscrabble reservation held appeal, and he had figured out every angle, except for stubborn women.

Navajo society was beset with contradictory crosscurrents. Politics were irreducibly patriarchal. No female has been elected president, and the reservation's Big Men swaggered. A former president used to insist on having a few seats reserved courtside for him and his entourage in the Wildcat Den. Liquor and despair led too many men to strike too many women. Yet Navajo culture was matrilineal, with descent traced through the mother's family. After a wedding, a husband most often moved near his wife's family and remained there throughout his life. Women worked the steadiest jobs, balanced the checkbooks, and rarely held their tongues.

Rita and other Navajo women in Tuba, in Page, in Flagstaff,

mapped a strategy and wrote long letters to the wonderfully contentious pages of the *Navajo Times*. They lobbied medicine men and women and talked of the damage this development would do to holy lands, and those associations voted to oppose it. They forged alliances with sheepherders and farmers and the famous World War II Code Talkers, elderly veterans who commanded deep respect. Younger Navajo women helped form Save the Confluence, a marriage of Navajo and Anglo environmentalists.

Jealousies and rivalries arose, Rita acknowledged that. But the women were strong enough to set those aside. Speed was essential: Navajo had to understand this was not another greased inside job.

Rita took charge of the petition drive and traveled across the Navajo Nation week after week, rattling drives down washboard dirt roads to flea markets in Dilkon and Greasewood, into the world of Black Mesa, and through the northern desert to Mexican Hat and up and over the Chuskas to Shiprock. She drove through sandstorms that descended like curtains; she set up her little card table at a Rough Rock rodeo when the temperature hit 99 degrees and moisture beaded on her forehead and her face turned red; she drove to the Chinle Christmas market in subzero temperatures. Navajo would gather around her table and she would answer their questions and ask a few of her own.

Do you know how many electric lines we could put up with $65 million? How many roads we could pave and fix with that money? How many college scholarships we could fund for our children? Let me tell you of our ancestors' spirits who walk this land. Are we going to respond as warriors? She and the other women netted eighty-six thousand signatures, on paper and online, roughly half the population of the reservation.

The developers, she said, flaunted mastery of bonds and loans, a financier's argot. So the women obtained Whitmer's four-inch-thick master plan and passed it around and read and underlined sentences and scribbled notes in the margins. Rita memorized near every line. The developers had enough self-awareness to feel a creep of nerves, and they thought it was wise to ask of these women, What do you need to make a deal?

The Navajo women shook their heads. No price. We will beat you.

Whitmer's development team averted their eyes when they saw Rita. And she learned to smile without a glint of humor. You wanted a battle? "We will give it back to you ten times over again."

One by one the Navajo chapter houses took up debate, and arguments erupted like lava pouring from a mountain's gullet, cousin against cousin, auntie against uncle. The desire for jobs in a land with crushing unemployment collided with the urgency of preserving a sacred heritage. In the end, every chapter house voted against the proposal. In November 2017 the Navajo Nation Council in Window Rock took up the question. Seven years earlier, council passage had appeared the merest formality. The proposed project lost by a vote of 16–2.

Whitmer took a front-row seat in the Navajo council chambers. The vote finished, he stood and stared at the council delegate who, along with Rita and all those women, had crafted the demise of his project. He appeared to scratch his ear; he was in fact giving his opponents the middle finger like a clever middle-school child.

Before the developer could get into his SUV, before he could drive back to the Valley of the Sun, Rita walked over to him and made sure her eyes caught his like flies stuck in ointment. She expected he would try again. Powerful white men rarely accepted defeat with grace. "You've gotten a taste of what we can do," she told him. "We'll do it again."

Weeks passed and Rita and her fellow activists climbed into the bay of a pickup and traveled out to the confluence, bouncing and jostling until the truck heaved to a stop. Rita was in her seventh decade, and she climbed out sore as a cowpoke. She walked to the canyon's lip and saw a world open beneath her feet, the grandest cathedral nature could conceive. She felt her head grow light and her body heave with emotion.

"Even now I have no words to describe it. That's very rare for me to have no words."

We paid our bill at Denny's and drove to Rita's home along a road sandy as the Sahara, careful to drive in the middle lest we slide sideways into those fine white drifts. We passed the home where her nephew and his wife lived. He pursued a PhD, and his wife was a doctor, and they tied a GO PENN STATE banner to their sheep fence.

Rita's plot sat near the top of a hill amid four or five cars in states of disrepair. Last year she gave her trailer to her daughter and son-in-law and toddler grandchild and ran a thick electrical line from the trailer to the prefab shack that functions as her home. Rita's shack has running water, but great quantities of the ground-water here, 770 million gallons, were contaminated with uranium, molybdenum, and selenium. And while she bathed and used water for her dishes, she never ever drank it.

What about that handsome blue pool I spotted north of Tuba? Was that a community pool? She could not help laughing at my foolishness. To dive into that pool would have been to assure my skin fell off in sheets. It was built on the site of a Cold War uranium mill, and it was a containing pool for radioactive isotopes— and those will cool in another few millennia. Periodically the federal government tacked signs on the doors of hundreds of nearby homes advising Navajo that the radioactivity in the ground-water was spiking.

Cancer settled like a plague into the pores of this land. Last year one of Rita's sisters lost several feet of her colon to tumors. The previous week Rita accompanied another of her sisters to Flagstaff Medical Center, and they held hands as a doctor delivered her sister's test results. She had pancreatic cancer. That was a near invariably fatal diagnosis, and the sisters locked arms and held each other's heads and rocked in their sorrow.

So why, I asked, do you live . . .

Rita knew the direction in which my question was headed and she did not wave it off as foolishness. She invited me to walk up the rise behind the house. We climbed atop a red boulder that was a natural crow's nest and she pointed to where her land ran toward the lip of a canyon. "Those are the houses of aunties, uncles, great-granddad, a few cousins." She pointed to the southwest, where land and sky met in a marriage of dreamy blue haze, the snow-capped San Francisco Peaks rising as spikes into a cloudless sky. "Those are the westernmost of the sacred peaks of Navajo."

"This land swims in my veins. It's our sacred place and all we have. No one can push us off it."

We said our goodbyes and Rita imparted a last steely order: "There's one more place you must see." She scrawled a map on a yellow pad with lots of jots and lefts and rights and I waved to her and maneuvered my car west along sand tracks that yielded to rutted dirt that yielded to bedded sandstone. I bounced a few hundred yards more, as though descending a marble staircase, and then surrendered and pulled over and parked. I walked the last mile across sand and schist that glittered as if the land had been seeded with diamonds. I reached the edge of a crumbling scarp, and hundreds of feet below, a jumbled pile of red sandstone boulders called to mind the tantrum-tossed blocks of a giant child.

The Painted Desert rolled outward for hundreds of miles, glistening and sun-scorched.

The sun dangled above the horizon, a fireball. Far to the west I could make out the blue ridges and blue cones of the Grand Canyon and the evening mist that found solace in its crevices. Out there was that mystical confluence where the land split and fell away.

I spread my arms, palms turned outward, and closed my eyes and felt the caress of evening currents wash over me. I advised my chattering mind to sit a while in this silence and concentrated on the rise and fall of my breath. I was a cistern filling. I opened my eyes and turned and walked back toward my car and drove across that scarred and beautiful land to Tuba City, where those sometimes-confounding Navajo teenagers from Chinle played a basketball game that night.

CHAPTER NINE

Christmas came and on a balmy late-December morning the Wildcat players climbed onto their bus and rode south to a holiday tournament in Pinetop, at the edge of the White Mountain Apache Reservation. Hours passed and the boys watched as red buttes and magenta escarpments and the arid sweep of their land slid away to be replaced by streams and forests that grew thick and deep and curled like beards around mountain peaks.

Decades ago Mendoza's life journey had taken him to these Apache lands, where he worked as a counselor and achieved another measure of coaching fame. These tribes are ancient kin and they are familiar and strange to one another. Millennia ago, when the Athabascan people journeyed south from arctic lands, some wended their way to what is now eastern New Mexico, southern Arizona, Texas, and Oklahoma. Over the centuries, these bands fused into the Ndee, the loose-knit people known as the Apache. They became the fiercest of warriors and held tight to their bloody reputation until the cusp of the twentieth century. The White Mountain Apache did not live dispersed in far-flung corners like the Navajo, preferring towns and villages bunched near the yawning cut in the earth known as the Salt River Canyon.

Other bands settled to the north across New Mexico, Utah, Colorado, and Arizona and they became known as the Diné, the Navajo. They, too, were formidable warriors. But unlike the Apache, they became farmers and herders of sheep. Sheep occupy a place in the Navajo soul without analogy in that of the Apache. (Traditional Navajo say, "With our sheep we were created, and this is why, when they are killed without need, we weep and mourn.")

The tournament offered a gauntlet of five games in three days and promised a showdown between the Wildcats and the Alchesay High School Falcons, the most formidable of the Apache basketball powers this year. The prospect of a battle with their kinsmen was already on the minds of the Wildcat players.

A few days earlier I sat in the bleachers in Chinle and talked with Chance, the Wildcats' defensive stopper and a slashing scorer. He was a handsome teenager with baby-soft skin and black hair flecked with premonitions of gray and glistening eyes that were catnip for the teenage girls who checked him out in the hallways and flirted on game nights and congregated on his Facebook page. We talked a long while of college dreams and his family's horses and his upcoming trip to Monument Valley in January to purchase a new mustang that he would race bareback this summer. Then he fell silent and after a while he told me this week held special meaning for him.

Why is that?

"It is anniversary of my father's death."

We sat with that a while and I asked what happened. He told me it was years ago and there was a crash, but Chance would walk no further down memory's path. This was a precarious time, as the Holy People slumbered in winter and could provide no succor to their children if they stumbled. He knew the importance of protection. "When I play the Apaches, I pray and roll bitterroot in my playing sock to protect myself."

The cosmology of this high-desert tribe and its beliefs was tangible and viscous and defined by polarities of male and female and sun and earth and a search for balance. All in this world was kin and all possessed soul—bears, lizards, rocks, soil, deer, canyons, sky, sun. All were Diné. The Navajo were a thread in this quilt of collective consciousness, the *diné bila' ashdla'i*, the five-fingered Diné. To insist that life was about material reality alone was to place a hand over an eye: You saw half of what was there.

Precautions were taken. So Shaun Martin, the athletic director, brought in a medicine man earlier this past autumn to conduct a ceremony to bless the Wildcat Den, which was built to reflect symmetry with the four sacred Navajo peaks.

The Wildcat boys won two of their first three games in this tournament, pushing their record to 7–5. Then they faced off against a team from Florence, a town of thirty thousand that lay southeast of Phoenix where exurbs meet sun-blasted desert. Its eight federal and state prisons made a company town of Florence, and its players came rawboned and tough. Mendoza assigned Chance to cover Florence's six-foot-four point guard, a rangy black kid with quicksilver moves and brilliant hops and a mountainous Afro. Chance gave away six inches and frowned, dubious. Mendoza offered Chance a faint measure of encouragement.

"The kid's a brother and he can jump. Stick with him and guard his kneecaps."

As happened so often, the Navajo boys were at their most cohesive and determined when facing a non-Navajo team. Chance was fleet of foot and competitive and kept his body between this teen-ager and the basket, hands darting and pecking at his dribble, flash-ing a grin as his opponent grew irritated. Chance held this talented player under his scoring average. Cooper remained a scoring stal-wart for the Wildcats, edging into the gullies between those broad bodies from Florence and discovering space to fire off his jumpers. He hit a layup as the Florence boys slammed against him, and he tumbled like a wayward top. Angelo used footwork to dance around Florence's six-foot-six, 225-pound center. Perhaps more surprising, given his diffident early-season wanderings, Angelo showed glimpses of becoming a floor leader. When Elijah let his attention wander on court, Angelo clapped in his face. He yelled encourage-ment to Chance and hit Cooper with one sharp pass after another. Angelo's senior teammates noticed when he and Cooper exchanged slaps of the palm as they walked off the court. The big man's taste for melodrama appeared as a tide receding, and he asked out of games far less often than he had in the past. Perhaps those one-on-one sessions with Mendoza's office had an effect.

"Way to go, 'Shlow. Way to go."

Mendoza entered the locker room clapping and calling out to his man-child center. Florence was big and good but not as good as they thought they were. The Wildcat season was a month old and the coach divined signs his team might yet become a better version of itself. Sleep well tonight. Don't stay up talking. Get ready for Alchesay.

"Be ready to go play your Apache cousins. Mañana at high noon!"

Mendoza and the coaches and the players awoke early the next morning and crowded into a hotel room that Will, a senior, shared with two freshman players. Reservation trailers are drafty boxes, and in midwinter, true warmth is an elusive shadow. Before Will jumped into bed the previous night, he had set the room's temperature at 97 degrees, leaving windows fogged and bathroom mirrors dripping with condensation. Mendoza walked in and staggered backward and looked around, frowning.

"It's like the Yucatán in here."

Will jumped up and lowered the temperature.

The boys listened carefully as Mendoza laid out the game plan against the Apaches. "Don't try to run with Alchesay, and don't get into a shootout. Chase their shooters off the three-point line and keep moving the ball. Find the seams and you'll win." The coach looked at Dewayne, whom he'd once accused of being unable to guard a garbage can and who, of late, had shed his tentativeness like an unwanted sweater. Mendoza nodded at him. "You're my jack-of-all-trades, a shooter, a point guard, and you're playing tough defense. I guess you could say I'm happy."

That was a startling compliment in Mendoza-speak. Dewayne allowed himself a smile and Angelo, sprawled on the rug, raised himself up on his elbows and smiled sardonically. Angelo said loudly, "I guess you can guard a garbage can now, Dewayne."

Even Mendoza flickered a smile.

The coach turned to Josiah. "You're concentrating on defense and setting up his teammates rather than taking those wild drives to the hoop. This is your team. You've earned it. Don't be afraid—don't back down to the Apaches." Josiah nodded, legs vibrating.

"Throughout the school year, you take tests. This is a test today. Are we ready? Can we do it? Believe in yourselves."

An hour before game time, the boys gathered in the locker room at Pinetop. Some walked into the bathroom stalls and one retched. The rest bounced on the balls of their feet and sang along with the Black Eyed Peas.

Time to go. Beau Natay, a twenty-nine-year-old assistant coach and former Wildcat star, reached into his leather jacket and drew a rawhide pouch filled with corn pollen, *tádidíin,* made of tassels of corn, which holy teachings dictate that only a woman should collect. The ground pollen put Navajo in touch with the Holy People and offered safety when their path became precarious, crossing the trail of a coyote or a tough native team. Beau held the pouch out and the boys filed by and dipped index fingers and sprinkled the power on heads and shoulders. A few put a taste of the powder on their tongue.

Only Cooper, an evangelical Christian, and Will, a Mormon, declined to dip their fingers.

Mendoza packed his black game bag with his back turned to Beau and betrayed no sign he had seen the pouch. He disliked the intrusion of magic into his locker rooms, seeing in pouches and herbs the opening of doors to fear and doubt and to division between Christian and Traditional players. He did not view magic and the immaterial as superstitious nonsense. Not at all. These worked all too well and should be kept at arms' length, and he would broach that most sensitive of subjects with the boys another day.

The Wildcat players whispered to me about the Apaches, whom they saw as experts at the magic arts and whose medicine men were known to stand in the bleachers and cast spells of confusion. Last season, they said, the medicine men targeted Nick Begay, the Wildcat point guard, who grew exhausted, his head swirling during the game. On the bus back to Chinle that night, he was wracked by trembles and fever, and the bus driver nearly detoured to take Nick to the hospital.

Every player on this year's team knew Nick's story. It was worth noting that the Apache players were no less wary of Navajo magic and fortified themselves with their own herbs. Kyle Goklish, the Apache coach and a former star player under Mendoza, shrugged. "Everyone fears everyone when Apache and Navajo meet."

The Wildcat boys sprinted onto the floor between bleachers that rose steep as canyon walls and were packed with Apaches and Navajo, who greeted them with a din of competing chants and foot stomps. Little brothers and sisters and cousins scampered to hug the players. The Wildcat boys affected insouciance, taking warm-up shots and layups without a backward glance at the Apache team.

The Wildcats could not fool themselves. They wore anxiety like a necklace.

Alchesay was undefeated at 15–0, and its leader and top scorer was Harley Upton Jr., a six-foot-three senior with a sinuous black braid of hair that extended to the small of his back. He was a Traditional, as those who follow the ancient beliefs were called. The buzzer sounded—time for the pregame handshakes. Not a single Navajo or Apache extended a hand to the other. They feared that medicine men had put magic potions into the palms of hands to transmit spells through handshakes.

The boys carefully raised and bumped forearms with each other, hands untouched.

The day before that game with the Apaches, Mendoza and I met for eggs and bacon in the Apache casino restaurant. It was just past dawn, and sunlight trickled like rivulets of water through the pines as a procession of cooks, waitstaff, former students, and parents walked to the table and paid respects to Mendoza.

They shook his hand and recalled his good works with their sons and daughters, his renown as counselor having matched that of his work as a coach. Mendoza remembered some of their faces and names and swapped memories and stories and asked after families. When he could not recall others, he amiably faked it. He leaned in toward me and smiled wryly: "Not everyone was so friendly when I left." Mendoza's teams won season after season when he was in Alchesay, but his teams did not grab a state championship, and jealousies and resentment bubbled up like geysers over politics and playing time. A councilman grew furious with him, as did a powerful medicine woman whose son was on his team and remained too often on the bench.

To counsel and coach the White Mountains at that time was to feel darkness enveloping. The Apaches had experienced a great rash of teenage suicides, and booze, pot, meth, and crack inhabited the land and its children. Mendoza found his stride in that moment, fortified by temperament and his feel for the immaterial. His Tohono O'odham were a desert people who understood magic, and he had wandered that wilderness and inculcated its ways. When his Apache kids began to knock on the door to his office, when they stammered and talked of pain and bewitchments, he nodded.

He had watched the pupils of an assistant coach in the White Mountains roll back in his head during a game, a sign that the man's astral self was roaming far afield. Another night his Apaches played a Hopi team on Black Mesa. The Hopi were the most ancient of the Pueblo people, and all tribes respected their understanding of the unseen. Mendoza's players played in a delirium that night, arms and legs weighted as though by iron bars. Mendoza kept shaking his head and drinking water, feeling so sluggish. His players whispered to him that they saw a cloud hanging over the court. After his team lost, a friend told Mendoza that the Hopi medicine men had burned sprigs of snake weed in the locker rooms and concealed magic dolls, kachinas, in the four corners of the arena. Then those men stood high in the stands and chanted softly throughout the game.

Another season his best player began to drink and smoke pot. The boy's mother knocked on Mendoza's office door at school, distraught, imploring him to help. Mendoza called the boy into his office. What is bothering you? The boy turned his face away and refused to make eye contact. So they sat there, and Mendoza talked of his own boyhood struggles and days when he feared he was lost forever.

Finally the teenager spoke.

"Three shadows follow me. They follow me to school and to home. They never leave me alone."

"Tell me," Mendoza said, "about those shadows."

"Remember that game where I did so bad?" the boy said. "One shadow is tall and stands by the basket and swats the ball away. A short one stops my passes. The middle one makes me so anxious my skin feels on fire. Now it wants me to kill myself, and I can't take it anymore." Mendoza summoned an Apache dancer to purify the gym and took that teenager for walks, and they read biblical verse, talking over hours and days. Slowly the shadows slipped away.

Traditional beliefs become sun-faded in an internet age; some boys know only fragments of their cosmology. But belief in the unseen permeated life in a way I have witnessed in few communities.

Mendoza was a member of the Assemblies of God, a fundamentalist variant that holds the Bible as inerrant, God real, Heaven glorious, and Hell eternal. It was a faith hard-edged enough to survive in the crucible of his southern desert. His beliefs made some natives uneasy. Who was he to talk to a medicine woman's son?

I asked Mendoza if he worried about the perception that he was trespassing as a Christian, and he nodded. He knew he walked a tenuous road. But belief in the power of magic was profound, and if he was going to banish firewalkers and dark spirits, he had to engage. He accepted that reality. When he visited a witch's house in Alchesay, Apache friends told him they saw black-winged figures rise over his truck. More mysterious still was Mendoza's account of a trip he took one night after a game.

That night was ice-tinged and moonless and he kept his eyes fixed on the road. As if conjured of darkness, an alabaster owl swooped down, wings spread and talons extended, toward the windshield of his pickup truck. Mendoza flinched and braced for impact. The owl rose as if sucked upward into the night sky. Mendoza looked in his rearview mirror and saw it loop down again toward the roadbed. Mendoza's daughter Veronica followed in her car this night in the White Mountains. She saw that white owl curl over the top of her father's truck and descend in a blink. Its talons touched asphalt and it shape-shifted.

An alabaster man bolted into the frigid forest.

Father and daughter have talked of that night with no hint of self-consciousness. Theirs was not a campfire story; they drank no alcohol and they did not try to persuade. They simply knew what they saw. The immaterial was immanent in that land. "The owl is a symbol of death," Mendoza said. "The witches were angry at me."

So the question arose: Had such encounters rattled him? Was he scared? He shook his head.

"You can't walk through life frightened."

Mendoza tried now and then to persuade me to accept the balm of evangelical Christianity. I traveled to Chinle the summer before the season began and late one night, as we sat in a Laundromat watching the spin cycle, his pitch grew more insistent. If I died without admitting Jesus and God into my life, I could be lost for eternity. Perhaps I would like to read the Gospel with him. Perhaps I would like to attend a men's group at the church in Kayenta. I felt a twist of concern and wondered if this presaged months of evangelizing. I told myself to stanch my worries and appreciate the attempted intervention. We enjoyed each other's company and he wanted to save my eternal soul. If his beliefs were mine, I would do the same.

I was not an atheist, I told him, but my beliefs were an unmade bed and I needed to walk my own path. He smiled and let it be.

The Wildcat players knew Mendoza was a Christian, although belief was a porous membrane on a reservation where many families mixed the practices of Traditional, Christian, and the peyote-infused Native American Church. The Navajo was a pragmatic and acquiring tribe, and so they accreted cultural and religious rituals.

Nachae Nez recalled a game against a fierce rival last year. He sat on the Wildcats bench before the game, his head lowered, girding for the struggle. He felt fingers run across his scalp, and when he spun around, he saw an older man with a not-so-friendly grin disappear into the crowd. His scalp began to burn as though fire ants were racing back and forth. Mendoza saw all this and quickly walked over to Nachae and muttered a few words and brushed the hex off his head. Other boys reported similar experiences.

"He doesn't practice Traditional, but Mendoza sees and believes," Nachae said.

The taproot of the immaterial runs deep here. Before the holiday tournament, I drove to visit sophomore Curtis Begay's family, who lived in mesa- and canyon-carved land northwest of Rough Rock. His father, Vernon, was an accomplished rodeo bull rider with the shiny championship buckles to prove it. His wife,

Jodonna, was a first-grade teacher; he worked at the hospital in Chinle and recently built with his own hands a handsome two-story home on their isolated land. Vernon and I stepped outside and walked past their horse and sheep pens. The great prow of Black Mesa rose out of the desert behind us.

A few winters ago, Vernon told me, a blizzard blew down upon them. The house was not yet finished, so he grabbed his wife and children and they huddled in their hogan as winds ripped out of the mountains and barreled across the desert and rattled the walls. He stoked the woodstove and Jodonna prepared a soup and then they heard it: footsteps on the roof. This was impossible, a trick of sound; no person or animal could stand up there as snow fell blinding and slantwise.

They heard the footsteps again.

The children began to whimper. Vernon slipped on coat and boots and leather gloves and hat and scarf and picked up his shotgun. He was a hunter, a good shot and comfortable in the skin of this lonely country. He pushed against the door and stepped squinting and bent into the maw of the storm, peering here and there. He saw a shadowed and hunched two-legged figure slide off the roof and fall six feet to the ground.

Thump.

He shouted as the creature took six, seven, eight bounding steps, animal-like, and disappeared into swirling whiteness. Vernon told me this story much as Mendoza spoke of the alabaster owl, not in hope of eliciting a shiver of fear. Some Navajo had become jealous of his success in life and whispered that he was undeserving and prideful; hexes and such creatures were to be expected. That was his life and it happened.

There are more such tales, arising unexpected, in conversation and casual chats. One evening, Nachae and his father, Felix, drove home from Many Farms along a dirt track that ran south of Sheep Dip Canyon through shrub and piñon and patches of bare rock. A hundred yards ahead they saw a great figure, twice the size of a man, with fur and feathers, and it crossed the road in three strides.

Nachae looked at his father. "What was that?"

Felix was a college-educated man who has passed many hours driving and walking remote corners of his land to work with Navajo sheep farmers on developing better strains of wool and meat. He had heard tales and seen mysteries. He looked at his son and shook his head.

"Better not to talk of this. Let's get home."

A final such story: My tour guide at Canyon de Chelly, Ben, told of driving to a fire dance in the company of his nephew, a Chicago-educated medical doctor and a student of Traditional belief. The dance was intended to restore a sick woman to health and to spread fertility in a land left fallow by drought. Ben and his nephew poked around unmarked roads until they found a sacred enclosure built of juniper and cedar. A great bonfire leaped and crackled, and medicine men gathered around with many other Navajo chanting and singing and dancing. Ben recalled that the air felt electric, as though atoms had been set to dancing. The medicine men placed eagle feathers around the fire.

Then those feathers rose up and moved about the fire.

"I looked with my own eyes, and those feathers stood and danced with the dancers," Ben recalled. "All these years I heard about the fire dance, and you never really see something like this. But I saw it with my eyes, as did my sisters." I talked with his siblings and they told the same story.

I understand what is problematic about subjective accounts and how eye and imagination can bewitch. I have talked with Richard Dawkins, the evolutionary biologist, and listened to Sam Harris, a neuroscientist, both thoroughgoing atheists and devotees of Western rationality. They see in such beliefs and talk a vestige of a time of enchantment and magic, an encampment from which rational man long ago escaped, and thank goodness for that.

I sought the counsel of Robert McPherson, that white-haired Anglo historian in Blanding, Utah. He had bounced across many back roads to attend Navajo ceremonies and funerals and marriages and seen hints and signs outright of phenomena that defied rational explanation. More than once, Navajo friends told him of conversations with a dead grandparent, a passed uncle, much as we would recall a chat with a neighbor.

McPherson is a man formed by Western culture and science. He would not, however, deny the reality of what he had heard and seen. He once asked a medicine man: Why does it so often seem that only the Navajo have a direct experience of these realms?

Think of shortwave radio, the medicine man replied. Anglos are on one frequency. Tune in a different channel and you see a different reality.

Days later I got to talking with Josie Tsosie, the sophomore team manager, and she was the full and complex spin of a Navajo. She embraced Traditional belief and country music and danced a cowboy two-step. When she felt surges of anxiety, she found peace by listening to Beethoven. She told me her grandfather was a medicine man and well read. She asked if I would like to talk with him. I nodded, yes, please.

The call from Josie came a few days later. I was to meet her grandfather the medicine man at the Burger King in Chinle on Sunday afternoon. I walked into the fast-food joint and found a cowboy gentleman with blue jeans and a handsome suede vest over

Raul Mendoza, married to a Navajo but not quite Navajo, coolly professorial before a game.

Raul Mendoza rarely stomps, and even more rarely yells during a game. But his raptor-like gaze misses little . . .

Chinle is not a pleasant place, an administrative center and town of three thousand, with a few diners and Laundromats and a supermarket. The nearest theater is an hour's drive away and shows a single movie that changes with the seasons.

The Navajo Nation, a reservation the size of West Virginia, is a place of primeval buttes and mesas and winds that can rock a team bus like a baby in a cradle.

Homes and a hogan, the traditional eight-sided Navajo home, set against a white-limestone and red-rock mesa.

They are everywhere, the feral wild horses of the rez, nibbling at grass in Chinle, cantering through Canyon de Chelly and standing astride back roads.

Cooper honing that metronomic jumper as his little brothers rebound the ball outside of his family's home in Rock Point in the red mesa lands north of Chinle.
(Caitlin O'Hara)

Angelo Lewis—'Shlow—the Wildcat man-child and all-league center, walks to the floor before the game.

Wildcat warm-up during the 2016–2017 season, with (*left to right*) Elijah Lewis, team captain Nachae Nez and Dewayne Tom.

Canyon de Chelly, the grandest and most holy of the great Navajo gorges, inhabited by native Americans since the time of ancient Athens.

Game time! (*Left to right:*) Coach Raul Mendoza and assistant coaches Beau Natay and Ned Curley.

In the moments before a game, tensions rising, Wildcat players meet alone for a final exhortation.

Chinle flea market, hay and horses and endless horizons beneath an azure sky.

a flower-print shirt, a new bandanna knotted just so around his neck. He had a Stetson cowboy hat and finely wrought boots with silver spurs.

Her grandfather had dark strong eyebrows that defined a handsome face, and he introduced himself as of the Red House People Clan, his mother's people. "My name," he added with a trace of a smile, "is Valentino Domingo, and, yes, that speaks to something beyond Navajo clans." We retreated to a corner table at a distant remove from Whoppers to talk realms of mystery.

Domingo insisted on calling himself an apprentice medicine man. There was no fixed endpoint to his studies, which stretched into valleys of culture and history and botany. Ceremonies like the Blessing Way, Fire Way, Protection Way, Enemy Way, could extend to five, nine, fifteen days, and consisted of words that must be understood and intuited and recited from memory with emotion and precision. Forget a line or a step and the patient would not heal, would not recover joy.

"I am freer to talk of our Holy People and their stories than I would be in summer, when all are awake and walking the earth. In the Anglo world, stories run linear. We Navajo locate ourselves in timelessness."

His teachers insisted that Domingo learned the precepts of Western medicine. A wise medicine man acknowledged that cancer treatment often relied on radiation or surgery or chemotherapy. In which case you sought the correct song and incantation to shore up the immune system and bolster the spirit.

To question old practices, to turn your head to the side and think why and where it came from, was to learn. Nothing should be sung, no herb offered, without knowledge. "I notice that the Christian ways don't always question what they are taught and preach. I have to think about what I am told, and I have to ask questions about everything. I can't just say, 'I'm an Indian and I'll do the ceremony.'"

Domingo was raised in Greasewood, a town at the foot of a low-slung mesa. He came of age in a dense netting of family, riding bulls, and roping horses. Domingo wondered what had become of his biological father and, at the age of twelve, found him working at a barbershop in Window Rock. Domingo walked in and sat in a chair. No, he told the older man, I don't want a haircut. I'm your son and I want to find out who you are.

His father cast his eyes down, rattled. "He did not say, 'Oh, okay, I'm glad we met." Domingo laughed and waved his hand in a que será motion. "Let it go."

Domingo tried on religions like shirts. His parents were Catholics who came to embrace Pentecostalism. One day a Mennonite preacher asked young Domingo if he wanted to attend their summer camp. He asked his parents. Sure, go ahead, maybe it will do you some good. Domingo attended a Mormon-run boarding trade school in Utah, where he learned to weld metal and play football. He was a halfback and he bounced off tackles like a man of rubber. One day Brother Roger said to him: "Domingo, you've done very well. I think you're ready to lead our Mormon sacrament."

"Brother Roger," Domingo replied, "I will be honest with you. I'm only here because of the cheerleaders."

He became a rodeo cowboy. The money was good "and there were all those women . . ." Domingo saw no need to finish that thought. Always when he returned home he fell into conversation with his grandfather, who was a medicine man. "It was like putting a blanket over myself."

He married and became a steel man, another of those Navajo welders hanging from the side of skyscrapers in Chicago and Las Vegas. He lived in separate worlds connected by long drives through tunnels of nighttime darkness. Then he went to work for the Union Pacific Railroad, another well-trod path for Navajo. "My brothers were already working there, and they put a good word in for me."

Sometimes he drove to Gallup and hopped a freight train to a work site. Sometimes he nosed up through mountain passes to Oregon and Washington. All those road trips gave him time to read and think. He meditated on *hózhó*, the Navajo sense of balance in life, and learned to accept good and bad not as a referendum on his soul but as the turning of life's wheel.

Domingo was intrigued by origin of the Navajo's Traditional beliefs and the resemblance to those of Tibetan Buddhists and Siberian animists. Navajo, Tibetan, and indigenous Siberian tribes have no word in their languages for religion—from a Latin word that literally means "to bind back to God." Navajo spirituality was not rooted in the past. It was lived experience, *anima mundi*, a world soul inhabiting all.

As the anthropologist Gary Witherspoon put it, Traditional Navajo do not go looking for beauty. They try to generate within and project it onto the universe.

Navajo elders taught that the Diné emerged with the help of the Holy People between the four historic peaks. Domingo's readings took him in an iconoclastic direction that hewed closer to that of archaeologists and historians. To trace the Diné roots was to go back to Tibet and Siberia in high mountain valleys and along the forested coves of Lake Baikal.

Tibet has similar latitude to that of the Navajo land, twin altitudinous desert lands. The Tibetans have the mandala with openings to the north, south, east, and west, and the Navajo have those sacred peaks. The Diné wandered a thousand generations and ten thousand miles. Who was to say that when their ancestors, who navigated by and built their cosmologies around the stars, arrived in the southwest desert and peered at the sky, they did not feel themselves in a familiar land?

He peered at me, perhaps expecting a skeptical rejoinder. "I try not to get into arguments," he said. "I believe we came in the second great migration from Asia and that we had horses too."

Linguists discern connections between Sino-Tibetan and other Asian language trees and the Athabascan languages of the Eskimo, Navajo, and the Apache. As to horses, they evolved and roamed the North American continent for millions of years before disappearing. The cause of that extinction, which claimed a host of great beasts, from mastodons to camels to saber-toothed tigers, had many theories and resided still in mystery.

How, I asked Domingo, did medicine men handle death and dying? Life's end was a fraught subject for the Navajo, who seldom talked of it.

Death arrived when the last wind left the fingertips, and Navajo turned their face away from its presence. In the old days when a Navajo died in their hogan, their relatives broke a hole in the north-facing wall of the house and removed the body and abandoned the home. To let your thoughts tarry on the departed and the cause of death was to risk getting sucked into despair's vortex. That was another tradition he did not embrace. "By not talking of death, we allow our young people to get swallowed up in grief."

A few months ago Domingo's nephews and nieces lost an adored grandfather. At the memorial, elders advised that he was in a more beautiful world and the children should not to talk of him too much. Domingo walked over and sat beside his nieces and nephews and put his hands on their shoulders.

"No one knows where your grandfather's spirit has gone. That is the mystery. All we can say is that he's in another state. We don't know if it's a better place. Remember this earth is good, a holy place, and you should breathe in the dawn and shout to the Holy People. Love this life. Love this world."

He had read ancient texts, the works of kindred cultures, and mixed Tibetan and Chinese herbs with Navajo ones. I asked to talk of those crosscurrents and he smiled and shook his head. "We don't try to explain everything."

Domingo said that he and two other men had just finished a healing ceremony under the guidance of a medicine man, a respected elder. A Navajo woman who had lived decades in Los Angeles returned to the reservation with diabetes and high blood pressure and labored breathing and legs so sore she had to be carried from car to hogan. She was old not of body but of spirit.

They filed into the hogan and men sat against the south wall and women against the north. Logs were piled and burned in the prescribed manner, and the medicine man applied intense heat and herb concoctions. They blew sacred smoke into her lungs and chanted and sang. By the third day, the woman sat up. By the fifth day, she walked.

Domingo and his fellow apprentices grew tired, their backs stiff and aching. Maybe, Domingo thought, I'm too old for this. Late in the afternoon of the last day of the ceremony, the medicine man led his apprentices up a steep path to a mesa top. They sat, legs dangling, gazing at Dinétah as the sky burned vermilion-blue. A wind swept across and lifted fatigue like a cloak from their backs. Domingo slapped his hands as he described that moment. "It all had been washed away," he said.

They sang that night with the strength and vigor of young men. We're done, the medicine man told the woman. We've sung the oldest song, the female-healing song. It's up to you and the Holy People. You are loaded with energy. Don't shake hands. Don't cook. Don't carry babies. Stay within yourself.

Weeks passed and Domingo drove to the Chinle flea market to buy hay for his horses. He saw the woman's brother-in-law, a boisterous man. He slapped Domingo's back—*whap!* She's well, she's healed! "I was like, 'Easy. Easy.' Everyone was looking in." Then Domingo saw that woman. She was walking with the vigor of a forty-year-old, breathing deep and smiling.

We left the Burger King as the sun fell toward Black Mesa. Do you believe, I asked, in magic and in the miraculous? Domingo searched my eyes. "There is more in this world than science knows."

He has not decided yet if he can embrace this calling. Navajo look to a medicine man as a parish does to a priest, and much more and his life would not be his own. Domingo must decide if he and his wife have enough retirement savings to afford this. They are raising several grandchildren, and they often give money to less fortunate friends. Josie lives with them, as she and her mother are in conflict.

"I've got five months and I turn sixty-two and I can retire with a pension," he said. "After that, I can study nothing but the old ways."

Domingo held up his hand—*basta.* "If you have more questions, call Josie. She knows where to find me."

Domingo and his granddaughter ambled to his pickup truck. At 3:30 a.m. the next morning, he awoke and drove into the glimmering dawn toward Oregon to lay metal on track beds.

The kinship game in Pinetop, Navajo and Apache face-to-face, was fierce, the pace relentless. The Wildcats came out at once over-amped and tired. They had played four games in two days. The long, lean Alchesay star, Harley Upton Jr., took advantage. He spun and twirled without a wasted motion, often passing when you'd expect him to shoot. His drives to the hoop called to mind a surfer riding a wave.

Curtis Begay kept the Wildcats in the game, venturing into the land of the giants and pushing a floater over outstretched hands. He hit a jump shot. The Apaches, no bigger than the Navajo, kept on coming, their defensive press a breathing animal, their offense featuring whipsaw passes and radar-guided three-point shooting. Chinle trailed by two points at the end of the first quarter and eleven points at halftime.

Mendoza was rarely predictable. Often he lashed the Wildcats for their mistakes and uneven effort even in victory. Now his players were tired and wheezing and losing and Mendoza played cheerleader.

"Hey, great effort. That's an athletic team, the best we've played so far this season. They are going to make us better. This game will be good for us," he told his charges. "Don't be intimidated and don't look like you've seen a ghost. Don't unplug for even a minute."

The second half began, and Will—who loved football and more than any player on the Wildcats would dive recklessly across the floor for loose balls—twisted his ankle and rolled in pain. "You're okay, Will!" the assistant coaches yelled. That was a command rather than question. Angelo was in foul trouble and they could not afford to lose a player. The pace was relentless, and that played to the advantage of Josiah, the tireless distance runner. He stripped the ball from an Apache and hit a three-pointer.

"Son, play deeeeeeee-fense!" "C'mon, 'Shlow—your brain, use your brain!"

The crowd was insistent, a roar of voices. The Apache fans were no less imploring of their stars. Alchesay's point guard, a cocky kid who played with brio and a perpetual smile, went by the name San Juan Slick.

"Be slick, Slick!"

The Wildcats pulled to within seven points at the end of the third quarter. Mendoza was a mad scientist with his lineups, pulling players in and out, trying to find the right combination. Dewayne, quick as a cat, hit consecutive three-pointers. Then he leapt for a pass and collided with an Apache and slammed to the floor. He landed on his hip and had to be helped off the court. Dewayne's loss deflated the team. Cooper looked haggard and his jumper fell short, bouncing off the front lip of the hoop. Chinle twice pulled to within two or three points only to recede. They lost 70–65.

The Wildcats would play a final game that night, against another big team from Marana, a town north of Tucson. They hung tough, Angelo an indomitable force in the middle, Chance and Dewayne pushing the tempo. By the final quarter, though, they were a spent force, and Marana pulled ahead for the win. Angelo's face was beet red, his chest heaving, as he shuffled to the locker room.

"Fuckin' tired," he muttered. "Fuckin' tired."

Players rested heads and arms on each other's backs in a locker room that resembled a hospital ward. Mendoza looked at his team and made eye contact where he could. He was pleased. "Remember, guys—patience. This is a grueling stretch."

The team had arrived at the end of December with a record of eight wins and seven losses, and Mendoza was okay with that. His bet all along was that he could use this month to get these boys in shape and focused and playing as one. He just might have found an unexpected point guard in Dewayne, Angelo and Cooper were working more tightly together, and Josiah had learned to swing the ball in all directions, not least to Cooper. If their engine flipped over in January, the team could accelerate into the February play-offs. This night he talked to the boys of toughness. He had seen too many native teams settle too easily for okay when they were capable of more.

This world, he told them, was not one that natives made. Yours is a collective culture and it's not easy to want to be the best, the one who sticks out. This season was to become a test of Navajo strength and will. "You have to learn to be ruthless," he said. "You have to play mean and open no door to fear."

He stepped afterward into the dark and the biting cold and walked across the parking lot toward the Wildcat bus. The stars offered so many stamped and frigid points of light, and Mendoza looked around and his mind strayed to what it had been like to work here in the late 1990s, to a struggle that extended beyond win and loss. He rarely spoke of his accomplishments, but those years were another matter. Conversation fell into a lull as he waited for the boys to file out, and Mendoza looked at me.

"Do you know what I'm proudest of in this life? Not a single one of those teenagers I counseled committed suicide. They lived, every single one of them."

CHAPTER TEN

Cooper Burbank was an enigmatic kid from up north, the soft-spoken outsider. It was not as if he and his family moved here from the Valley of the Sun or hailed from a Las Vegas subdivision. They lived in Rock Point, *Tsé Nitsaa Deez'áhí*, the place where the creek slips under the rocks. Theirs was a town, a hamlet really, of maybe six hundred Navajo if your count was generous and your census extended to sheep camps in gorges and trailers and hogans hidden in remote curves of the land. It was only forty-nine miles away, but it was far enough to mark him as not of Chinle.

Cooper knew those mesas and sheep paths and washes like a grandparents' face. When his parents packed up the pickup truck and moved to Chinle two years ago, Cooper passed his first weeks there watching and listening so carefully with his outsider ears and eyes.

His new life was exciting and wearying. When basketball try-outs opened in 2017, Mendoza decided that Cooper would skip the freshman team and the junior varsity and play on the varsity. The other boys noticed and whispered among themselves. A few weeks later the coach slotted Cooper as a starter, promoting him over a senior guard. He was young with an old feel for the game, a kid who knew when to pass and cut and when to unleash a jump shot.

That season started and Cooper heard hisses of static from the stands.

"Coach, you going to play your favorite again!?"

"Where's your pet, Coach? Where is he? He can't do anything wrong, right?"

Parents, uncles, aunties, cousins of other players set to twitching whenever Cooper stepped onto the court in the Wildcat Den. The kid from Rock Point had edged out their son, their nephew, their cousin. Nachae was the leader of that team, but Cooper was the leading scorer. Cooper did not preen and strut, and that earned him props. Not with everyone though. On nights when the Wildcats struggled and Cooper missed a jumper or one of his twisting layups bounced awry or a rebound bounced off his outstretched hand, the sniping and catcalls crackled like bonfire.

"How come you never pull out him, Coach?"

A year had passed and Cooper had befriended teammates and achieved a détente with near all. The holiday tournament in Pinetop, those tough games back-to-back-to-back-to-back, had bound together the boys in something that resembled harmony. But to go home at night and read social media, to absorb the chatter on Facebook, Instagram, and Snapchat, was to sense tectonic plates that shifted precariously still. Earlier in December when the Wildcats were losing too often and players were growing frustrated, Josiah had taken to Facebook and complained of Mendoza: *"He doesn't believe in any of us, except like two players."*

Everyone knew who Josiah was talking about: Curtis Begay and Cooper Burbank, the sophomores from the high plains to the north.

A few days after New Year's the players rode the bus north to Kayenta, twenty miles from the grand opera of geology that is Monument Valley, a land of buttes and mesas beloved by directors of old western flicks.

The boys stretched on the wood floor of the cavernous Monument Valley High School gymnasium and watched the Chinle girls play their game. Dewayne's four-year-old sister scaled Josiah's back, and the little point guard grabbed and carefully tumbled her forward in a storm of giggles. Two children chatted happily with Angelo, and Big Daddy put his arm around them and talked with a loose-jawed ease he seldom flashed around adults. Several younger brothers of players doubled as Mendoza's assistants, and they scampered about picking up water bottles and fetching bandages and tossing off ensign salutes to the old coach.

The seniors sat as contented spiders in a web. They have known one another since elementary school, their families and clans close, their lives a shared blur of summer leagues and rodeos and horse races and friends and cousins.

Their parents ran chillier, their radiators emitting little warmth when around their sons' rivals. A few days earlier Mendoza and athletic director Shaun Martin had called a meeting with the parents to address still-simmering tensions. Fourteen adults filed into a hot little conference room in the Wildcat Den, and again the parents complained of what they said was Mendoza's too-harsh manner and the primal unfairness of his coaching decisions. No boy should be forced to sit on the bench throughout a game, they said, and suffer embarrassment. Two mothers did most of the talking, offering words bitter and stinging while husbands and boyfriends and uncles sat in chairs set against the back wall of the room, baseball caps on, arms folded, a mountain range of big and broad and silent men.

"It is humiliating, *humiliating*, to watch a boy remain on the bench and fail to play," a mother told Mendoza and Martin. "This is not what high school basketball should be. Everyone must play. Everyone!"

It was yet another reminder that in a familial culture where Navajo numbered siblings and cousins and nieces and nephews and aunties and uncles in the hundreds, to see your son embarrassed was to feel a knife sink deep into the skin.

The most consequential charge remained at once unspoken and clear. The parents resented the attention given to younger players and to Cooper in particular. This subtext was the more remarkable as Joni and her husband, Darrick, sat in that meeting, and they did not remain silent. When the mothers lashed and poked at Mendoza, the Burbanks parried and defended and complimented the coach's steady hand. Mendoza, they stressed, had his eyes set on ensuring that these young men would be capable of thriving in the world after high school. Sometimes Mendoza kept their son sitting on the bench and sometimes he pulled hard on Cooper's reins. Cooper was the better for this discipline. "We tell him to be a sponge, not a rock," Darrick said.

"I tell my son, 'We come from Red Mesa. Everyone looks down on us,'" Joni said. "We have to work to make sure that every arrow on this team is pointed in the same direction."

The couple spoke carefully, deploying allusions rather than confronting criticisms head-on, aware that their clans and cousins were found not here but to the north. And still some parents rolled their eyes as the couple spoke.

Mendoza and Martin, the lanky ultramarathon runner and himself an outsider in Chinle, treaded no less delicately, offering answers that occupied a diplomatic land short of candor. We strive to help every youngster, they told the parents, and we will work to communicate better. But we need a reciprocal commitment and an acceptance that playing time was precious and must be earned. "To me, I want to compete for a championship every year," Mendoza said. "Don't get angry if I get on your boys. The work, the sacrifice I require of the kids, is not just physical but mental."

Martin stood and offered his take. "I ain't gonna lie: We want a state title. But all I expect is effort. I love your children like my own, but none of this comes easy."

Martin emerged from the room wagging his head. Some of these parents, he said, their boys were barely passing classes, hanging on to eligibility by their fingertips. Their boys would soon enough enter an uncertain world. Was playing time really their biggest concern?

Mendoza knew the answer to that question. A coach who fell short in wins, who failed to manage parental anxieties and expectations, put his job in jeopardy. No need to wait for a formal season-end evaluation. Fans would march into the school board and demand your head. One year, he told Shaun, he had piled up a handsome number of wins but his team fell short in the playoffs.

He walked into in the postseason school board meeting and the room was packed, near vibrating. Voices rose and fell and murmurs built to crescendos. Talk lapsed into Navajo, a language of which Mendoza knew just a few words. His wife, Marjorie, served as his translator.

They are grumbling and insulting you, she told her husband. So are those two board members over there. Her eyes narrowed. They are stupid and small-minded. Mendoza put his hand on her knee and whispered: Don't worry. Don't take it personally.

Mendoza had allies on the board, and they remained patient as bobcats on the hunt. When conversation flagged and critics ran short of the nouns and verbs of complaint, they pounced. Mendoza, the board members told the audience, is one of the most successful coaches in state history. He rarely had a losing season. Send him walking and we're going to lose a lot more games and people will say we're idiots.

"That quieted the grumbling—for a couple of months," Mendoza told Martin.

Martin and Mendoza chuckled and headed home.

The Wildcats opened their game in Kayenta with a surge, their urgency no less powerful than in the holiday tournament. Chance cut in a blink to the baseline for a layup. Angelo blocked a shot and took a pass at the top of the key and whirled and hit Elijah with a pass for a layup. Dewayne drilled a three-point jumper. The crowd roared, that three-hundred-strong Chinle contingent who'd driven up here after work.

Just as suddenly that tide receded and the Wildcat boys ran aimlessly and tossed up jumpers, failing to look for Cooper as if they had forgotten the name and number of their best scorer. A less-talented Monument Valley team shot itself back into the game, and the Wildcats jogged at halftime into a chilly locker room. Angelo's legs had cramped, rock hard, and Lenny, the assistant coach and a paramedic, stretched him out, kneading knotted thighs. "You guys got to slow down," Angelo complained to his teammates. "I can't keep up."

Mendoza was acerbic. "Stop this nonsense. You can't pretend you don't know where you are and who you should pass the ball to. It is January, and it doesn't matter who we play. We have to beat them. Keep that intensity, but slow it down!"

Those were Mendoza's last words as the team took the floor. Chance promptly tossed a sloppy behind-the-back pass that the Mustangs intercepted and took for a layup. The game stayed close as it dwindled to the final few seconds. Then Angelo and Josiah hit free throws and the Wildcats pulled out a 61–56 victory, the margin of victory once again tighter than it should have been. Mendoza forced himself to offer up a dollop of reluctant praise.

"Guys, you did what you had to do. We beat guys we had to beat."

I drove back to Chinle in Mendoza's company, rolling past the mesas of Sweetwater and White Top and descending across Trading Post Wash, mile upon mile of darkness and milky fields of stars and the flickering lights of isolated trailers and hogans. The coach talked of the impenetrable mystery that was the mind of a teenage boy and of the tensions that parents with too many disappointments in their own lives imposed on their children.

"I love the sport because it takes five people playing together like musicians. What's so difficult about that to understand?"

He fell silent and stared into the emptiness.

We pulled into the Chinle High School parking lot past midnight, and I dropped Mendoza at the Den, which loomed immense as a spaceship in the moonlight. He swung his leather bag onto his shoulder and unlocked the door to the gym office and settled onto a couch to wait for the bus to arrive. He would not go home until the last boy got a ride home. Some boys would not fall into bed until 1:30 a.m., and they would catch the bus back to school at 7:00 a.m.

———

The Wildcats played a game the next night out west in Pinon, where asphalt yielded to washboard dirt roads that led many miles on to the ancient Hopi villages that sit like Aegean towns far above the blue-yellow sea of the surrounding desert. To the north of Pinon were the southernmost limestone flanks of Black Mesa, where townspeople kept cattle and sheep camps tucked into its scalloped folds.

The land was breathtaking and that truth coexisted with another: Pinon, a town of nine hundred, had too few jobs and too many teenage parents with tough prospects. School buildings and tribal administration offices were cordoned off by fences topped with razor wire. Hard-eyed Navajo teenagers loosely affiliated with the Crips, aspirational gangbangers in blue gang colors, marked their territory with graffiti tags and enforced their writ with bats and knives and the occasional revolver. From time to time, blue-clad young men rode horses and cars through town, poseurs with enough menace to cause parents to clench their jaws and herd their children inside.

The Wildcat boys took the court in Pinon and again started off slowly, doing their best to keep an outmanned inferior opponent in the game. Mendoza peered at his players at halftime, incredulous. "Again? You're not hustling, you're not playing defense, you are statues. Are you kidding? Wake up!" He sounded like a man trying to flog a gallop from a listless horse.

The Wildcats left the locker room, and as suddenly, the cohesion Mendoza chased materialized. Their defense constricted like a python. Angelo swatted balls and grabbed rebounds. Chance and Josiah harried any Pinon guard foolish enough to attempt more than a dribble or two. Cooper roamed the court, probing, deciding how and when and where to attack. He was in such minutes sure of his every step and scored a surgical twenty-five points. The Wildcat lead expanded and expanded again.

Dewayne, who was born in Pinon, was the star distributor this night. He roamed the court lithe and coiled and tossed artful passes on the run. Like a sports car, he tended to overheat, and when that happened he tugged on his jersey. Josiah, the other half of that two-headed beast of a point guard, ran in to replace him and distributed the ball and played tough defense. The boys were seniors and close friends and their shared assignment offered no flare of resentment and rivalry. On the back of that dominant quarter and their willingness to find Cooper with their passes, the Wildcats trounced Pinon 68–44. It was another vision of what could be.

The Wildcats' record now stood at 11–7 even as another storm front approached. Those White Mountain Apaches from Alchesay would arrive in Chinle in a few days for a rematch. The Apaches' record had swollen to 20–1, a native juggernaut. "Get your mindset right," the old man warned his boys. "If you don't come out aggressive, if you don't come out cohesive, Alchesay will hit us so hard we'll have whiplash."

The coach would prove prophetic.

In practice the next day Mendoza lined up the boys and paced the floor and spoke softly of fear and fatigue and manhood, a therapist attempting headwork on his patients. He often tried to reach the boys and when he hit his mark, they leaned in and strained to hear an old coach's wisdom. When he grew longwinded or didactic or annoyed, the boys looked away distracted, watching the girls finish practice at the other end of the court. This was such a day. The boys were television sets tuned out. Mendoza stood in a pool of silence.

"Mrs. Burbank is going to talk to you."

Joni Burbank sat in the bleachers talking with another parent, planning a potluck dinner for the team. She was about to leave and drive her younger son and daughter home and plan her next day's class when she heard Mendoza call her name. She turned and he was waving to her. "Mrs. Burbank, come over. Talk to the boys."

Joni walked across the floor, a woman accustomed to a classroom stage. This was nowhere near as daunting as that meeting with the parents a few days earlier. She had coached Cooper and his basketball team in middle school, and they beat teams from Chinle and Tsaile stocked with these same boys. Angelo and Cooper had played on summer all-star teams, and Darrick had driven them to far-flung games, ranging as far afield as Colorado and Oklahoma. She had made dinners for the team this year and listened as the boys chattered and joked and vamped, observing who was happy, who was frustrated, who was filled with doubt. No need to tiptoe.

"When I look at your coaches, I see men who put enormous hours in this gym when they should be home with their families. When I see Coach Mendoza, I see a man who does not sleep when you lose. And you are not paying attention to him.

"Don't ask if you scored enough in a game. Ask if you have dived often enough on the floor, if you bounced off enough bodies, and if you grabbed enough rebounds. Look into yourselves." She talked of the clan and family demands that sit at the edge of awareness. "The crowds are demanding, right? They are insistent and unforgiving, right? Well, how could they not be? You are their golden children.

"The people come and watch you and some don't have enough

money to buy hay for their horses. They don't have enough money for gas—that's why they hitchhike to your games. When they look out on the court, what they see is the peak of their lives. It looks great to them. It may not be fair, but you carry the weight of their dreams."

The boys listened and slowly their shoulders loosened and they nodded. Their society venerated mothers and grandmothers, and they recognized the elemental reality that Joni, like most Navajo women, knew her hoops. Many of their grandmas and female cousins and mothers, ponytailed Joni among them, had played varsity basketball. Quite a few of these women had fought deeper into the playoffs than these boys.

"People will knock you on social media; they will try to set you against each other," Joni said. "Tune that out. It's useless. It's toxic."

She stopped and caught their eyes, peering into one after another. She clapped, her spell was broken, and the boys bounded off to run layup drills. I walked out of the Den with Joni. Your talk seemed to hit the right note. How long did you think about what you were going to say?

She looked at me and laughed. "I had no idea he was going to ask me to speak to them. Mendoza surprised me. To talk with them, I just relied on the life I've lived. Nothing comes easy."

You could knock on Cooper's door a long while before he cracked it open. Tall and slender, with eyes that probed and asked questions he declined to put into words, he was as polite and as self-contained as his father, Darrick. Joni was chattier, spiritual and restless and willing to contemplate a dive off life's high board.

Two years ago Chinle advertised for a prekindergarten teacher.

Joni was teaching at Red Mesa Elementary and Junior High School, one of the smallest schools on the Navajo Nation. She applied and aced her battery of interviews. The principal offered her a job, and she and Darrick faced a decision: Could they and their children leave all that they knew and start again?

Such worries might sound odd to an outsider, she acknowledged. Their proposed move would take them just down the road, a long dog leg around a set of blood-red buttes. But they had come of age in Round Rock and Rock Point, and love and loss had lashed them together and defined them to their core.

When Darrick was four years old, his dad drank and missed a turn and the car skipped off the road, rolling like tumbleweed. He died and Darrick's mom was cut loose, drifting to Phoenix and away from her little boy. His grandmother took him in and Darrick clung to her as to a tree in a windstorm.

"My grandmother prayed and watched over me. She was my everything."

Darrick did not talk much, but his hands were wondrous. He could fix a bike or a car, build a dream of a tree house. As he grew older, he hopped on the backs of 1,600-pound bulls that bucked and bounced him like a rag doll. The grip of that skinny teenager was so powerful that spectators wondered if they'd have to drag him off the bull's back.

When Joni was eight years old, her father drank heavily and he, too, died in a car crash. Her mom, Virginia, refused to break. She had as a child survived a distant boarding school where her mouth was washed out with soap whenever she spoke Navajo, and she had graduated college and become a schoolteacher. She was Tangle Clan, *Ta'neeszahnii*, and born for the Folded Arms Clan, *Bit'ahnii*, strong and resilient people. She held tight to Joni and her brothers; Their family studied and read and prayed together.

"We called ourselves the Fantastic Four. No one could separate us."

We talked of all this as we bounced along a dirt road on a rolling yellow prairie. Joni drove the pickup truck, taking my wife, Evelyn—who was visiting—and me to see their family hogan atop a distant mesa.

She and Darrick met as students at Rock Point elementary school, and she thought he was a pest. Middle school brought about an outlandish metamorphosis: He became a good-looking guy and kind of cool. They became friends. In high school that gave way to something deeper and more mysterious. They recognized in each other an ineffable connection and could not bear to be apart. "We were magnets attracting, flying together," Joni said.

Navajo Nation has many thousands of teenagers who go through unplanned pregnancies and thousands of too-young moms and wayward-boy fathers, although fewer than on many other reservations. Virginia would accept no such fate for her daughter Joni. She and her family laid down the rules and the teenagers' romance evolved slowly and in accordance with tradition. Darrick dated Joni, which meant the boy could come by on weekends and visit with her mother, brothers, aunties, uncles, and grandparents. He was respectful, and he knew how to toss a lasso around the neck of cow and to repair a car, and the family took a liking to this boy.

But holding hands was forbidden. "Kissing was impossible," Joni said. "We kept it on the down low."

Virginia let Joni—who went to high school in Flagstaff—attend Darrick's high school graduation and maybe they snuck in a kiss. Soon after, Joni, whip smart with good grades, won a coveted Chief Manuelito scholarship and left for Flagstaff and Northern Arizona University to get her degree. Virginia moved there, too, to get her master's degree, and mother and daughter shared a small university apartment along with Joni's grandmother. The three women cooked and studied and talked each night of plans and past and future. "Those were the best years ever," Joni said.

Darrick was the first in his family to graduate high school, and he lacked the confidence and context for college. He strapped on a carpenter's belt and built homes in Flagstaff and Phoenix and Las Vegas and made a name, too, in the fierce and competitive world of rodeos, winning championship buckles and cash. The wages of his rodeo life numbered a broken arm, a busted rib, a sprained knee, a bruised back, and a punctured lung.

Life's winds could well have sent this couple spinning away from each other, but Darrick kept driving to visit Joni in Flagstaff. Once on a whim after Joni graduated, they hopped in his car and drove across the desert and curled up through green-bristled mountains and redwood forests to San Francisco. They arrived at midnight and walked to the harbor as ten thousand whitecaps ran across a cold black chop. They breathed deep and felt salt air fill their lungs and in the Monet sunlight of early morning they drove across the Golden Gate Bridge and stood on the Marin headlands and watched as the mists receded into the Pacific. They vowed to remain in each other's arms forever.

They married atop Carson Mesa outside Rock Point, speaking vows within sight of the razor-edged Carrizos and the red Chuskas. Darrick has since built a handsome blue hogan on that spot. Joni began teaching in Rock Point and Darrick drove off to build more homes, his work hours long and his drives home longer still. Joni gave birth to Cooper and one night she turned to Darrick and said, "Our life has to change. You are a husband and a father. We need you here."

What did she mean? Panic pinched at Darrick. He adored Joni

and Cooper, his baby son—they were his all. But he was a skilled craftsman, his hands his salvation, and wasn't he providing as a man must? Navajo men travel far and work hard and send money home; that is their way. Joni shook her head. No, Darrick, she said. That path leads to splintered families and sons raised by grandparents. It must not become our life.

"I knew my job was to give my children a dad, but I had no model. I didn't know what that meant."

He looked for work on the reservation, which was like wandering in search of a desert spring. He caught on as a school bus driver and earned little more than minimum wage, many thousands of dollars less than he had grown accustomed to making. Was this his future, to work and scrape for pennies and become a man dependent on his wife's salary?

Soon after, his grandmother died. He awoke in predawn and climbed into that school bus and felt himself hollowed out. "I had a hard time getting used to making so little money. I felt bad about myself." Joni stroked his back and shoulders and took his face in her hands and reassured him: We are more than our paychecks.

One night a dream swept him in a powerful undertow. Darrick found himself standing in the desert, wind blowing cactus and piñon, the land as vivid and strange as a photo negative. He saw his grandmother's house on the far side of a wash and he felt happiness course through him: There it is, she will be there, I will see her again. He ran toward it but a shadow kept passing in front, and he could not make his way there. In his sleep he felt an ache and tears.

"I couldn't cross. I couldn't make it."

He felt warmth in his hand and looked down and his palm held a Bible and he sensed something more and turned around. "Joni was standing behind me. She was smiling and reaching out toward me." He was bathed in light and an overwhelming sense of this woman's *nizhóní,* her balance and harmony, her beauty. He awoke, eyes blinking and tear-filled. "I knew God had given me this family and this woman. I still struggle with my life sometimes, but my job is to give these kids what I never had: a dad."

Soon after he found a job as the Red Mesa school custodian, which paid better, and then as a skilled carpenter and electrician at that school, which paid better still. He came to watch over Joni's family, building a corral for an uncle, keeping a protective eye on Virginia. One of Virginia's beloved brothers died, and Darrick obtained a backhoe and expertly filled and smoothed that grave. This was his family and he would watch over them all.

Change came.

Joni and Darrick desperately wanted Cooper to go to college and get a four-year degree and to live a life of many possibilities. Rock Point's high school had no extras—no drama or chess club— and a handful of certified teachers; their village had a post office and general store with shelves that rarely held more than a few fresh fruits and vegetables. A tiny diner sat in Mexican Water, twenty-two miles to the north, and the nearest movie theaters were in Durango and Farmington, a four-hour drive round-trip in good weather.

If they moved to Chinle, Cooper could take college-level courses and play basketball for Coach Mendoza, who had that championship ring and who put so much care into raising young men in a tough world. Joni talked to Cooper about navigating that new land: We are Navajo and we must start here to make it down the road of our lives. We are from Rock Point and people may look down on us. Are you ready, son? Cooper nodded.

"I prayed and prayed," Joni said. "Finally I said to myself, 'Joni, you have to show your children that you aren't scared of life.'"

Virginia watched as Darrick and Joni and the children piled into the pickup truck and edged onto the asphalt and drove south to their new home. She waved until their car was a dot on the horizon. As an educator, she knew this was the right move even as she felt pain in her heart, for Joni, her grandchildren, and Darrick.

"My son. I never call Darrick my son-in-law. He's my son."

The Burbanks moved into a three-bedroom apartment in the suburban-looking compound that Chinle built for its teachers. Chinle School District, as is true of schools across the reservation, recruits from across the nation and overseas, Pakistan and Switzerland and the Philippines and Rock Point too. When school started in early August, Cooper slipped a book bag over his shoulders and walked across three parking lots to the high school. Cooper's middle school in Rock Point had 112 students; Chinle High School had 1,050 students.

"Mom, when the bell rings, it's like a swarm of ants pouring out of a hill."

Joni and Darrick taped biblical verses over the door to Cooper's bedroom. Romans 8:28: "And we know that all things work together for good to them that love God, to them who are called according to his purpose."

Basketball season began and the hostility began to build. *"Your golden boy struggling, Coach?"*

Cooper would have had to put in earplugs not to hear it. Mendoza shrugged and took the boy into his office. "This is about their unhappiness, not yours. Pay attention to what you can affect, which is your game and actions and how you hold yourself as a young man." Cooper nodded. He never snapped and never complained; he just kept running and practicing that jumper. Some nights Cooper walked home and finished his homework and sought out Joni and Darrick. I'm frustrated, he told them.

They talked late into the night, taking inventory of their new life. Darrick, who once could find so few words for himself, helped lead his son through. "I know this is hard, son. You will make it because you are a strong and we will armor you in love."

Joni and Darrick walked a gauntlet too. The parents who sniffed and spoke too loud sat rows away in the Wildcat Den. The couple tried to ignore them, although patience was not a trough endlessly refilled. "The old me would say something to them," Joni said. "We have trained ourselves to have selective hearing. Be thankful for what you have and for your gifts."

Each weekend Joni and Darrick drove back to their home in Rock Point, and Cooper woke up, ate breakfast, checked the NBA scores, and trotted over to his grandmother's trailer. She hugged him and he stretched on her couch and let her massage his legs and feet as he haltingly talked of his new life.

Joni and Darrick took pride in Navajo culture and dress and felt a visceral connection to family, clan, land, sky. Traditional belief was not part of their world. They declined to believe that to cross a path with a coyote was to court bad luck or that a sneeze could loosen a windstorm. Such beliefs made them fearful of that which was beautiful, they said. They attended God's Grace Fellowship Church, which sat at the end of a rutted dirt road two miles north of Rock Point. A few dozen parishioners filled the church, men in jeans and dress shirts, cowboy boots and hats; women in flowing calico dresses and turquoise jewelry and cowboy boots; young children carrying picture books and dolls. Two men and a woman played Christian country melodies on fiddle and pedal steel guitar. They read from Navajo-language Bibles that the female pastor translated for me. Her sermon that day roamed into the dark corners of her life, a voice-cracking tale of pain and despair and drink and a redemptive climb to salvation. The service ended, and all shook hands and embraced, and Cooper excused himself and walked to the pastor and held his hands out, palms up. His voice was a whisper, and the pastor leaned in to hear him.

"I need strength, Pastor. Would you pray with me?"

She laid her palms on Cooper's palms, her neck and wrists and fingers bejeweled with silver and turquoise that reflect the desert sky, which is God's domain. She and Cooper prayed that he might find the wisdom to accept stiff challenge and to feel cocooned in His love.

Cooper had grown perhaps faster than he realized in the last two years. A girl had succeeded in catching his eye, and he walked the halls with her, their hands dangling, touching, not quite clasped. Nachae Nez was the Wildcats' natural alpha dog, and while Cooper had not replaced him, he did urge teammates to play a tougher defense and bear down. He was finding a voice in his sophomore season to match his jump shot, and the other teenagers listened to him even if their parents remain unpersuaded.

The boys seemed to intuit that this season's playoff run could rest on the slender shoulders of this quiet young man.

Once again, the Apaches from Alchesay were setting young Navajo nerves to dancing. Will could not stop his legs from vibrating before the rematch. And once play started, Curtis Begay and Chance could not get their rainbow jumpers to fall. The Wildcats fell behind quickly, as if they had tumbled off the back lip of a truck. The Wildcat defense was porous, their offense a game-long slumber, and the Alchesay players again whirled the ball about, barely let it touch their hands as it passed from one side of the court to the other.

That was the way Mendoza wanted his own team to play, the way he drew it up on the whiteboards. Shot after shot fell through the nets, and the old man rumbled, disgusted. In the fourth quarter, he benched every starter save for Cooper.

Out, out. You sit now.

Cooper again was asked to unpack his full game.

"C'mon, Cooper! Wake up!"

Joni cupped her hands and pleaded with her son from the stands. Several team parents pursed their lips at the sound of her voice and mention of her son. Other parents, though, started to clap and soon joined Joni in pleading with Cooper to breathe life into the team, to save the Wildcats. In that moment the team became his.

For the second time in two weeks Cooper led a squad of younger bench players on a furious counterattack. He dribbled, facing down the Apache star, and spun to the hoop. He grabbed a rebound and hit a butter-smooth jump shot. He scored and scored and tossed a scare into Alchesay. On this night, though, the Wildcats were a car that had skidded into a too-deep ditch. Toward the end, Mendoza waved for Elijah, one of his seniors, to go in and the teenager shook his head. The assistant coaches leaned over and stared at Elijah, astonished. The teenager thought better of his insurrection and trotted into the game.

Parents milled about afterward on the floor of the Wildcat Den, whispering, funereal as five thousand disappointed Navajo filed out, shaking their heads, grumbling, and flipped on car high beams to begin the dolorous drive home. In the locker room Mendoza could barely bring himself to look at his players, his seniors in particular. It was the team's first loss in January after three victories, but to lose badly, 75–66, on their home floor and for a player to refuse to join the younger players in their attempted comeback . . . "Look, I'm very disappointed. We should look forward to games like this, and we just let it slip away, scared. You can't look at a good team and think, 'Wow, man, can I have your autograph?' You have to grab a game by the throat. These are your games. This is your life.

"Who are we? Can you guys even sense how far this team could go if we played as one? Can you sense how empty you will feel if you look back later in life and know that you did not give it your all and we fell short of our goal?"

Mendoza would wake up at 4:00 a.m. and stare at his ceiling and ask himself the same questions he asked the boys.

CHAPTER ELEVEN

What sets a fire to crackling in a young mind? How to find the courage to step out of Dinétah and into the unknown? I asked Nachae who it was at Chinle High who filled him with a desire to venture beyond his world? He led me to Parsifal Hill-Smith, the English teacher and a former surfer dude, and Parsifal in turn led me to Keanu Gorman, a shy, almost bashful boy. This kid, the teacher said, was worth getting to know.

So I sent a message to Keanu and asked to talk. Days passed and just before midnight I received this text:

Can you visit tomorrow morning?

I had tried to get in touch for several days running, and as dates and appointments aren't easy to pin down in the Navajo Nation, I tapped a quick reply:

Yes, definitely. When and where?

He sent instructions:

Drive south, take the road to Pinon and turn left at the
first windmill. Wait there. I will come to get you.

Another text followed:

It might be the second windmill. Don't worry, just turn off
and I'll find you.

Which is how I came to stand in midmorning by a windmill—
it appeared to be the only one for many miles—that called to mind
an arrow shot to earth, tall and silvery with a feathery vane that
shimmered and glinted. It rose in the middle of a vast plain beneath a sapphire sky. No trees, not so much as a gnarled pine: just
red dirt and sand and sagebrush and snakeweed and that slow,
creaking windmill dredging water from the depths.

I walked around the concrete cistern and studied archaeological
layers of graffiti: NO JUSTICE NO PEACE and SMILE MY NATIVES and
WATER IS LIFE and I LOVE YOU CHARLI, along with abstract jots,
squiggles, and bursts of spray paint like the universe exploding. To
the north Black Mesa rose in piles of broken white sandstone, and
to the east I could make out the gray clay bluffs that overlooked
the desolation that was Pleasant Valley, a leafless depression of salt
licks, phosphate mounds, and white volcanic ash with dust in a
perpetual whirl.

I could see no sign of Keanu or any living thing. I closed my
eyes and breathed the desert musk and concentrated on the encompassing silence.

A half hour passed and I spotted a distant dot that trailed behind it a red cloud like a marble rolling across a dusty horizon. In time that dot cohered into an old sedan and it turned toward my windmill bouncing like a dune buggy, shocks gone. It pitched to a stop and a heavyset kid with a shy aspect and big black glasses stepped out and blinked sleep from his eyes and offered a soft handshake. Keanu had stayed up late completing a paper on Oscar Wilde for his English class. As he owned no laptop and the electricity in his trailer flickered like a candle in the wind, he had tapped out the essay on his mobile phone.

Keanu Gorman, valedictorian of Chinle High School, asked me to follow him in my car to his home.

That drive extended down dirt road after dirt road, and eight miles on we pulled onto a single track that led to an old bruised trailer near the foot of Balakai Mesa, which means "the place with reeds on it." Medicine men prized Balakai's 7,300-foot summit as a sacred site for the Healing Way ceremony, which ensured good luck and blessings. Keanu's mother greeted us outside the trailer. She was of the Bitter Water People Clan and spoke fluent Navajo and broken English learned while attending school from the third grade to the eighth grade. His grandmother was next to step out the trailer door. She was petite, tiny even, and wore a blue calico dress and cowboy boots and necklaces and bracelets; a turquoise clasp held in place a soft and luxuriant coil of white hair.

She was born under a peach tree behind the trailer, and Keanu figured she was in her ninth decade. She possessed no birth certificate, and neither she nor anyone else in the family was certain of her age. *Yá'át'ééh*, I said by way of greeting.

She peered up at me with a quizzical look and spread her arms and in singsong voice commanded: "Speak Navajo!"

With a shrug and hapless hand gestures, I tried to explain to her that this *bilegáana*'s knowledge of Navajo had expired unceremoniously immediately after "hello."

She laughed merrily and climbed into a fossilized pickup truck to drive to the market with her daughter. Keanu was fluent in Navajo and he often tagged along and translated when they had appointments with a doctor or government welfare or food stamp bureaucrat or when it was time for parent–teacher conferences. "My mother speaks some English but she gets nervous and trips over the meaning of official words."

Keanu watched as they drove to the road and the truck turned left and disappeared around a bend. He explained to me that his "mother" was really his grandmother. And his "grandmother" was really his great-grandmother. His biological mom lived in Flagstaff with his siblings. He saw her once in a while, but they weren't really close.

We walked behind the trailer to a pen constructed of logs bleached gray-white by the sun and held together with baling wire. The pen was home to a few grouchy goats and twenty or so sheep, common American and Spanish Churro and two desert bighorn sheep, which an uncle of his had found and captured years ago on the mesa. That uncle had passed away and all these creatures became the property of his grandmother and great-grandmother. Balakai Mesa harbored cougar and bobcat and coyote, and a few weeks ago Navajo shepherds reported that a Mexican red wolf had wandered north of the interstate onto the mesa. The sheep and goats appear to have incorporated an awareness of this unwelcome news into their core as they huddled more tightly than usual in their pen and had taken to loud bleating at night.

Rez dogs, mutts of dozens of genetic flavors, acted as hair-trigger sentries and patrolled the perimeter of the corral, the hair on their scruff raised like mohawks.

We walked back to the trailer and took seats at a small table at the edge of a tiny kitchen while Keanu's little sister sat in the living room and watched a movie in Navajo. The trailer had lacked running water until Keanu turned thirteen years old, and he used to haul in five-gallon jugs of water to flush the toilet. Today the water that flowed from the faucet spit and coughed and came out milky and fizzy and tasted like aluminum foil. Electric service remained spotty, and when his family fell behind on payments, Keanu read Greek mythology and Charlotte Brontë and Wilde and Homer by the light of religious candles purchased at the dollar store.

I asked of his plans after graduation.

"I really hope I get into this college called Swarthmore."

The borders of his life were nearly as tightly circumscribed as those of his sheep; he had not traveled as far east as Albuquerque, as far west as Las Vegas, or as far north as Salt Lake City. "I have never really seen the outside world. I've never seen a lot of things."

He discovered Swarthmore while leafing through catalogs that his English teacher, Parsifal, left in piles around his classroom along with university pennants and flags. Keanu examined photos of gray stone buildings and leafy oaks and chestnuts and poplars and lawns of startling green intensity. Were those real? He read and reread the thumbnail biographies of professors and descriptions of classes in ancient Greek philosophy, Kant, F. Scott Fitzgerald, and Henrik Ibsen. He was entranced.

"It's so beautiful, I mean, wow," he said. "I really want to experience that world."

The life of a top student here could prove confounding. A few years back, Keanu's math teacher persuaded him to apply for a fellowship to attend an elite summer math camp at the Phillips Academy in Massachusetts. If he was accepted, and he was a strong bet to get in, the program would cover his travel and dorm bills for the summer. His biological mother heard that he had applied and sent word to his grandmothers that he could not go even if he was accepted.

"She said it was too dangerous for me to get on a plane. I told her that it was a lot more dangerous to drive around the reservation."

Mother was unyielding, and Keanu passed that summer working at the Burger King in Chinle, reading and doing algebra problems in his head.

Keanu spoke mostly Navajo until he was five years old and school officials placed him in a bilingual school. "I knew English but I had an accent." His class was filled with kids from the rural reaches of the reservation, children of shepherds and farmers, and instruction and expectations were not rigorous. Keanu grew bored and sorted restlessly through bins in the library and picked up and read books in English, one after another. And when he reached a word or sentence he did not understand, he read the chapter over again—or he read the book again. When his grandmother watched television shows in Navajo, he switched on the English subtitles and forced himself to read those.

Novels, biographies, histories, Greek myths—he inhaled them all. He turned eight years old and teachers moved him to a regular class and had him skip a grade. Not long after, his biological mom moved to Phoenix and he and his sisters followed. By hanging out at bodegas and talking to Mexicans, he learned passable Spanish. Not long after, his mom moved the family to Winslow, a city of eleven thousand people on the sun-swept plains along Route 66 and I-40, a blink-and-you-miss-it stop for gas and a taco on the highway between Albuquerque and Flagstaff. Winslow is equal parts white and Navajo and Mexican, and a spark of tension could light a prairie fire. He entered his classroom at midyear, and a couple of white kids eyed the new boy, small and thin and with big glasses, and smirked.

"Oh, here's another Injun."

"Hey, teepee man."

A white boy ordered Keanu to stop speaking Navajo and burped at him. Keanu punched that kid and the teacher forced him to sit out the class. He was developing a deep dislike for Winslow when a South Asian student, a Sikh boy, befriended him. Keanu's family lived in a single room in the Motel 10; the Sikh boy's parents owned the motel.

Keanu sat with his new friend and ate dinner, chicken and jasmine rice and chutney, chili and saffron, coconut and turmeric and coriander firing on his tongue as he listened to his friend's mother and father tell tales of a far-off subcontinent, of aunties and uncles and cousins, of tribal languages and history and magic and Shiva intertwined. He decided that India sounded like the Navajo Nation and that he liked this family very much.

Not long after, he had to say goodbye. His biological mom had met another man and this time she was driving her children to Flagstaff. No. Keanu had had enough. No more floating on the wind. He went to his grandmother and great-grandmother and said: Please. Can I live with you and go to high school in Chinle?

"Life is getting too chaotic. I can't get my head around the idea of just giving up."

Chinle High School offered a complicated swirl, its challenges an exhilaration or headache, depending on the child or the hour. Each year a couple of top students, teenagers like Keanu, gained admittance to top liberal arts colleges and the Ivy Leagues, and those boys and girls adjusted, thrived even, and graduated on time. Like all schools on this remote swath of land, Chinle High School had trouble attracting and holding certified teachers. A few weeks earlier, school board members devoted their winter meeting to trying to figure out how to patch over the hole that had opened beneath their feet when two Anglo high school teachers packed up and quit during the vacation week between Christmas and New Year's.

Some Anglo teachers, those like Parsifal Hill-Smith, take to the embrace of this land and culture, hunting, hiking, running their rez dogs across its mesas. Other teachers wrestled fitfully with the isolation and lack of cell service, the distance from family and friends, the absence of movie theaters and restaurants and stores. Much of the meat in Bashas' was marbled white with fat, the vegetables passable at best, and depending on the day, a run for a six-pack of beer could consume two and a half hours round-trip.

Chinle's principal, Clete Hargrave, was a fresh-faced and reserved man who worked hard to set high standards and attract teachers. He and his wife were Mormons who had done missionary tours overseas, where they and their children had come to embrace the richness of life in a culture radically different from their own. Being principal at Chinle meant Hargrave had to sail into the idiot wind of education requirements piled high. Ours was an age of data rapture, standardized tests, metrics, rubrics, and annual grades for every school. That could prove deeply at odds with the jagged and nonlinear way learning happened here.

State and national education officials promoted distance learning and online tests as ways for remote schools to broaden their resources. I asked Hargrave about computers and distance learning for homework assignments and only his natural reserve kept him from laughing in my face.

Many teenagers at Chinle High School toggled between homes, an auntie this week, a grandparent the next, maybe a parent visited from Flagstaff or Las Vegas, or maybe a foster care family helped out. Other children were functionally homeless and relied on school and the athletic center for showers and meals and with luck an adult who might put a hand on a rudder in rough waters. Even the many children from stable families often arrived home in late afternoon and had sheep to feed and hay to pitch and wood to chop and dinner to heat up for a young brother, sister, or cousin as their parents finished hours-long commutes home. Distance learning? Hargrave offered a thin smile at mention of the latest buzzword. "We concentrate on teaching as intensely as we can while the students are at the school. 'Distance learning' is not always a useful concept."

Traditional rhythms, too, aligned awkwardly with those of a state-school calendar. A few weeks back a revered roadman in the Native American Church pulled into Pinon, and the parents of two Wildcat players let their sons attend an all-night peyote ceremony, cedar and piñon logs burning and crackling, with singing and old stories told and intense heat inside the teepee as the peyote buds ignited their electrodes. The night cleansed the boys' bodies and spirits and opened wide holy doors of insight; it also left them tired and washed out.

In biology class, some students refused to dissect frogs, as tradition taught that opening up a frog or a snake was dangerous and forbidden. An English teacher who talked casually of a character in a novel who behaved like a snake might notice that Traditional students averted their eyes, nervous and embarrassed by the allusion. A snake was a powerful creature in touch with the spirit world and to talk of one was to risk that your hands and heart might swell dangerously.

Basketball's golden children and an athletic season that dominated all others presented another challenge. Josiah, the little point guard and cross-country runner, had stumbled through academic thickets in his freshman and sophomore year, distracted, fooling around, piling up too many Ds and Cs. Slowly he felt the tug of ambition and of his future in a broader world and he settled down and his grades arched upward to the point he scored a high B average in his senior year.

His performance in those early years haunted him; he worried that his overall grade point average could hurt his chances to attend a four-year public university. He rummaged in a shoebox and pulled an old report card when I visited him and he studied his freshman- and sophomore-year grades as if in hope the letter grades would offer a new answer.

"Damn, I think about those first couple of years all the time. Damn. I was a fool." His voice trailed off.

The travel and the unending intensity of the hoop season, elation and despair rising and falling like successive ocean swells, posed challenges emotional and intellectual. Athletes often skipped afternoon classes to travel to gyms in distant towns, and the rhythms wore on even the most disciplined. Early one morning I walked to the high school and took a seat in the Advanced Calculus class of Mohammad Raza, the Pakistani-born teacher who had lived in Chinle for two decades and was so well respected that kids called him a Navostani, a blend of Navajo and Pakistani. He arrived at school just after dawn and left late nearly every day, ever willing to tutor and explain and push a student to excel. I watched as Dewayne, who sat on the far side of the classroom, repeatedly rubbed his temples and eyes. A studious kid, he was trying with middling success to forget the previous night's loss and focus on his equations.

Dewayne had arrived home the previous night at 2:00 a.m.

Arizona regulations dictate that grade eligibility for athletics is determined week by week. For those like Angelo, who struggled with grades and sometimes cut school altogether, this led to recurring difficulties. On a Monday afternoon in January with a game that night, Mendoza and Shaun Martin stood in the athletic office in the Wildcat Den and made stabs at small talk as the secretary peered at her computer screen and clicked on grade charts and announced which player's grades had fallen short. Angelo's grade in math had tumbled to a D, and that meant he would miss this game. Martin sighed and Mendoza rolled his eyes.

Angelo came strolling into the office and looked at the men and sensed trouble, no words needed. "You're out, Angelo," Mendoza said. "No grades." The big man looked sort of but not really surprised.

"Wait, Coach. Wait." He held up his hand.

The big teenager did not wait for Mendoza and Shaun to interrogate him. He loped back across the parking lot to the high school and to his math teacher's classroom and knocked once, twice on the door. Her face appeared in the window. She rolled her eyes and invited him in. It wasn't the first time he'd visited. His grade problems owed to lack of interest and to his inability to see a future where such things would matter, rather than to his incomprehension. "Could we count my late homework assignment or an extra-credit assignment?" He talked fast and smiled and she conceded his point. His grade average nosed up to a C minus, which was enough to let him play. She figured maybe basketball kept this young man in school.

He trotted back to the Wildcat Den and roamed the hallways looking for the coach. The opposing team already had dressed and walked out to the court to take layups. He asked two janitors if they'd seen Mendoza and they pointed down the hall. Then he spotted the old man and, grinning, waved the paper signed by the teacher. "Mendoza! Look!" The coach squinted, skeptical, examining the signature like a jeweler too often fooled. "Okay. Get suited up."

The weekly sprinting, wheedling, and begging made Mendoza and Martin uncomfortable. They preferred the previous system with grade eligibility settled once each month. Blow your grades and sorry, kid, you missed games. That forced restless teenagers to get serious.

"I will never call a teacher on your behalf," Mendoza often warned his players. "Never ever. Expect no favors."

The same day that Angelo persuaded a teacher to bump up his grade, Mendoza summoned the big man, his hope for the playoffs, and told him to take a seat in his office. "'Shlow, your grades and attendance are wobbling and bouncing, a mess. You don't show up in class enough. What is going on?"

Angelo studied the carpeting. He remained silent and then: "I'm too old. I don't belong here. I should graduate with Dewayne and Josiah and Chance this spring. They are my friends and my age. I have been left behind." Angelo stopped talking and you sensed a familiar shroud descending, as if he knew precisely when an adult had tread too close to his vulnerabilities. His eyes glazed.

Mendoza began to talk. "I was just like you, 'Shlow. I turned nineteen during my senior year in high school. You know what? Even then I was not mature. Even then I was not ready. Sometimes you have to wait and find out what life holds for you. Just stay afloat and try to get away from Chinle. There's nothing wrong with being nineteen when you graduate."

Angelo nodded. Yes. Sure. Yes. He made a quiet joke and rose and edged around the corner and pushed through the office door. It swung closed and I asked the coach if he thought his words got through to Angelo. "I have no idea," Mendoza confessed. "His life is chaotic, and the reservation is a bad place to float. I want to see his light go on."

Keanu was a classmate of some players who were excellent students, but those who came running into classes to try to persuade teachers to hand out passing grades made him uneasy. He rooted for the team and even tutored a player or two, but the wheedling did not feel right. "Teachers feel so much pressure from the community to make sure athletes play," he said.

That did not happen in Parsifal's advanced English class. He took no crap.

"Don't bullshit me! Where are your papers?"

Parse, as he's known to his students, had walked into his darkened AP English classroom clapping his hands. "Let's go, let's go. Showtime!"

A half-dozen girls sprawled on the rug conferred on Oscar Wilde. A male student typed on a school laptop, teasing out his thoughts on a Buddhist interpretation of *Jane Eyre*. A boy curled an arm around his girlfriend, snuggling as they reviewed their essays. The classroom chairs were arrayed in a crescent moon around an old blue armchair, Parsifal's throne, where he sat like a laid-back king, glasses pushed back on his head, white curly locks falling in a mass down his nape. The lights were perpetually set on dim, and a wood statue of a horse hung from the ceiling along with quotes from William Blake, a string of Christmas lights, and posters explaining how to file the common college application.

Nothing was off-limits; his was an intellectual gymnasium. Navajo and white people? Sex and romance (within reason and as refracted through novels)? Bring your sharpest thoughts and no bullshit. Parsifal stood six foot five and had a gliding walk. He pivoted and said loudly, "You are lucky you can stand up, man!"

Parsifal glared and pointed at a teenage boy, who grinned back, uneasy. Oh man. What does Parse want now? The boy wore a T-shirt with a Nike swoosh, and his hair was pulled back in a traditional knot wrapped in white yarn; long hair on a young Navajo signified the root of thought and abundance. Parsifal turned to the rest of the class and, still pointing at this boy, explained: "This bastard sends me a text message at midnight! I'm worried it's something about my wife and daughter and it's just you, *you*, wanting to ask about *Hamlet*!"

Everyone laughed—the boy too.

"An eight-page single-space analysis of *Hamlet* is due Thursday at six a.m. If you want to stay up all night writing, knock yourself out." Twenty minutes later, Parsifal led the class, tugging, prodding, through a talk that segued from a nineteenth-century novel to slavery to the complications and entanglements of white people and Native Americans. The only verboten answer was anything easy, anything clichéd. Navajo teenagers have a reputation for being reticent, but few shied from this fray.

"What's pride? Should I be proud of being white?"

"No!"

"Are you proud to be Navajo?" "Yes!" Why? "Our culture and ethnicity derives from our traditions," a girl said. Parsifal pressed. "Can you be truly proud of something you were born into by default or only by something that you have earned?"

The students came back at him. "Some of us are proud that we are still here after what our ancestors went through. Our culture, our sense of ourselves, derives from our traditions. We're still here, and that makes us proud."

Parsifal nodded. Now he shifted course.

"Is everyone here able to succeed at the best college?"

They nodded as one.

"Then will you sign up for the goddamn SAT, man? C'mon, c'mon, what are you waiting for? None of this Navajo putting-it-off stuff."

Parsifal pulled this maneuver every week. These were Chinle High's better students and he wanted the dream that they might attend top colleges and college ambition to rattle around in their brains. Year after year he cajoled and ignited and got his best students into top colleges, often in possession of full-scholarship rides. Nachae's cousin, a Parsifal alumna, just graduated from Cornell.

The class pivoted again and dived into *Pride and Prejudice*, debating motivation and flirtation and the nature of love. One student was adamant that Darcy, the principal male character, was guilty of rape.

"You're a crazy bastard," Parsifal replied approvingly.

They segued to the nature of gendered roles in dating and sex. Parsifal turned and looked at Keanu, who yawned. The teacher wrinkled his nose, disbelieving. "We're talking about love and sex and you're yawning, Keanu? You are working too many hours at Burger King?"

The class drew to a close, the bell about to sound. "Are you guys keeping all of this in your minds? Because I won't be here tomorrow. I'm taking my dogs and bows and going hunting in a canyon, dig it?"

They did.

Parsifal had an earlier incarnation as a world-class cliff climber, those long curly locks of white hair blond back in the day. If you nosed around Google, you could find photos of him clinging to toe- and handholds on high and sheer cliff walls. He was in his sixties now, old enough to worry about what would happen to kids like this when he retired. Professional mortality spoke with sotto voce urgency.

Parsifal did not intend to teach English, and God knows he never planned on teaching high school. It just turned out he knew how to set a young brain on fire. We met days later at his apartment in Many Farms, a place filled with Navajo rugs and photographs and hunting bows and rifles along with fossils found on camping and hunting expeditions into the hidden canyons and mesas of this land. He had a couple bottles of fine whiskey salted away.

"We're going bouldering," he said. Cool, I said, lying flat-out. I loved to hike, I loved to explore canyons and mountaintops, but I'd never been taken by the idea of hanging by my fingers and toes with too much air between me and the earth. Off we went in his pickup truck, bouncing toward a cut in the earth known as Owls Nest Canyon.

I asked what drew him to teaching.

"I fucking hated high school. I was bored out of my goddamn brain—it was stultifying. I got Ds in every class. I had very few friends and did no real introspection."

Parsifal enrolled at the University of Arizona and felt his brain boot up. He earned a degree in literature and strapped on a backpack and took off for Europe, hopped trains, stuck out a thumb, slept in railway stations and on mountainsides, drank lots of wine and flirted with all the pretty women. He climbed anything vertical. He enrolled at the Sorbonne in Paris and got a master's before heading back to Arizona to get his PhD. He kept climbing, hunting, finding secret places from Patagonia to the Rockies.

He taught at the University of Arizona and got bored. His father, another Parsifal—"It's a family curse"—was the college professor. He felt drawn ineluctably, as if riding the tides, to teaching high school. "With all these degrees, I thought maybe I could see what bored the hell out of me in high school."

He took a job as an English teacher at a prep school on a bluff outside San Diego. He coached the surfing team, teaching those boys to slip inside breakers. It was a sweet life and he needed to quit. He liked those kids but he'd catch himself looking at them and thinking: You're smart and articulate and your families have lots of money and tutors and all the advantages of wealth and class. That's cool. You just don't need me to get where you're going.

Maybe it was a climbing buddy, maybe a former colleague in his doctoral program, he's not sure, who mentioned that the Navajo reservation was looking for teachers. Parsifal applied online to Chinle High School, was interviewed over the phone and promptly hired. He shooed his dog Buttercup into his car and drove to the high desert to conduct a reconnoiter. He walked through the school, ate at the Junction Diner, saw the canyons and hogans and cliffs and all those kids. He was a fish on a hook. "I realized this is a place worth staying."

"You never have to worry here about waking up in the morning and asking yourself, 'What am I doing here? What is my purpose?'"

He was no starry-eyed fool. His students have few libraries and books, they sit on the bus for hours. Families were splintered, some fathers had gone missing, some kids had roamed so far into life's wilderness that they lost sight of the path back. "You pick any of the social problems that exist, it's here."

We crossed Sheep Dip Creek and climbed slowly across plains toward the Chuskas. "Whenever I start worrying about that, I say to myself, 'All I can control is this classroom. All I try to do is set a brain on fire.'"

He married an Anglo woman, Carissa, a speech and language

therapist while on the reservation after years of wandering in and out of relationships. She yearned to live in her native Nebraska, to have a farm and a child. But this land had embedded itself in Parsifal; he could not leave even as he and his wife had no desire to split up. So she lived in a Nebraska farmhouse with their daughter, and he drove there many weekends, a thirteen-hour drive snaking through the Rockies. He spent much of his summer there.

Life was a vagabond journey.

Hours passed and we drove back from bouldering, which consisted of my watching this sixty-three-year-old man read a boulder like a book and pull himself up near-invisible finger- and footholds. We descended toward the improbable blue of Many Farms Lake, a dammed-up pool in the desert. An old pickup truck rolled toward us in a cloud of dust, and a middle-age Navajo woman in a cowboy hat waved. Stop.

She and Parsifal exchanged *yá'át'ééh*s.

"I've had sheep taken by a coyote, the same trickster who has bothered us before, I am certain of it. I am tired of this varmint. Could you . . . ?"

Parsifal nodded, agreeable. He was a formidable tracker and hunter and from time to time the Navajo turned to him for help. He walked across their land and camped and hunted in lost canyons, and it was the least he could do. She thanked him and we drove on. "It won't do any good. There's a lot of coyote out here," he said. "But she'll feel better about those lost sheep."

Parsifal required every student in his AP English class to apply to three private colleges and three public universities. They could pick just a single college in the Four Corners states of Arizona, Utah, New Mexico, and Colorado. They had to ratchet open their doors of the possible. All must sign up for SATs and ACTs. I told Parsifal of Nachae Nez's experience: He drove to the test site, sat in the parking lot in his car, and pulled away without taking the test.

Parsifal shook his head, deflated. He liked Nachae. "Shit. I can make them sign up, but I can't make 'em go. Nachae's a bright kid, self-aware. He can still remedy this if he can get himself to pull away."

Parsifal talked with each student in the class about college. It was Keanu's turn, the brightest kid in a bright class. Parsifal asked him where he wanted to go to school.

"My mother wants me to go to Diné College. It's close—"

Parsifal cut him off. "I didn't ask where your family wants you to go. I asked where you want to go." Keanu frowned and drew a breath. Then he said the word: Swarthmore.

So let's figure out how to make that happen. Keanu took his SAT and scored a 1290, which was superb on the reservation and damn good anywhere. Keanu was worried; elite schools wanted scores of 1400s and beyond, and so he signed up to the take the test again along with his ACT. Some days Keanu felt like he was running a race blind. He had no tutors and no one in his family even knew where those colleges were.

Why, he asked, would they want a kid like him? Keep going, Parsifal replied. "Believe in these kids," Parsifal said, "and they will not disappoint you."

Keanu typed college essays on his cell phone and transcribed these when he got to school. Some ideas came to him in dreams, a power line that transmitted in English or Navajo, depending on the night. "When the dreams are in Navajo, I sometimes have a hard time expressing myself because a lot of our words do not really exist in English." His dilemma, what to do with his beautiful verb-saturated Navajo language and its dozens upon dozens of conjugations, became the subject of one of his college essays.

Keanu was dipped in Traditional and Christian ways and he wrote of that too. He attended a fifteen-member Black Mountain Mennonite church and he loved Daniel, a Navajo preacher who kept his hair pulled back in a white knot and had a beautiful baritone voice, the services held in a white tent held up by great wood beams, as they burned cedar and sang of Christ. It was Keanu's place of comfort. His grandmother and great-grandmother told him Bible stories and tales of the Navajo Holy People and Changing Woman and Spider Woman and the Coyote Trickster, and some nights he and his sister put on their turquoise and hopped and spun and danced in the Traditional way.

I asked him if his grandmother had accepted that he might leave. Keanu squinted at me, nodded tentatively. "I think so. I think she has. I really want to show my younger siblings there is more to the world than the rez." We stepped out of the trailer and walked toward my car. The limestone walls of the mesa glistened and the sheep and goats milled restlessly.

"I will miss it so much," he said.

He grew nervous as he talked of what was to come, his sentences flecked with conditionals: if I get better scores; if I can write the essay I want; if those colleges want a kid raised in the shadow of Balakai Mesa. If I go east, if I become a doctor and ready to serve my nation, first I will take my mother by the hand and lead her out into that world. He looked me in the eyes. "My life plan is to travel with my mom. She hasn't seen this world. I want to make that our adventure."

CHAPTER TWELVE

Too much listening without hearing, too much nodding without understanding, too many teenagers on the cusp of manhood who acted like silly rez ballers. It was mid-January and the Wildcats had let a mediocre team from Window Rock, their traditional rival, sneak back into a game and almost tie the score. The boys slept on defense and looked uninterested in waking up. This was the stretch lap before the state playoffs, and although the players had lost just a single game this month, Mendoza was twitching. All season he had played the "kid whisperer," invited Angelo, Cooper, and Dewayne to sit in his monastic cell of an office in the Wildcat Den and talk strategy and life, talk about looking around the corner of senior year into the world beyond.

Sometimes the boys engaged and sometimes they stared and mumbled and glanced at the door.

Now he saw bad habits not kicked, oblivious passes to oblivious cutters, and play too lazy to even be called defense. Mendoza walked to the locker room at halftime, sorting the possibilities. Their record stood at 14–8. The team was certain to make the play-offs, but their rank in the state remained uncertain. If the team came into the postseason with a mediocre record, they would have to play playoff games far from the reservation against top-seeded teams.

Maybe, he thought, the boys are not ready for the playoff, maybe they are too immature, maybe I overestimated them. I am too old for this. He pushed open the locker room door and felt a wall of sound, Jay-Z and a thumping bass line echoing off the white tiles and gray concrete floor and bathroom mirrors, players yelling and laughing. He had had enough, no more, no *mas*.

"Turn that thing off!"

Click and silence.

Mendoza stooped and picked up the wireless boom box speaker and peered at it, an archaeologist examining a peculiar artifact. He turned and reared his arm back like a baseball pitcher, cradling that speaker in his hand. The boys' eyes popped wide as Coach prepared to hurl that mighty little noisemaker against a tile wall and shatter it into 1,004 pieces.

"How much does this thing cost?"

Mendoza's question registered as a low growl.

A player whispered, "Four hundred dollars."

Seconds of breath-holding silence passed.

"Okay, that's too much." Mendoza placed the speaker back on the floor. "I don't make that kind of money."

Dewayne smiled uneasily, hip to what he hoped was a coach joke, and squinted at the whiteboard where Mendoza began to scratch diagrams and point out mistakes. Angelo clapped his hands, impatient, competitive, and instructed teammates to pay attention. He could be as focused during games as he was flaky in practice. Cooper stared straight ahead, his face a frieze. Josiah and Chance and Curtis studied that board, studious as monks.

"Guys! Get serious," Mendoza said. "Everyone on the rez can shoot the ball; we have plenty of shooters. Don't be prideful. We win with defense. Period."

Elijah pulled off the protective goggles he wore to cover his eyeglasses and listened as Coach listed mistakes in general and his in particular. Elijah's slumbers on court were maddening, especially as they arrived without warning, like a cold front slipped down off a mountain range. He would stop moving and stop looking to take his silken mid-range jumper, the best on the team. He leapt higher than anyone on the team, yet he drifted clear of rebounding scrums. He was a fine athlete, but his defense too often devolved into a toreador wave.

"Elijah, do you plan to wake up?" Mendoza asked.

Elijah nodded. Yes, he saw the virtue of awakening.

Maybe he was just spacey or maybe he had fallen too hard for that pretty girl from Many Farms. Most midwinter evenings now, Elijah and his girlfriend, Shawntay Yellowhair, with those glistening eyes, typed out Facebook posts thick with declarations of love and peppered with heart emoticons and exclamation marks. She ran down out of the stands after a recent game and they kissed at courtside and the players cracked up. "Whoa, whoa, Elijah. Man, you a killer, bruh."

"Pack your cologne," Mendoza advised the boy by way of postgame dating advice for the lovestruck.

Elijah leaned in as he exited the locker room in Window Rock and whispered, "Mendoza's telling us what we need to hear: the truth. You don't need to take it personally. What he says, you just have to listen."

Not all the boys weathered upbraiding so easily. Months ago

when Mendoza pulled that garbage can onto the court during practice to make a point to Dewayne, the boy felt his cheeks grow hot. Navajo are communal; to be embarrassed before peers carries a cactus sting. Dewayne rode the school bus back to Pinon that evening, watching purple ridge lines roll by and later told his mom he was considering quitting. His mother felt a surge of anger and wrote the letter that ended up singeing everyone's feet.

A few days before this Window Rock game, I drove to Pinon to check in with Dewayne. His mom told me to wait at the far end of the Bashas' supermarket parking lot and they would guide me to their home. Slouch low, she advised.

Slouch low?

There was a shooting two days ago, she told me; a Navajo gang-banger took a bullet in that parking lot. There was talk of blood for blood, and everyone was on edge.

I slouched low in my old Subaru.

Not so many minutes later we turned our backs on a glorious desert morning and bolted the door and sat in Dewayne's kitchen and talked. He was a good student and gave no hint gangbangers caused his nerves to jump, other than to say that he had tired of sitting around and watching television.

He adored family cookouts and Traditional songs and ceremonies. He loved to sit with his grandfather, a cowboy who had given up the horse and taken up the walker, and listen as the old man wove stories of growing up before Bashas' and asphalt, before the modern world leaked into this land. The government drafted him in the 1960s and shipped him to Vietnam. Ask what he saw and about those he lost, and he fell silent.

Last summer Dewayne and his cousin Ziggy, who played on last year's team, herded their grandparents' cattle in the canyons north of town. Early one evening as the bellies of cumulus clouds flared crimson, the boys heard the roar of a mountain lion and it caused the hair on their necks to stand on edge. He dreamed of becoming a mechanical engineer in Phoenix, but he would miss his land, he knew that.

Dewayne's thoughts now were on the playoffs, his nerves jumping during class, his sleep restless, his dreams filled with visions of success and failure. How do you get along with Mendoza? His fellow seniors heard in that question cause to tiptoe. Dewayne was not sure he agreed with them anymore.

Mendoza anointed him as starting point guard in late December, and Dewayne told his father and they began to watch one college game after another, an extended graduate course in point guardism. Notice, Nate told his son, how the best guards keep their eyes fixed up court, probing, watchful, a golden eagle after prey. You must see the game better than everyone else.

Dewayne liked this challenge. He was a fine shortstop, the fulcrum of a baseball team just as a point guard is in basketball. He made another discovery: The coach had insight. "Our relationship has gotten better. I talk to him a lot more now about my playing style. I think he trusts me." He had skipped Mendoza's practices in the Den last summer to play baseball, and joined Chance and Josiah on weekends for those marathon rez ball games. That, he acknowledged, may have been a mistake.

"Mendoza knows a lot. I might have learned more with him."

Dewayne no longer waved at defenders. He stayed in a low and springy crouch, perched on the balls of his feet, and attacked ball handlers like a raptor. When he sprinted and went airborne for a steal during that winter tournament in the White Mountains, he whacked his hip and writhed on the court. He talked of that bruise with pride. "Mendoza forces us to play defense. When we do, we win."

Halftime ended and the Wildcats trotted back into the five-thousand-seat Window Rock arena as the local fans hooted and urged their boys to run the Wildcats out of the building. The Chinle boys quashed such dreams straight-out. Angelo faked, spun on those surprisingly deft feet of his, and got fouled by the Window Rock's center, a talented kid who wore a scowl like a shirt. There were steals and stutter steps and on-the-button passes. Elijah cut smartly and his shots began to fall into the hoop. It was as if a hard-of-hearing team had begun to hear Mendoza.

The Wildcat defenders became a locust swarm. Every corner of the court became claustrophobic for Window Rock, and the Wildcats claimed an easy win.

Perhaps Mendoza's worries had gotten the better of him, perhaps a coach cannot quite see his team's precise place in the narrative stream of a season. Angelo had broken his early-season pattern of making stupid fouls, and Josiah had made peace with passing and playing tenacious defense. He learned to shrug off those cousins and friends who told him to ignore old man Mendoza and shoot. You could be a shooting star! He rolled his eyes and kept on passing.

Cooper was an immutable force, game after game his effort and smarts consistent whether his shot fell or not. Curtis Begay had looked fawnlike early in the season, wide-eyed and jumpy. More often now his high-arching jump shots rose like baseball pop flies before falling through the hoop, the net leaping. He was gangly and perhaps he would grow a few more inches and fulfill his father's dream that he would play big-time Division I basketball for Arizona State.

The parental rifts remained half-healed, tensions and rivalries set aside if not discarded. Joni Burbank organized an evening game between players and families; mothers and fathers and cousins and most families showed up in the Den and ran and passed and shot, and laughter echoed in the empty arena. A few nights later the parents catered a pregame dinner for the coaching staff and players, making their best Navajo tacos, beans, rice, and barbecue. The meal fell a touch short of jovial. Not everyone sat at the same table, but no parent came accompanied by a food taster.

Josiah's mother, Rosalyn, stepped away from the tables and I caught up with her and we spoke in the shadows beneath the bleachers. She was that rare Navajo mom who encouraged her son to take flight, to leave the reservation and maybe not come back. "I tell him he should attend a four-year college. My friends say I'm crazy, that I should tell him to stay."

She shook her head. Josiah needed to depart even if she remained behind, even if she cried at night and her chest grew tight again. He had so much potential, so much. What was here for him? She paused. Her voice dropped a few registers: "I'm struck by how quickly it's over."

Her eyes were wells of sadness and residual wariness. She still believed Mendoza should have played Josiah and his senior classmates as a unit more often, that group of boys she regarded as her sons and as extended family. Her worries still built like storm clouds until her voice grew tight and choked. She could not easily forget slights, and as I spent much time in Mendoza's company, perhaps she was suspicious of me too.

She started to talk of that and then shook out her hands and nodded toward the hall that ran under the stands, as if to show such thoughts the exit. "Josiah told me it was time to let it all wash away. We have to come together for our boys. We had to think of what was best for the team. He's right. I'm trying."

Mendoza had not joined the parents and staff for dinner. I walked down the cinder-block corridor and pushed through the swinging door to his office and found him with a plate of food in his lap. Joni Burbank had brought him rice and beans and tacos. He was invariably welcoming, and a laugh arose easily within his chest, and he would make time for any parent who wanted to talk. But he wrapped himself in a serape of aloneness.

I asked why he didn't want to sit with the parents.

"I learned a long time ago not to get too involved with families. They always want something, they're always watching what you say to other parents and their kids. Talk to one and everyone else wonders what you are saying."

I mentioned that Dewayne considered himself an enrolled student in the School of Mendoza and that his father spoke well of Mendoza too. The old coach smiled, not bitter, not annoyed, aware of the human comedy offered up by each season. "Dewayne's dad and mom kept complaining to me last season and early this year, asking me why Dewayne wasn't playing. Finally I said, 'I can't play him because he won't play defense. He won't pass. He just isn't ready.'"

Dewayne played defense and rebounded and passed, and their boy had become a team mainstay.

Mendoza looked around his office at the whiteboard and the rosters of the various teams his Wildcats could face in the playoffs and all of his scouting notes and videos. He had NBA tapes he turned to for inspiration, Larry Bird and the Celtics, Steve Nash's Phoenix Suns, the Lakers with Magic, his talismans. He knew so many coaches, old rivals who had over the course of four decades become friends as well as protégés who remained loyal even as they coached their own teams. The Alchesay coach recently passed along scouting reports to his old coach and mentor. Mendoza had passed a lifetime living in Navajo lands without being Navajo, and he was at peace with his duality. Just don't ask him to pretend.

He pointed to the walls of his office.

"In here I'm safe."

Mendoza had stepped across a perilous line that week. Before practice he told the boys to file back into the locker room and to take seats.

"You could grab a top seed in the playoffs. I'm proud of you. But I've watched you and we have a problem."

He told of seeing the pouches of bitterroot and corn pollen and the boys rolling up arrowheads in their socks. He had watched their legs vibrate and seen them come up flat in practice before big games. Too great a belief in magic, too much worry about the hexes of another team, spoke to weakness.

"These are signposts of fear. We're scared."

Mendoza illustrated his point, as he often did, with a personal story. "My parents abandoned me as a little boy, and my brother and I lived with my grandmother in her adobe hut. She doused that kerosene lamp each night and darkness became total. I ached to yell, to scream, to ask for a hug. I pulled a thin blanket over my head and prayed. 'God, if you're real, I'm trusting you to protect me from demons tonight.'"

He looked at the boys.

"I guess I was afraid of my family disappearing. I was afraid of dying. I was letting fear eat at me like an animal. Do you understand?"

The boys nodded after a noncommittal fashion, Yes, not really, maybe. They knew of Mendoza's evangelical beliefs and his reputation for seeing the unseen. Last year's seniors swore by his ability to sweep away demons. These boys were more wary.

"Everyone in this life knows fear," Mendoza said. "Witchcraft is real, and it can scare you."

Mendoza parceled out words like bread crumbs for wary birds, trying to entice the boys into a conversation even as he was aware of stepping perilously around the vastness that was Navajo cosmology. He saw the shadows and demons of Navajo and Apache traditions as acutely as a medicine man. He did not deny magic so much as he saw it as dangerous and possibly the devil's work. He did not say that; he was neither insensitive nor reckless.

"I am not questioning anyone's belief," Mendoza said. "I just prefer your rituals are observed outside of the locker room. Fear can make you not think right. You'll throw a bad pass. You will not see things as they are."

The assistant coaches sat expressionless, arms folded. Julian was well read and well traveled and reflective, and close enough with Mendoza that the men roomed together on team road trips. They saw eye-to-eye in their evaluation of the kids. But Julian's beliefs were a Navajo mixture of Traditional and Catholicism, and he had no interest in letting one elbow the other aside. At night in those hotel rooms, Mendoza read his Bible and prayed. Julian was okay with that even as he made very clear that he did not want to talk of evangelical Christianity.

He watched Mendoza through wary eyes.

Mendoza soldiered on. "I have a cousin who lives in southern Arizona," he told the boys, "a powerful *bruja*, a witch. We have not talked in years, but I know her power and it's fearsome. I have had medicine men line up before games to shake my hand and pat my shoulder, and they try to palm off spells on me, and one time my arm went numb from my shoulder to my fingertips. I wiped it off, shook it off."

In a high school locker room in New York, such talk might sound crazy, but here no one flinched, no one rolled their eyes. To live in Navajo lands was to talk to sensible people who have had matter-of-fact experiences that in a different context might sound unimaginable, a hallucination. When I told such stories to friends from back East and added that I found some plausible, real even, they nodded vaguely and no doubt figured I had gone around one too many bends.

Mendoza talked a while longer, and the boys wore blank-faced stares and he shrugged. *Enough.* He had tried to open a door. "Some of you guys won't say anything. I get that. We're in a locker room, you're in front of your friends. Just remember: Shake off fear. Don't live with it."

The boys filed out to run their sprints and shoot layups, and the assistant coaches followed and said nothing. I sidled over to Mendoza. What if a player or an assistant coach construed your talk as an attack on their beliefs? Mendoza allowed that was a possibility if unintended. "Fear starts in the mind. If you want to leave here, if you want to go out into the larger world, you have to go without fear."

He walked out to the practice floor.

I sat in a crowded row of seats behind the Wildcats bench at the Window Rock game, nestled next to burly Joe Yazzie, another of those Navajo who had a coach's eye and feel for the game. He attended nearly every game and knew the players, their tendencies on the court, their attitudinal tics, their ability or inability to stick a jumper in traffic. Like Mendoza, like everyone in Chinle, he worried what the stress and tension of the playoffs might hold for this mercurial crew. What happened when they collided with those big Valley teams? Would they snap and crack? How far could they go into the state playoffs, and could they carry Chinle with them?

Yazzie's hair was salted white, his skin wind-cured and coarse as sandpaper. He had the oft-heard Navajo work history: construction worker and shepherd and now stablehand, a man with a gravelly voice and a self-deprecating sense of humor. As the game wound down and the Wildcats took victory in hand, he asked if he could get a ride back to Chinle with me and the coach.

Three hours earlier the temperature in Window Rock had fallen below freezing, and frosted air had nipped like a dog at my skin. I asked him how he had planned to get back if he couldn't snare a ride. He held out his thumb; that was how he'd gotten to the game. He nodded at my unspoken question about the cold. "It's dangerous. Usually I get a ride."

We walked across the parking lot to my car, Mendoza, Yazzie, and me, the air frigid and dense, and the bald pate of the high cliffs dusted with snow. We rode north through the fields and pine forests that ran across the feet of the Chuskas. A new lunar cycle offered up a bare sliver of a moon, *tł'éhonaa'éí*, "the one carried at night," and a million stars claimed the night sky. My passengers advised me to exercise care on the empty road. This was free-range land, and cattle and sheep roamed where they pleased, as did bear, elk, bobcat, and coyote.

We passed Wheatfields Lake, the surface a ghostly sheen of ice. Its waters poured down millennia-old crooks and rivulets into the belly of Canyon de Chelly. Joe peered into dark stands of ponderosa pines and spruce and firs and remarked that Sasquatch lived back in there. Bigfoot sightings are widely reported and often believed here; the creature fits easily with Navajo tales of shapeshifters and giants.

"Sometimes I hear their cry," Joe said, "or my nose picks up their foul smell. They stink! In such moments I sing softly to the Holy People and ask for their protection."

"Do the Holy People answer you?"

"I don't know how good their hearing is," Yazzie said. We rode on as he chuckled to himself.

It took an hour to curl around the perimeter of that vast gorge, and Joe talked of his friends and neighbors, several of whom I had come to know. He was friendly with Cecil, the jeweler who set up his table in the canyon to sell his fine-wrought bracelets and necklaces and who tutored me with so many stories of life here, and Ben, the burly guide who took my son Aidan and me into remote canyon corners. When he could, Joe got rides from these men to the games. On nights when he could borrow a car, he returned the favor and became their chauffeur. No one wanted to be caught out walking a dark road in winter.

"You can stop here," he told me. I pulled to the side of a two-lane road that curved in an arc down toward Chinle, the lights of which glimmered in the distance. Joe cared for the horses that carried tourists into the canyons, and the owner let him sleep in a one-room shack nestled in a fold of sandstone and cottonwoods. The dark was dense as ink, and we heard horses snorting and rustling unseen in the corral.

A coyote howled; she was nearby and her cry was akin to a mother's shriek.

Joe waved good night and ambled into the dark. The coach and I blew on our hands and drove on toward Chinle.

CHAPTER THIRTEEN

Early Saturday morning, fortified by a plate of blue corn pancakes and hours before the boys gathered for practice, I drove *ha'a'aah*, east. My drive rose steadily upward, past a wayward mustang and a jangly band of coyotes returning from a nighttime hunt, until the facing wall of the Chuskas dominated the horizon. I turned and drove through sagebrush and juniper to a small parking lot and set off into Canyon de Chelly for my daily three-mile walk.

This morning I walked alongside Cecil Henry, who carried a cloth satchel filled with his expertly crafted silver bracelets and necklaces of turquoise and jet and abalone shell, the holy stones of the Navajo. As a teenager, he disdained this switchback trail as too easy. The canyon was veined with precipitous and hidden paths and his feet and fingers were sure as those of mountain sheep.

Cecil was no longer young, his gait stiffer, his hair a lush black forest receding, his face weathered as a canyon wall, and so he joined me as we skirted sinuous walls of ochre-colored sandstone. He patted the stone and advised that we remain silent a moment and imagine when these rock walls were mountains of sand whipping and shifting in lost geologic eras. We passed a team of young Navajo runners clipping up the trail at a great rate of speed, and when we reached the wash at the bottom, Cecil set up his card table along the embankment and laid out his jewelry before stuffing his hands in his leather jacket.

I asked if he was cold. Cecil shook his head. The chill blue shadows will flee soon enough when *Shá hiinaah*, "the sun rising up," glinted over the canyon rim. "I find the sun and remain in its light." His voice was inflected with the lilting, up-and-down vowels that were the inheritance of those who spoke tonal Navajo as their first language.

We exchanged notes on Wildcat basketball, sharing our wary optimism about the boys' winning streak and the coming playoffs and shaking our heads at their confounding habit of not engaging until the outcome of a game was in doubt. Cecil and his brother Ted played basketball at Holbrook High School a half century ago, and it remained the sport closest to his heart. He was related by clan and bloodlines to several Wildcat players, and he worried about the playoffs, which started the following week. Were they ready? These boys, sometimes they listened to Mendoza and sometimes they go deaf.

He cracked a joke about the cluelessness of youth and laughed and that made me laugh in turn. He repeated the punch line and we giggled again. His aunties, sister, nieces, cousins (the precise map of relationships was difficult for this *bilegáana* to penetrate) set up shop at nearby tables as we talked. Some mornings I waved at Cecil and his gaggle of relatives and walked on, seeking solitude. Today I tarried and examined their work with an eye toward a purchase. My eldest son, Nick, and his wife, Caitlin, were expecting their first child, a baby girl. I had been in Navajo Nation for five months, and the nearness of my first grandchild's birth had stoked longing. I thought of Nick often and desired to give him a memento to mark our long-ago walks into this canyon and the birth of his daughter.

"Sons, children, are important, the stars in our sky," Cecil told me. "My son Terrance, he loved this canyon."

My gaze turned to a silver bracelet, the Tséyi storyteller. Cecil was a master of this Navajo silver-making form, which included every symbol of Canyon de Chelly—conquistadors in their terrible armor and petroglyphs and Massacre Cave and those peach trees and Navajo wagons. I was in my running clothes and didn't have my wallet. I asked if he could set the bracelet aside so I could buy it when I had money handy.

He waved a hand, dismissive of my foolish fastidiousness, and instructed me to take the bracelet. "I will see you again. We know each other, we laugh at each other's jokes. You will pay me later." He also had no idea where I lived or my last name.

I spent the remainder of the day visiting an old farmer near Rough Rock, twenty miles to the north, who showed off his Churro sheep and demonstrated how his whistles made his sheepdogs twist and turn and come to a halt, the canines silent and obedient as Buckingham Palace guards. A hawk began to loop and dive in the sky above, and the farmer's calico cat slinked away, looking skyward like a thief caught in a spotlight, and took shelter in the hogan. Later I walked the northern plains and peered into the gullet of the Carrizo Mountains, trying to read its crags and ridgelines. For a moment or two I thought that I had spotted a mountain lion, then decided I was a fool; those fierce felines did not give away their game to amateurs.

I arrived back in Chinle as afternoon faded to the contused purple-blue of early evening and drove to the Thunderbird Lodge, where Cecil told me he would eat dinner. This was the first of the Anglo trading posts established at the mouth of the canyon in the nineteenth century, though it was now Navajo owned. Cecil was settling into a plate of mashed potatoes and meatloaf in the cafeteria along with a younger man who had the stringy and tousled look of a fellow with hard miles on his odometer. They joked and laughed and made clear that they had raucous stories to share. I begged off sitting with them, as I had to meet a friend for dinner. I handed Cecil $130.

Cecil counted the cash and shook his head: "I have to be honest. You gave me too much. It was one hundred and twenty."

Oh man, I said, those stupid Anglos can't count, and that drew a laugh from them. Cecil, a man without a car to his name, a man who might have to walk miles home tonight, returned my ten dollars and thanked me for buying his bracelet. We shook hands and I stepped outside and peered at a night sky freshly inlaid with the brightest of its stars. I pulled my jacket tight. The desert temperatures had begun their sharp step down into the iced reaches of early morning.

My cell phone rang early the next morning. It was a local number, which was rare.

Hello?

Cecil's niece was on the line and she apologized for bothering me and asked if I had paid her uncle the night before. Perhaps she was giving voice to a family concern, as that was a handsome bracelet I'd walked off with the previous morning. I assured her that I had seen him and settled up.

There was a long pause.

"What time did you see him?"

Early last evening. "Is there a problem?" I asked. "Is Cecil okay?"

Another long pause. "He died last night. My uncle froze to death."

The next minutes were confused, as I fumbled, asking for details, mumbling offers of comfort and condolence. Cecil was within sight of his cabin when he died, he had asthma, maybe he choked on sunflower seeds. She and her family wanted to make sense of his death, what happened, she was so sorry to bother me.

Cecil died not of seeds but of drink, as his relatives later told me. He had an appetite for booze, and he used the money I paid to buy too many drafts of too-powerful liquor. There was no judgment implied, in my reckoning. My father, a boozer until he sobered up late in life and worked hard to make amends for his considerable sins, once said that if you shook the Powell family tree, drunks would fall off most branches. Alcohol was the great carnivore pursuer of Navajo, a beast that had chased generations to the ground and throttled too many. I rarely met a family that had not lost a brother, a cousin, a father to booze.

Indians are five times more likely than Anglos to die of alcohol-related diseases. That statistic cannot be explained as genetic predestination; recent studies have found that Indians harbor no special DNA weakness for alcoholism. Navajo take peyote carefully and with reverence and love for the spiritual world it reveals and largely without falling prey to abuse. There's more to their haunted relationship with liquor, an outlawed substance, a product of despair and perhaps of inchoate protest against the melancholy and harshness of post-invasion existence. By federal law, alcohol is banned on reservations unless a tribal council decides to legalize it.

As it happened, I had breakfast a few days earlier at the Junction Diner with Navajo police captain Michael Henderson. Henderson was a thoughtful and phlegmatic man bored by evasion and bullshit. Yes, crystal meth was a plague on the reservation; yes, heroin was found here; and of course there was an abundance of marijuana. But booze was the whirlwind, the destroyer of the Navajo spirit. If Captain Henderson had his way, he'd legalize the stuff. Educate teenagers about it, work with parents and schools and grandparents to teach safe habits and use, demystify it, regulate it, talk about it. Nothing was accomplished by playing cops and robbers with moonshiners and smugglers except to toss men in prison and ensure that they'd emerge with felony records and yet more hardened. His was a lonely voice.

Many Navajo are fearful of letting alcohol into their homes or to acknowledge that it might already have taken up residency. The Blanding historian Robert McPherson recalled discussing alcohol with his Navajo students. He asked them to debate the question of prohibition and to vote at the end. The debate was intelligent and anguished, and prohibition won by a considerable margin.

I could not shake the shadow of haunted loss and the swiftness of Cecil's end. With no clear purpose other than to pay respects, I drove that evening to the Parish Hall, the aluminum-sided recreation center that rose behind Our Lady of Fatima Church. I stepped into a dimly lit hall used for bingo games and sewing circles and youth leagues and found a place jammed with 250 people sitting at long tables and standing against the walls. Cecil's brother and sister and niece and a cousin or two sat or stood at the front at a small card table set up beneath an orange basketball hoop.

They would gather here for four consecutive nights and throughout this evening. Cousins, uncles, friends, and neighbors walked to the front table and picked up an old microphone wrapped in masking tape. It produced a scratchy, muffled sound, as though the speaker had tuned in from a neighboring dimension, but they paid that no mind, speaking of Cecil's humor and generosity in Navajo and in English and a marriage of the two, in hope that plainspoken words might ease his passage into the next world.

Families brought Navajo tacos, posole, lamb ribs, doughnuts, coffee, tea, soda, and sweets, the platters piled high on tables at the back of the hall. I sat to the side on a bench until Cecil's family found and led me over to shake hands with his extended family. As it is taboo for Navajo to save for their death expenses, a stream of old men, young women, and children wandered by and pulled dollars out of wallets, purses, shirt pockets—one dollar, five dollars, ten dollars, twenty dollars, spare change maybe, anything to help pay for Cecil's funeral and burial costs. Hours passed and I bade goodbye, and still pickup trucks and vans and cars pulled into the church parking lot, tires crunching across gravel under a frozen sky.

Cecil roamed the fields of evangelical Christianity, but he was born and died a Roman Catholic, and those beliefs remained central to his identity. The next morning I returned to Our Lady of Fatima, which was run by Franciscans, and knocked on the rectory door. Brother Bernard invited me in. Cecil's laughter made me smile, I told Brother Bernard, and his stories left me wiser about life and the ways of this nation. Would you, I asked, tell me about the nature of Christian faith and death on the reservation?

"Let's stand on the porch," Brother Bernard said. "I need to catch a smoke."

Brother Bernard had a tangle of gray hair, angular features, and sky-blue eyes fixed as though on a distant point. Although temperatures hovered in the mid-40s and morning had come up gray with a chill, he wore a brown habit and sandals and sat on a wooden rail as we talked. Brother Bernard had rolled into Chinle years ago, his personal pilgrimage having reached a temporary end-point in this high and desolate desert. He and a Filipino friar conducted services in four churches on the reservation every Sunday, the times staggered just enough to give the men time to shake hands with parishioners and catapult into their car for the drive to the next church.

Brother Bernard took care of the driving, fast and with wrap-around shades over his eyes.

There has been one iteration or another of Our Lady of Fatima in Chinle since the nineteenth century, and, as was their wont, the Catholics incorporated aspects of Navajo culture in service of a grander project. The current church was built with logs in the eight-sided-hogan style with a hole to the sky in the middle. The masses attempted to marry separate millennia-old traditions, the Holy People and God and Christ. We "strive," the church bulletin stated, "to walk the sacred pollen path of Jesus and his message."

Brother Bernard and the other friars performed baptisms without many marriages, communions without lots of questions, funerals for whosoever's soul required it. He shrugged, his voice as dry as gin. "We have a missionary dispensation; it is an experiment in reaching beyond boundaries. If you were a traditionally bound Catholic, you'd commit suicide here."

In these winter months, he said, more than half the funerals performed at Our Lady of Fatima were for men and women who got drunk and froze to death. Some struggled through alcohol's haze to rise and flee, and others appear to have sighed heavily and laid there as cold ran its icy fingers into throat and lungs and heart. Families scraped and struggled to pay for the funerals and a nominal fee for renting the hall, and the church helped financially when it could. Traditional Navajo lived providentially, believing it sinful to store away too much money for the future when those around you have need. "I come from a taught culture of poverty," Brother Bernard said. "Theirs was an instinctive one."

We shook hands and agreed to talk again.

That afternoon, I walked down that canyon trail and fell into step and conversation this time with Cecil's niece Dee Steinem and Erick Begay, her husband. Erick was a jeweler of excellent reputation and the couple owned a handsome and well-regarded jewelry store in Boulder City, Nevada. More relatives waited on the canyon floor, a sister, cousins, granddaughters, and sons, and we sat beneath a molted cottonwood with bare branches that soared like outstretched arms into the sky, and listened to Cecil's story, layer upon layer. In days to come, Cecil's brother Ted and grandson Ravis, a park ranger, would unearth still more strata.

"He is our loved one and you became a friend," Dee told me. "You should know what sort of man he was."

Cecil was born into *Ta'neeszahnii*, the Tangle Clan, and born for *Tó'aheedl'inii*, the Water Flows Together Clan. He was the youngest of eight; the family called him the caboose. His brothers and sisters fed, clothed, laughed with, and raised him, and taught him to help herd the family sheep from the winter camp on the rim to the summer camp on the floor of Canyon de Chelly and to work the autumn harvests.

In old days, Navajo adults put turquoise and silver around their neck, hanging from their ears, and on their wrists before they set out to harvest melons and corn and peaches and maize. The Holy People taught the Diné that to wear beauty ensured a beautiful bounty. Cecil and his siblings could run their fingers through the sandy dirt of ancient fields and now and then find shards of turquoise and silver dropped by long-departed aunties and mothers and fathers.

"That canyon was so filled with life back then," said Ted, Cecil's brother. "My God, it was beautiful." I met Ted for lunch at the Denny's in Chinle. He wore a Cardinals football cap tucked tight over his scalp, and his piercing eyes and prominent Roman nose and mischievous smile reminded me strongly of Cecil's.

He told me how an Anglo photographer arrived during the Great Depression, passing weeks in a canyon he came to love, talking to the Navajo and climbing rock slides in search of vantage points. That photograper, Ansel Adams, shot a photo of Cecil's great-grandmother Rose as she held her baby boy swathed in white on a cradleboard. She offered the barest hint of a Mona Lisa smile. That photo, titled simply *Navajo Woman and Infant*, has appeared in collections around the world. Cecil and Ted's parents sent them to boarding school in Holbrook, where the boys lived in wooden barracks with other Navajo and children of migrant Mexicans and Chinese and blacks. The boys struggled to master English, their Navajo verbs strip-mined and replaced with the spare few provided by English.

"Boy, it was rough. We took a long time to learn English," Ted told me. "I told my daughters, 'I don't want you to go through that.' They learned only English. I regret that now."

After he graduated, Cecil, or Cee, as he was known to family, set off hitchhiking to Chicago, where he became a welder and union man and made fine money hanging from bridges and scampering up the side of half-built office towers. As a canyon boy, heights did not faze him.

The Navajo Nation remained a lover tugging at Cecil's soul, and in time he yielded to her blandishments. He returned, and he and Ted made jewelry, sitting together at a narrow work table, Ted at his right hand, hammering and polishing and soldering. To sell their work, they traveled a continent, walking Pacific beaches and the mountains north of Santa Fe. They strolled along the streets of Denver and Dallas and rode the New York City subway. Sometimes Cecil took along his son, Terrance, who smiled and listened as his father and uncle told so many tall and wonderful tales.

Ted pointed at the wall behind me in the restaurant. I turned and saw on the wall a print of a famed Edward Curtis black-and-white photograph, Indians on horses riding single file across the sandy bottom of Canyon de Chelly.

"That's our grandfather on the lead horse."

That book of photos went by the title of *The Vanishing Race*. Ted pushed his hat back and his eyes caught mine full on, his good humor draining like water from a trough. The implied erasure stung; the Navajo are a living people. "We did not vanish. That's our canyon still."

Cecil and Ted made nice bundles of money and as often gave much of it away. They paid for a sister's dental visit, a cousin's electric bill, a niece's trip to an amusement park, an auntie who had never been to Las Vegas. They struggled with the bottle, and then Cecil kicked it and traveled as a lay preacher, wandering north to Yellowknife, in the forested vastness of the Northwest Territories, where he preached God's word to the Athabascan. One late night near the Arctic Circle, he called Ted, his exuberance a knife cutting through that scratchy telephone line:

"Ted, it's Cee! You're not going to believe this! They speak the same language we do. We understand each other. We really are cousins!"

Back in Arizona, Cecil married a woman named Evelyn, and he loved her so intensely. She left him for another man, and that decision left her nearly as unhappy as it did Cecil. She became pregnant and that boyfriend deserted her. In her desolation, Evelyn called Cecil and he drove to her home and cared for her and they fell in love all over again. Her water broke in April at the time of the holy winds, the *Nitch'i Diyini*. Trees crashed and rocks tumbled and dirt and sand rose like clouds of smoke off the desert floor. His wife's labor had complication piled atop complication, and the road was an impassable bramble, and an ambulance could not reach them.

Evelyn died along with her baby.

Tragedy was not done with Cecil. One night his son Terrance from another woman walked home along the roadside, and a truck wobbled and veered and struck him. He spun dead into a ditch. Cecil and his extended family laid Terrance into the earth in Black Rock, the family camp atop the towering peninsula that rises ribbonlike between Canyon de Chelly and Canyon del Muerto. Cecil put aside his Bible and began to fall.

Sadness seeded within, although he was not easily reduced to another broken Indian. Cecil drank too much and carried the heaviness of loss, but he made jewelry of astonishing quality and showed much love. Whenever he walked into the Canyon de Chelly National Park Service office, he called out to Ravis, the young park ranger, "Hey, grandson!" Ravis stepped around the desk and wrapped Cecil, his grandfather, in a hug, and they talked a tumbling stream.

Ravis was a young man comfortable in many worlds and cultures, and in the winter, when the Holy People slept and tourists appeared infrequently and the National Park Service furloughed him, he became his grandfather's apprentice. They traveled to shows in Santa Fe, Flagstaff, and Durango. Ravis was courteous and well read and Traditional, and I several times sought him out.

Turn too quick down a conversational path too personal and he could grow reticent, a flower reluctant to reveal its colors. He adored his grandfather, though, and worked to make him known in the fullness of being.

Not long ago before his death, Cecil had put an arm around Ravis's shoulders. "Grandson, I had it all. I had a nice truck! I had a good job, I had a home, I had a beautiful wife and children. I've traveled the world. I've been to the Arctic Circle, I've seen the Pacific Ocean, the Atlantic Ocean, I've been to cities and met a lot of good people.

"Grandson, don't end up like me, whatever you do. You do better than I did and remember where we came from."

Cecil served as caretaker of the Henry camp in Black Rock, living in an eight-by-ten wood cabin with a bed, a small TV, a log stove, and a workbench where he made his jewelry. On those nights when he could not find a ride to the Wildcat Den to watch Angelo and Cooper and Josiah, he listened to the games on his radio, clapping his hands.

Ted and Ravis and Dee and the rest of Cecil's family celebrated Cecil's funeral mass in Our Lady of Fatima with prayers and incense and joy that he was keeping the company of Christ and Holy People.

We walk this way to bring about the reign of God in our midst so that all may begin and end in beauty.

Afterward the family climbed into trucks and drove to Black Rock along a dirt road that passed under the eyes of the Chuska and through groves of juniper and mesquite and onto that bare peninsula between the canyons. There they chanted and recited Traditional words learned in thousands of years of traversing this planet, and lowered Cecil, fifty-nine, into his grave. He was laid shoulder-to-shoulder with Terrance.

Ted felt a yawning hunger for solitude and could not bear to remain in Chinle after the funeral. He drove through desert and ponderosa and cactus wilderness to his daughter's home in Phoenix. In accordance with tradition Ted walked into the hills and took his knife and cut yucca root and went home and ground it and washed the suds into his hair, leaving it streaked red.

The next morning, on the fourth day following the funeral, he recited Traditional words of mourning to the *hayiilka*, the morning twilight. Ravis and the rest of the family did the same back in Chinle.

That night Ravis went home and tapped on his laptop a recollection of the day his grandfather died. Old friends of his had come to visit, and Ravis had taken them on a long walk through the canyon. "We were the only ones down there, as it usually is during the winter. Birds were chirping, the wind was whispering, the water was trickling, and even the coyotes echoed their cries for us to hear.

"I later realized that the howling coyotes were trying to tell me something if only I had listened a bit more clearly. . . . As we exited the canyon that afternoon I received the news of my Grandpa's passing."

CHAPTER FOURTEEN

Like an animal alive, the approaching playoffs ate at Angelo's innards and seized his dreams. He sat on the team bus as it bounced and swung along an old Indian route rolling through a raw and nearly deserted corner of the reservation, past Horse Thief Mesa and Mormon Ridges and Many Ghosts Hill. The bus nosed northeast for three hours under a low-slung winter sun toward the boys' final regular season game in Page.

Saddle-sore, yawning with hunger and jangled, Angelo and the other boys sat on the bus as it entered Page. The Page Sand Devils had bewitched the Wildcats over the years; this past December they had beaten the Wildcats in Chinle in overtime, a loss that caused Angelo to stomp in disgust with himself and ask how he could have fouled so much and so stupidly and why he could not get his shooting untracked. He had let down his teammates and himself and slept fitfully that night.

The Wildcats were 18–8 now. The team had clinched a playoff

spot, although its precise seeding remained uncertain. Angelo's legs vibrated. He hungered for this rematch, the last game before the regional tournament, a tune-up before entering a playoff time of promise and danger. Would he rise to the challenge and make family and clan proud and prove that he was . . . what? Going to succeed, whatever that meant? His future remained shrouded. "I tell myself these are all just another game. Sometimes I believe myself."

Page was another town of the borderlands, sun-scorched and tinder-dry, occupying the western edge of the traditional Navajo world. It had seven thousand residents, 60 percent white and 35 percent native and with no small number of children of mixed parentage. Page originated as a 1950s work camp for the men who built the grand Glen Canyon Dam. The town's eastern border sat on an upland desert plain, and the streets sloped steadily downward past tourist motels and a Pizza Hut and beachwear and curio stores to the shores of Lake Powell, a surreal inland desert sea beset by drought and shrinkage. The marina overflowed with white yachts and speedboats that glinted in the sun, and if rain and snow failed to fall before summertime, they might not make it out of dockage.

Mendoza chatted a moment with the driver and the bus kept rolling past the high school and across a curving bridge over the shadowed vastness of the Glen Canyon Dam to a stone-strewn mesa that overlooked the lake. The boys stepped out of the bus in their road-trip dress shirts and black pants and ties and ambled, talking and joking, toward the lip of the mesa. A setting sun bathed lake and buttes and vermillion ridges in a silken light. They fell silent.

Mendoza stood by the bus. "They should see things of wonder. It's important for us natives to realize what this world holds."

I had driven this way a few days ago and pulled into a dirt parking lot in the desert and made arrangements with a young Navajo guide to see Antelope Canyon X, a slot canyon. I walked across scrubland until I began to step down a sharp, sandy incline into a sandstone maze smoothed by eons of rains and floods. There were hallucinogenic curves of pink and red and purple rock, and I slipped through shadowed passageways so narrow I had to squeeze sideways, moving from antechamber to antechamber. Here and there shafts of sunlight lit the sandy floor as if flashed by a cosmic stagehand, another place of wonder. These natural chapels, my guide told me, are where the ancestors whisper at night.

Some nights, he said, he climbed down in the darkness and sat and listened to their chattering. I suggested I'd like to join him, and he smiled and shook his head. I don't think so . . .

The bus returned to Page High School and the boys walked into another gym, where fans sat shoulder-to-shoulder without a spare seat to be found and a din rose in enveloping decibel waves. The Page Sand Devils had gone 9–1 in January, a ferocious team blowing out opponents by thirty- and forty-point margins. The Wildcats looked mathematically no less fearsome, accumulating a record that month of 10–1, but victory or defeat, their games tended toward narrowly, tensely fought affairs.

The Wildcats had yet to achieve escape velocity, that mix of intimidation and inevitability that coalesces like an aura around dominant teams.

The Page coach, a man with a barrel chest and the glowering swagger of a defensive lineman, had five words of growling advice for his team, all but a few of whom were Navajo: "Beat these Chinle guys. Now!" They nodded and clapped loud. On the far side of the scorers' table, Mendoza offered counsel to his teenagers. "Page is going to come out tough and cocky. Stay within yourself.

This is our chance to show them what we're all about and for you to learn what you're made of before the playoffs."

Mendoza, even now, did not know how his boys would answer that challenge.

The Wildcats, it turned out, were a coiled snake this night, vibrating and ready to strike. The game opened with a Wildcat whip pass and another and another and back again to Dewayne, who launched a mortar shot of a three-pointer. Good! Josiah jumped to his feet on the bench, loosening a banshee howl. Cooper offered a short lesson in hooping to his defenders, three straight baskets, a jumper, a fallaway, and a spinning layup, the last off a silken dribble pass from Angelo.

Chinle led at the end of the first quarter. Cooper, still hungry, came up with a steal. Angelo had a big rebound and a block; little Josiah put up one of those looping-from-the-heavens three-point shots that fell clean through. Chinle led at halftime, 38–20. Chinle had unleashed a disciplined destruction, and the Page fans had grown quiet as morgue attendants. "Hey! Hey! Hey!" Mendoza said to his boys in the locker room. "They're surprised at us. We're not surprised at us. Right?" Keep that ball moving with fast, intelligent passes, he told them. Stay ruthless.

Mendoza was too hopeful. The Wildcats soon set about handing back the game to the Sand Devils. The second half opened with a Chance inbound pass that floated like a knuckleball and a Page guard intercepted it and scored. The boys rushed their offense when they should have been methodical, shots clanked, and freshmen played like freshmen with much too little purpose. The Page Sun Devils, tough and cold-blooded, attacked and put Chinle on its heels.

A human refrigerator of a Sand Devil center, the six-foot-four and 270-pound Cheyenne Richardson, executed a handsome drop step and hit a spinning layup over Angelo. The Chinle lead shrank to five points, four points, three points. Joni Burbank put her hand over her mouth; Nate, Dewayne's father, rubbed his temples; Josiah's mom, Rosalyn, implored her son. "C'mon, c'mon, Josiah."

It was as if spirits, conflicting and wild, had come to inhabit this game. The game had run in one direction in the first half and now it came sprinting back down the hall at Chinle. Strength turned to weakness and edged toward panic. In the final minutes, Mendoza made a high-energy man-to-man picket fence of his best athletes, anchored by Angelo, and the Wildcats arrested their decline. With less than a minute left, Cooper dribbled the ball, casual, looking away, and whipped a sly no-look pass to Chance, who cut to the hoop for an elegant layup.

Chinle won 60–55.

Line up!

Russ Skubal, the Page coach, told his team to hurry and shake hands with the victorious Wildcats; league rules required good grace. But when he reached old man Mendoza, no congratulations, no smile. Skubal offered a quick handshake and flicked at eye contact. "We'll see you in the tournament," he said, terse. He spun on his heels and walked away. Mendoza allowed himself a barely perceptible smile as he walked to his locker room. He had splendid evidence that his boys had crawled into a competitor's cranium.

"Hey, listen," he told his boys. "There are the games we have to win, and this was one. Don't try to force things. Don't try to be a hero. Don't try to walk on water. That first half, that was you!"

Or so he still hoped to persuade them.

The door to the regular season had closed. Chinle had finished as one of the highest-ranked teams in the state in its class. We drove back, the coach and I, through that empty quarter, nothing to be seen in the encompassing darkness. Raul remained silent a long while before he said, "I started off thinking to myself, 'We're eventually going to be tough to beat.' A lot of nights I wondered if I was right. Now I know. I don't want to hear from parents anymore because I didn't play their kids. From here on in we're going with the best players.

"We're chasing a championship."

He was talking less to me than to himself. Not long after, I braked hard as four moon-washed steers strolled across the road. I slowed down after that. Playoff season was no time for the coach and me to get into a crash.

It felt like a dream, a fast-dawning joy.

The Wildcats had become champions of the Arizona North division, best of the rez, no better team to be found in the immense reaches of the Arizona side of the Navajo Nation. The Chinle boys had marched into their postseason regional tournament and shut down Tuba City and Window Rock. Now they were happy wanderers on the floor of their cavernous Wildcat Den, confetti tossed into the air, hip-hop playing, and long hugs from parents and aunties and uncles. Many hundreds of fans remained, clapping loud, exchanging high-fives. There was Josiah putting his arms around his mother, Rosalyn, who cried and smiled and cried. There was Chance with his glinting eyes and matinee looks, the fatherless boy who races horses bareback, posing for photos with cousins and his mother and lots of high school girls.

Tears rolled down his cheeks.

"Champions of Navajo," he said. "This is a dream."

Angelo and Elijah, childhood best friends, had printed and sold black-and-yellow T-shirts featuring their photograph and reading THE TWIN TOWERS. They took turns kissing the golden tournament trophy cup as their families snapped photos and applauded. The customized jersey business was a lucrative side benefit of a good season on the rez, and many of the Wildcat boys and their families designed and printed up dozens of T-shirts to sell to family and friends and fellow students.

Cooper walked by in his custom-made T-shirt, which read THE LORD IS MY STRENGTH AND MY SHEPHERD. MY HEART TRUSTS IN HIM AND HE HELPS ME. PSALMS 28:7. He fell into the arms of his grandmother Virginia, who hugged him tight and rubbed his scalp.

These boys were mountaineers arrived at an emotional peak, rez champions, a culmination of all those years of middle and high school hooping and those iterations of summer leagues. Their passion and relief was plain to see and Mendoza sat courtside and watched impassively. He thought to himself:

This means nothing, nothing at all.

The Wildcats' regular-season record had ensured they would make the playoffs even if they fell short in this tournament. To take too great a pride in becoming the best team in the Navajo Nation was to yank at a false door. You stepped through, and there was a long hallway to the bigger door that was the state playoffs and all the non-native teams that lay in wait for Chinle. That was the world Mendoza yearned to dominate.

"To become champions of that world out there, that is what we play for, not this."

The coach would wait until tomorrow, until the boys had gathered again beneath the basket in the Den for a playoff practice, to remind the boys of that cold reality. For now he let them cry and hug as applause washed down like a waterfall. This tournament had run two days, and at least five thousand fans had filed into each game, no matter afternoon or night. If you had a job, you called in sick; if you lacked a car, you cadged a ride. Dads walked down into the Den with little kids on shoulders, mothers with babies wrapped in light blue blankets, Granny and Grandpa following, gingerly, some on canes, some with walkers. That FedEx driver, the husky young man with the long ponytail who still got stopped on the highway by middle-age Navajo who remembered him as a star on the Wildcats team that reached the state finals a decade ago, found seats with his wife and kids. Steadily, one after another, gray-haired men and women stopped and asked if they could pose with him for photos.

Mendoza plotted his tournament game plan with his usual unbending emphasis on defense. Slow the rez game, toss a roadblock in front of teams that love to run and shoot and run, and you will slay your enemy. Borrowing from the old Indiana University coach Bobby Knight, who preached unrelenting defensive schemes, he went with a switching man-to-man defense. Zone defenses let the boys stand around and encouraged sloth. Facing Tuba City, whose star Tristan Yazzie was an ebullient and conscienceless shooter who, when hot, could hit from anywhere inside half-court, Mendoza took aside his best defenders, Chance and Josiah, and told them: You will be his shadows. Yazzie goes nowhere without you. Slow him and we'll see if the rest of his team can compensate.

The Tuba boys folded.

In the locker room afterward, Mendoza pointed to his defensive stars. "These guys were Yazzie's worst nightmare. Their coach told me no one has ever played him like that. Never. I've won a state championship because of guys who played defense like that.

"When you get old, when you are a grandfather, you can tell your kids you were the champs of the north."

"An *hacheii*." Angelo murmured the Navajo word for a maternal grandfather. Mendoza looked at his big man and nodded Yes, 'Shlow, an *hacheii*. You'll make it there one day.

Toward midnight custodians swept aisles and dimmed the lights and I climbed the steps out of the Wildcat Den accompanied by Floyd and Derek Simmons, itinerant radio and internet sports broadcasters and father and son. They had traveled the northland reservations all season long, putting in tens of thousands of miles, broadcasting nearly every big game for *Sports Zone*. The internet had allowed them to turn this reservation and Navajo diaspora into a great sea of an audience.

The Wildcats' first playoff opponent would be the American Leadership Academy team from Queen Creek in the Valley of the Sun. I asked Derek if he had seen them play. Are they good? He nodded, his look cautionary. "They are very big and talented. The Wildcats need to watch out. This is the best team they will face this year."

Are they better than Chinle?

He held out his hands, palms up. Who knows? Maybe.

Mendoza shrugged when told of this. Any playoff team could become a dagger in the ribs. This night he chose to worry about only his team.

We drove south out of the Navajo Nation across plains of yellow grass bent sideways in the wind. In the distance a stockade of cypress trees half-hid a small ranch house, and on a rise cottonwoods stood silhouetted against a pale gray sky. The coach had taken a day to practice with his team after the tournament and now he was driving out of the northern desert, taking the ten-hour round-trip to scout American Leadership Academy, which was playing an introductory playoff game on its home court.

We crossed the reservation and rolled into Holbrook. Years ago, when his Holbrook team played in the state championship game in Mesa, outside Phoenix, a many-miles-long car caravan of fans had followed the team bus there, as police squad cars sat with lights flashing at intersections and officers waved on hundreds of cars and trucks. When Mendoza's team walked into that arena, fifteen thousand fans rose cheering in the stands.

They clapped and stomped and hooted so loud that Mendoza's ears rang for hours. When the team returned as champions, a midnight parade snaked through Holbrook. There was another parade the next day. "We had three parades in all, right down Navajo Boulevard. Men on horses waving their hats at us, girls blowing kisses at the boys, and guys piling out of the Empty Pockets Saloon and cheering loud."

This day he stopped at an adobe Mexican joint for lunch. A half-dozen older residents of Holbrook wandered by to shake the hand of their former coach. He made eye contact with me.

"Life here is brilliant when you win."

His oldest daughter lived in the Mendozas' house in Holbrook. She had married young, but her husband developed a too-deep affection for the bottle and that marriage dissolved and she became estranged from her parents. Mendoza and his wife ended up raising her kids, a rerun of parenthood. His daughter has reached a far better place and reconciled with her parents and her children, who are in college and beyond. "I guess you could say I did a better job the second time. I guess I was a better grandpa than father. My daughter tells me, 'Dad, you've changed.'"

He stopped talking and I waited him out. "I hope she is right."

We followed a twisting road down through the Tonto National Forest in a driving rain, mist hanging like beards around the chins of mountains, precious water dripping off arms of saguaro cactus. We rolled hours later into Queen Creek, where the Phoenix exurbs expired in the desert and the Superstition Mountains rose gray and jagged to the northeast.

We leaned into the rain and ran across the parking lot and entered the American Leadership Academy gym. Mendoza let his eyes take a run of the sparsely populated place. There were at best eighty fans sitting in the bleachers and at least sixty-five of them were Navajo.

"Sitting room only," he noted.

The American Leadership Academy team, known as the Patriots, came running out onto the floor, big and white with the single exception of a black point guard. Their opponent in this first play-off game was the Holbrook Roadrunners, all of its players Navajo or mixed heritage gave away many inches and pounds and no small amount of talent. Holbrook had fielded a mediocre team this year and this game appeared a massacre foretold.

American Leadership Academy presented an interesting and very twenty-first-century American challenge for its opponents, native and non-native alike. The Queen Creek school was part of a network of charter schools in a state where regulation of charters was considered bad form. Arizona law applied no lash of conflict of interest and right-to-know provisions to charter operators, and as a result the state was regarded as the most charter-friendly in the nation. The regular public schools in Queen Creek were strong academically, better by most measures than the American Leadership Academy schools. But the charter's founder was a Mormon businessman and former Utah politician, and his marketing stressed Mormon-aligned values. Several Mormon parents spoke to me of getting pressured at church and in sports leagues to send their children to the "Mormon" charter.

If religion was one pillar, athletics was the other. Several of the

American Leadership Academy schools have come under scrutiny for recruiting athletes in violation of state rules. The Queen Creek branch offered its own baroque twist when it was revealed in December 2017 that a Patriots player who was a star tight end on its championship football team and a smooth-shooting forward on the basketball team had in fact graduated from high school the previous year in Alberta, Canada. He was living in Queen Creek with his uncle, who, as it happened, was a coach at American Leadership Academy.

American Leadership Academy officials executed a fine dance of dismay, proclaiming themselves shocked and saddened by this news. Its athletic director talked of confusing visa requirements and then acknowledged "holes in our process" and then stopped talking to the press altogether.

The school dropped its ineligible player from its basketball team and was forced to forfeit those games in which he played. But the Arizona Interscholastic Association curiously put off a decision on whether to bar the Patriots from this year's playoffs. The Patriots roster remained stocked with big top-flight players and so presented a formidable challenge.

I called officials with the state sporting association and offered that their failure to act struck me as a curious lack of consequences. They replied in voices dipped in a pool of reproach. You are, they said, awfully sure of your facts. I replied that American Leadership Academy officials themselves did not dispute that an athlete who should have been a college freshman had starred on its football and basketball teams.

My observation was met with silence at the other end of the line. Weeks later, after the Patriots' playoff run ended, the interscholastic association put the Academy's football and boys' basketball teams on probation for the following school year, which will prevent the teams from competing in those playoffs.

The Wildcats knew nothing of this controversy. As Mendoza noted, teams on the high desert existed in a world of their own, at a distant remove from the sports politics of the Valley. They could worry only about playing their best.

The American Leadership Academy Patriots easily disposed of the Holbrook team. The charter's best shooters were tall, lanky, and cool-eyed—and in particular a six-foot-seven guard with a soft shooting touch from twenty feet out caught Mendoza's eye. He jotted a few notes and put his pad away, as he had seen enough. We drove back that night through rain turned to snow, thick and damp, a skidding haul into early morning.

The following afternoon Mendoza leveled in a fashion that set his teenagers to rocking back and forth. This team you'll face is big and good. Those Valley boys can rebound and shoot, and they are quicker than they look. "To be honest with you, this might be the best team we've seen. We can beat them, but it will come down to concentration and relentless defense and blocking out."

Oh, and another thing.

"Don't be prideful. No heroes. You have to help each other. By the time we're done Saturday, will we have lived up to our potential? That's the question that should keep you up at night."

CHAPTER FIFTEEN

In the days before the playoff collision with American Leadership Academy, the waitresses walked by Mendoza's booth in the Junction Diner and made shy small talk and wished him well. Retirees and schoolteachers and Navajo ranchers in cowboy hats came strolling by, too, and shook the coach's hand and scanned his eyes for signs of worry or confidence. Mendoza went to the Laundromat and aunties quietly nodded at him as they folded clothes, and he walked across the parking lot at Bashas' and drunks clapped and cars stopped and drivers rolled down windows and yelled:

"C'mon, Mendoza, c'mon! Go Wildcats!"

He kept on walking.

It was no different for the boys, their minds chattering like caffeinated parrots. Cooper, the sophomore, was enough of an old soul to know that he should try to grab a championship when he had the chance. He walked into the gas station to buy juice and the cashier said good luck, and a man with an inlaid turquoise belt buckle and a white cowboy hat instructed him on the virtues of letting the game come to him. He stepped outside and took a breath. Josiah had more people calling to him than usual when he ran the red dirt roads behind his trailer and more on his mind as he tried to concentrate in math class. He was halfway through senior year, and he had college applications out. What would the admissions offices make of his grades and scores? What would it be like to leave his land? And all the while the playoffs ran on four paws straight at him. He awoke at night and ran his hands through his hair and stared at the ceiling.

"I can't stop. I'm thinking about it all the time."

Chance took a long ride on his horse, crouched forward, a jockey with legs gripped tight to flanks, taking in the horse's scent, galloping through a limestone canyon under a baby blue sky.

Their world was about to collide with the world out there and pressure pushed heavy on their chests. Once, years ago in Window Rock, Mendoza had a top-flight team, state-championship material. The tournament was about to start, and all the aunties and uncles and granddads and children were getting ready to double up in motels in Phoenix. Coach came into work and there were his two best players shifting foot to foot.

We drank this weekend, Coach. We got really drunk. We're sorry.

Mendoza loved those boys, but he suspended them right there and informed the athletic association, and later his team lost badly. Anxiety and a chaser of pressure had laid them low. "They told me it was too much, all of the family and clans. That was when I learned counseling was as big a task as coaching."

Early on the morning of the game against American Leadership Academy, having nothing better to do and feeling restless, I drove to Curtis Begay's home in the emptiness of the red mesa lands beyond Many Farms. Curtis's father, Vernon, had offered to drive me up to Black Mesa to show me where his father's people came from. First though, Vernon and his wife, Jodonna, sat me at their dining room table and brought out albums with Curtis's basketball photos from the age of five to the most recent hoops tournament, along with those of his rodeo and lasso contests.

Their ambitions for Curtis were many. They wanted him to excel at academics and attend a four-year university in the Valley of the Sun or farther south in Tucson. They wanted him to excel at basketball so that he could get a college scholarship. He was the oldest of four children and he could light a path for his three younger siblings. To stay or go, to make a way in that broader world—Vernon and his wife faced no such choices at that age. They were a high school couple, they fell deep in love, and in senior year she became pregnant with Curtis.

"I think of how young I was," Jodonna said, "and how difficult life became."

Baby Curtis was three months old when she graduated from Chinle High School. She came from a family of educators, and she declined to let life as a teenage mom put her on a road that expired in the desert. She and Vernon married, and she obtained her bachelor's degree and became a teacher. Vernon found a hospital maintenance job, and those jobs made of them a prosperous couple on the rez, able to afford to build a two-story house on curving mesa land.

With that success came gusts of jealousy. Build a two-story house? Did they think they were better than everyone else? "The Navajo don't always want to see you do well," Vernon said. "Maybe they wish ill upon you, and then you have to get a protection ceremony." He tried to associate with Navajo who dreamed big, who wanted to build and run businesses.

Vernon steered his truck up a dirt road cut into the flank of Black Mesa, edging around potholes the size of small ditches. We climbed higher and he showed me the spot where his father and other Navajo had rescued a drunk driver whose car skidded the wrong way at the wrong place and pitched over the side and bounced and tumbled until it was snared by tough-as-steel mesquite trees at the edge of a four-hundred-foot drop. His relatives say the Mexican wolf, *Canis lupus*, had made its way back onto Black Mesa, an omen loping onto its long-ago hunting grounds. He set the emergency brake and we stepped out and took in the sweep of the Navajo north, reds and yellows fading to a haze of purple-blue, wind washing our faces.

He spoke of longing. "We got married so young, we never had a chance to see what the future might hold for us. I wonder at the life . . ."

He left the thought unfinished, perhaps not wanting to hear himself complete it and to deal with the implications. We climbed back inside the truck and rode back down. The playoffs started in a few hours, and he had dreams for Curtis that he prayed he would see translated into reality.

The Wildcat bus rolled to the playoff game under a gray fish-scale sky, cirrus clouds scudding. A supposedly neutral site, Ganado arena sat on the Navajo reservation just thirty-eight miles south of Chinle. It had five thousand seats and nearly all would be filled by Navajo this night. The bleachers nearest the floor were kept partially retracted on three of the arena's four sides, which would leave the densely packed fans peering down into the court and lend a cockfight quality to the game.

Cooper watched the great sweep of prairie and the occasional sheep farm and windmill slide by. Angelo peered into his phone; Dewayne slept, slack-jawed; Josiah put his head back and closed his eyes. No luck. He was wired. The boys exchanged a cumulative five words as that aluminum tube slid into Ganado. They arrived hours early and the line of ticket buyers stretched two hundred yards long, curling along the side of the building. Children and teenagers and adults walked over and tapped the sides of the Wildcat bus as it slow-rolled by: "*Good luck, boys! Good luck—win!*" The boys passed into the arena and down to the playing floor and through the halls to the locker room, bare-bones, no towels, no uniforms hung and pressed at the ready. The boys pulled on creaky metal locker doors and dressed, telling nervous jokes: Oh man, let's start this game already. Boys folded tiny foil wraps of sage and cedar into their socks and stuck fingers into Beau's pouches, sprinkling his stashes of corn pollen and bitterroot on their heads and letting it settle on their tongues.

Holy People protect me tonight.

Mendoza observed them, quiet, their faces betraying no emotion. "Silence is a good sign. They seem ready."

This was not high school football in Texas, nor high school basketball in Los Angeles or Houston. No scouts would sit in the stands taking notes, no college coaches would drive five hours to this desert plateau to take the measure of a modest-size Navajo kid. If they lost, most seniors would see their competitive basketball life end forever. Win and their reprieve would extend another game, three at most. Maybe a couple of the boys would play a year or two for a community college team. Today's game was about now, a yearning nation of uncles and aunties and cousins and friends and high school alumni who traveled hundreds of miles to this game. It was about thousands more who would sit by laptops and radios in Las Vegas and Phoenix and Flagstaff and listen in.

Mendoza began to talk. Often during the season the boys would roll their eyes at coach's love of old basketball videos and his fondness for teams and coaches who had passed into history's shadow before they were born.

No giggles now. They leaned hard on his words and his whiteboard and all that experience of his and his quirks and tics comforted them. This isn't about the regional tournament anymore, he told them. "Champions of the rez? So what! This is the playoffs and this is what counts."

"You"—he pointed at Josiah and Chance—"you guys are my defensive hawks. Tonight you will take turns guarding their best shooter, he is a sophomore and wears number 23 and he is six-foot-seven. He's good. He will try to isolate on you, take you one-on-one and shoot over you. Do you care?"

Chance and Josiah, five nine and five four, respectively, shook their heads, legs rocking.

Mendoza sketched out a switching defense, a game plan predicated even more than in past games on thirty-two minutes of relentless play, a cumulative sanding down of these bigger players. "On offense keep cutting, go backdoor, and don't fear their height. Their big men are six six and thick, and they will block some of your shots. So what?

"I heard that some of you guys are knocking at the knees. Fellas, this is just preparation to go deeper into the playoffs. This is our thirtieth game of the season and the only playoff game we will play on the reservation. This is what you work so hard for. This is what you have to love."

Mendoza scribbled on the board, repeating, reiterating, reemphasizing. "'Shlow has to rebound just like he has all season long." Angelo stood up, ready to face what might come, starting to clap. Mendoza kept talking, his voice rising in volume.

"Look around you and say, 'I'm ready to go, I trust you. And you. And you.' We are ready together."

Dewayne got to his feet clapping, Josiah, too, and Chance. Elijah picked up a basketball and started to dribble it hard. Cooper rose and turned to his teammates and bounced on his toes. "'Wildcats' on three!" They jumped, ready. And they ran out of that locker room and down a concrete alleyway and onto the floor of Ganado arena as rockabilly blasted on the loudspeakers and thousands of fans rose cheering, stomping, howling. No future mattered—the desert wanderers had to win here, now, today.

The American Leadership Academy Patriots had arrived earlier after the long trip from Queen Creek. Big and long, as advertised, they joked and laughed and did little dance steps as they practiced and looked around at the sea of Navajo faces in this arena. Thousands had come to a first-round playoff game? Really? They shook their heads at an unknown world. Twelve of their fourteen players stood taller than six feet. Five were six five or taller. Some were being scouted by Division I college coaches. None looked worried.

The horn sounded and Mendoza waved his boys over and spoke to what was on everyone's mind. "Yes, they're big, and that does not matter. If we push, eventually something will open up. Play together and have fun. Enjoy!"

Chance walked onto the court and turned and jogged back. Mendoza peered quizzically as the boy held up his fist and forced the old man to give him a fist bump.

The Wildcats and Patriots began with a trade of baskets, parry and thrust, and then the Wildcats became a car fishtailing, nerves jumping. Angelo saw a rebound bounce off his hands, Chance cut to the hoop, quick and slick and went up, but one of the six-foot-six giants swatted away his shot. That tall white kid guard Mendoza had warned about, number 23, took a pass and turned and nailed a long jump shot in Chance's face.

Cooper curled to the corner. Dewayne found him with a pretty pass. Coop was wide open, and the crowd roared in anticipation. This was his money spot. His shot missed the hoop altogether, an air ball. He heard the blood chugging in his ears, the game a monster more unruly than he anticipated.

"I could not hear a thing."

Angelo made a balletic spin and *whap*! His shot was blocked. Curtis, five ten, tried to wave his arms and distract that tall shooting guard. It was like watching a grasshopper waving at a giraffe. Wildcat frustration hit an anxiety-laden peak when Angelo ran to get the ball late in the first quarter. He turned and looked to make a pass, but his teammates were frozen, not moving. In frustration he put up a long shot from beyond the three-point line. Mendoza winced and turned away, no need to watch as the ball barely glanced off the rim.

"Come on, Wildcats. Cowboy up! You're playing like scared white boys."

The first quarter ended with a blown Wildcat layup, and the Patriots had pounded on the Navajo to lead 17–4. After a long season and a great January run, the Wildcats had become a ship run upon the shoals.

Slow it down. Mendoza retreated to a cave of calm in such moments, no expletives and no panic. There were three quarters left, and rez ball quickness and speed and defense were equalizers. If they concentrated, if their desire was great enough, they could climb back into this game.

A minute into the second quarter, Angelo floated to the three-point line again and this time he tossed a no-look pass to Elijah, who cut to the hoop for a layup. Next Elijah ran to the foul line and rose with that elegant shooting form and tossed a jump shot into the hoop. Elijah was a senior, aware of what this moment meant. He had submitted no college applications. Lose and he would be left to the business of trying to divine his future. He would attack and attack. "I know I can't get back the time after it's gone."

Not long after, Josiah stripped a Patriot point guard and the Wildcats come down court. Cooper curled and caught a pass and again the Navajo in that fishbowl yelled in anticipation and Cooper nailed the three-point shot, net jumping.

Chinle pulled to within five points.

Nachae Nez sat on his couch in Albuquerque and loosened a howl. He had wanted to go to Ganado to root for his old teammates and friends, to swim in the kinetic currents of hope and desperation. A playoff game is a crucible. But four weeks ago, a surgeon again opened up his knee and again stitched together his torn anterior cruciate ligament. He had offers to drive him from his apartment in Albuquerque to see the game, but he would have had to sleep at his parents' trailer and their road this winter was a swirling brown mass of mud and their truck skidded like a drunk on skates. How could he walk around on crutches, what if he slipped and fell and twisted that knee again? Stay in Albuquerque, son.

So Nachae lay on the couch in his apartment, knee elevated as he listened to the Wildcats, his team making mistakes, falling behind, rattled. "Shit. I was one of the best point guards on the rez, one of the best shooters, and now I'm lying here." He balled his fists and cursed the shadows.

"C'mon, Wildcats! Play your fucking game!"

All season long the Wildcats had shown the ability to go on

runs, their defensive quickness a bear trap snapping on the foot of their prey. They did it again in the second quarter, Chance bellying up on that six-foot-seven-inch white kid, Angelo banging with the Patriot big men, his face red, his chest heaving like a heavyweight in a late round.

The Patriots were disciplined and talented and did not break. They kept swinging the ball, using their height to crash the boards. On the sidelines, their coach yelled again and again to push it. Go harder! Mendoza heard that and noted to himself that telling a team from a town near sea level to push the pace could be a mistake. He filed away that thought.

Dewayne drained another three-pointer. Chance grabbed a rebound and put it in high off the backboard against a player eight inches taller. Elijah juked, faked, and shot. Good!

Elijah's father sat and clapped and hooted in the northeast corner of the Ganado arena, a rough approximation of the seat he took in every game in the Wildcat Den. He needed a seat far enough from the floor to watch with dispassion, to see how the players moved and ran plays. He was a devotee of Mendoza; that man, he told Elijah, knows basketball. Listen to him!

He had worked just up the road for the past few months, helping to lay concrete and frame out a new reservation shopping center, and that had allowed him to see all his son's home games. That job ended a few days ago. "I got laid off." He shrugged; rez life meant making peace with migratory work. "My next job is going to take me a lot farther north, many hours' drive. My father-in-law has to take care of Elijah now."

The clock wound down toward halftime. Cooper hit a leaning jumper and the buzzer sounded and the Wildcats had pulled to within five points at halftime, 30–25. Panic had subsided, they had siphoned off the excess pools of adrenaline that made it so difficult to think. A reality remained: The American Leadership Academy team was very good, very tough, and they had weathered the Wildcats' run.

Throughout the first half, Mendoza stood, arms folded, at the far end of the Wildcats bench in his black-on-gray ensemble. He was Johnny Cash if Johnny had been reincarnated as a Tohono O'odham. His eyes missed nothing. He walked into the locker room. "We should be okay." The boys lifted their heads, surprised at his confidence. "You just need to relax. We're pressing, that's all."

Raul was insurance-adjuster calm, laying down facts. "We were so nervous in the first quarter we couldn't even catch the ball. Our half-court game was nonexistent. Again, guys, again: Relax. All season long, when teams think that we're out of a game, that they have you, they're wrong."

The boys trooped back out to the floor and ran through their layup drill and felt better about themselves. But the third quarter did not go remotely according to plan. The Patriots came out just as tough and relentless about pressing their height advantage. The game swung back and forth, and a Patriot guard hit a floater at the end of the third quarter. The Leadership Academy had pushed its lead to eight points.

The Wildcats had passed into the valley of shadow, the danger zone. The boys walked out for the fourth quarter to cheers deafening and imploring. Dewayne thought that he had never heard anything that loud in his life.

"Fundamentals, Wildcats, fundamentals!" "Wake up!" "DEEEE-fense!"

Martin, the athletic director, sat in the midst of all that anxiety in the single wall of bleachers that extended to the playing floor. The lean champion ultramarathoner, the Traditional, the son of a medicine man and a little German American woman, he had masterminded the theft of the old coaching legend from Window Rock in hopes of putting in place a coaching system that would produce Chinle winners year after year. The Wildcats' win total had more than quadrupled in just two years, and the players were graduating high school. Still, Martin did not kid himself. The design, the goal, the obsession shared by most of those within a two-hour drive of Chinle, was to win a state championship.

A season that ended here was not in the plan.

He and the principal talked often of the relentless and viselike pressure. Was there too much stress on the athletes and too much on the teachers, and what message did the outsize role that hoop madness played in this culture send to other students? Then he heard a countering voice: If we did not expect to win, what did that say about competing in life?

Show the world what the Navajo can do. He clapped hard and trained his eyes on the court. Win.

"C'mon, Wildcats! Play your game!"

Angelo opened the fourth quarter, perhaps the last eight minutes of the Wildcats season, with a dervish spin and a sweet up-and-under. The ball rolled round and round and in. The Patriots came running back down court and number 23, that long, talented six-seven kid with the dagger jumper, took a pass and turned to face Cooper. Cooper kept his arms raised and saw this kid was standing five feet beyond the three-point line. That's a bad-percentage shot. Sure, go ahead, shoot.

The tall kid shot and missed.

The Wildcat defense extended eighty-four feet, baseline to baseline, frenetic, giving no safe harbor to an opposing player, no place to dribble and regain your breath. Chance and Josiah climbed into the jerseys of the Leadership Academy guards, clapping, harassing. The Wildcats drew closer and closer, and Dewayne stole another ball and pitched ahead to Josiah, who got hammered by a defender and was sent spinning to the floor.

Josiah landed on his shoulder and writhed facedown. Fans put their hands over their mouths, wincing. *"Get up, son. Get up. You have to get up!"* An assistant coach helped him to his feet, and that assistant and Josiah disappeared into the hallway to the locker room.

Raul called a time-out and crouched, leaning into his players as the crowd keened and pounded hands. There were six minutes left, and the Wildcats trailed by four points, 43–39. Moments earlier Mendoza had glanced at the American Leadership Academy bench and seen the big men, hands on knees, chests heaving. They looked gassed. "We've got lots of time left," he told his boys. "Push them everywhere on the court." He paused and, voice loud, said, "Listen, guys: Finish it!"

Angelo flipped a geometric beauty of a long bounce pass to Cooper for a layup. Soon after, Cooper curled to the corner, received the ball in rhythm, and the crowd chanted as he released it. Yes! For the first time this game, the Wildcats had taken a lead.

Josiah came walking gingerly back out to the court, making windmill motions with his arm and shoulder, trying to loosen up and to forget his pain. Mendoza looked at him questioningly, and Josiah nodded at the old man and trotted out onto the court.

Josiah stood there in his purple sneakers and the oversize shorts that fell a quarter way down his calves and waited for the Patriots to come out of their huddle. He listened as their coach told his players to stop fiddling around. You see that kid—the Leadership coach pointed at Josiah—who is the size of your little brothers? Take him. Take him!

Josiah let those words settle over him. He had heard such talk for years, whenever he lined up with his dirt bike against guys taller and older, whenever he ran statewide cross-country races in Mesa and Phoenix against guys with far longer strides. He settled into his defensive stance and looked at that Patriot point guard and said, "You want me? Okay, here I am. Let's go."

Josiah stole the ball on the next play. Two plays later, a hound on the scent, he forced the Patriot point guard to toss a wild pass that flew off the shot clock. A Patriot big man took a long jumper that led to a long rebound and Josiah flew into the scrum and came down with the ball and took off dribbling at a gallop.

Shots fell short, passes went awry, the boys from Queen Creek were done. The Wildcat lead climbed and climbed, and at 58–48 the final buzzer sounded and Angelo heaved a great sigh. Fuck. Fuck. We did it. Fuck.

"Dude," Angelo said to Dewayne, "that game was scary."

Dewayne nodded.

"'Shlow, I thought I was dying."

The boys hugged, faces drained and pale.

Raul walked into the locker room shaking his head. "Hey, listen, guys, I don't know what happened in that first half. We could have been blown out by thirty points. We were scared—" He caught himself. As if stifling his inner drill sergeant, his voice fell a few decibels and his jawline softened.

"You decided you weren't going to give up. You never gave up, and you fought and fought. I'm proud of you."

Most of the boys walked out into the parking lot, vapor rising in clouds out of their mouths and off the top of their heads, and rode home with their families, whose cars and trucks stretched like a string of Christmas lights for miles up US Highway 191 toward Chinle. Josiah was one of the few who rode the bus with the coaches back to Chinle. He was exhausted, drained, and on the trip home he would fall asleep. First, though, he replayed his moment with that Patriot point guard.

"'Okay. Take me. Let's go.' Man, that felt great."

The boys would travel in a few days to Prescott, Arizona, a city set in the Bradshaw Mountains, and if they won there, they would travel to Phoenix. They had piled up twenty-two victories so far this season; twenty-five would make them state champions. Could these boys imagine anything more difficult than the peak they'd scaled this frigid night?

Did they have more climbs left in them?

CHAPTER SIXTEEN

What if desert wayfarers arrived in Oz and found the door to the inner sanctum locked? What if slow-accumulating confidence in the inevitability of victory proved as ephemeral as other human conceits? What if canyon dreams expired like a stream in a sandy wash?

The Wildcats rode the team bus six hours west, past Flagstaff, through blue-green forests of juniper and blue spruce and granite obelisks and mountain ridges to Prescott. They possessed an eleven-game winning streak and faced off next against a team from Wickenburg, an old gold-strike town in the Sonoran Desert. The Wickenburg Wranglers were hardworking and quick, Anglos all, but they lacked the imposing height and brawn of the American Leadership Academy team. Mendoza gathered his boys in the locker room beforehand and reminded them that thousands of Navajo had traveled here for the game and theirs was the last team from the reservation still playing. "The north loves good basketball, so let's put on a show for them," he said. "Towns like Wickenburg didn't used to respect Indian cowboys, but they do now. Let's go!"

The Wildcats came out fast-paced, no mercy, ball moving from hand to hand to hand, cutting hard to the hoop. Old jealousies and uncertainties were forgotten as they played in concert with one another. This time it was Mendoza who suffered a lapse; the coach kept his bench players on the court too long in the third quarter, and the Wranglers came crawling out of the grave and gave everyone a case of the sweats. The end, however, was not in question. Chinle was battle-tested and too deep and they claimed a 64–55 victory.

"Mendoza, what happened out there?" Angelo needled his coach.

"Okay. I may have kept a couple players in there too long." Mendoza shrugged. "On to Phoenix."

The Wildcats had reached the semifinals and the remainder of their season would play out at the vast Gila River Arena near Phoenix.

The words ran like an electric current through the rez: The Chinle boys are going to Phoenix. Pack lunches, put the bedrolls in the back of the pickup truck, find a cheap motel, call aunties and cousins and sisters and old friends and ask about a spare room, a couch, a spot on the floor. The day before the semifinals, a great migration of cars and SUVs and trucks edged down US Highway 191 and along those old Indian routes, thousands of fans driving south to Phoenix, the Second Rez, to cheer on these Navajo boys.

On game day, the Wildcat bus rolled into the parking lot of the Gila River Arena and edged down to the loading bay. Many hours before the game, fans had parked forty or fifty cars in the lot, and among those were three pickup trucks, bays piled high with bales of green hay. Apparently enterprising natives had found a deal in the Valley. "Cowboy up," Julian said, voice soft as he peered out the window. "The Navajo are here and ready."

The players wandered through subterranean hallways to the locker room. Angelo showed up with a new razor-cut hairdo, three serried lines cut along the side of his scalp, looking sharp and hip but feeling less so. "Man, I'm nervous." He frowned and rubbed his stomach. "Butterflies, man."

Chance looked at him, shaking his head, rueful. "I just try not to think about it. Not a word."

Josiah sat in a shadowed recess of the locker room, eyes remote and fingers steepled. I suggested, too glibly, that his seasons as a top cross-country runner had prepared him for this. He cocked his head and stared at me a moment and shook his head. No. In a race, your nerves jump and lungs burn but you feel in control, you set the tempo, you decide when to make your move.

No one player could control a basketball game, and besides, this was rez ball and hoop pressure was just different. "You can say, 'Oh, man, I need to get a steal.' But you can't just do it on your own."

"I'll be real, man. I'm nervous."

Mendoza walked in and the boys looked thankful for a retreat into ritual: the methodical unpacking of the black leather bag, the whiteboard pulled out, and the old man drawing lines and squiggles and jots. The coach had stayed up late watching video of their opponent, the Winslow Bulldogs, and laid out the considerable nature of their challenge.

The Bulldogs were a predominantly Navajo team from another of those high-desert border towns. Winslow had made it to the championship game before losing last year and had come back to compile a 26–5 record this season. The team was packed with seniors and juniors.

The Bulldogs liked improvisation. If a play did not work, the players would reverse the ball, Mendoza said, and run a variation and another one after that. If the Bulldogs had a weakness, it was a defense that flickered like a campfire. Keep passing and pushing and attack the hoop, Mendoza told them. The boys stretched, tied and retied their sneakers, listened maybe, and nodded. Chance wore a T-shirt: BELIEVE IT IS MY TIME TO ACCOMPLISH THE IMPOSSIBLE.

Did he?

Cooper sat by his locker and stared into space. He knew the arc of Mendoza's talks and heard the end approaching and stood and told his teammates to put their hands together. "'Wildcats' on three! Let's live the moment, fellas!"

Their cheer was loud without sounding buoyant.

The boys jogged through a shadowed hallway until they reached a black rubber-mat walkway, and security guards pushed back curtains so the boys could pass out of darkness onto the brightly lit floor of the arena. The boys' eyes popped wide.

"Shit, it's big," Angelo said.

"Man," said Dewayne.

Josiah grinned nervously.

"Cowboy up," Julian said.

The highest and most distant section of the arena, the nosebleed seats, was curtained off. Perhaps ten thousand fans sat in the stands as the boys ran out for layups, and breakers of applause washed over them and momentarily jellied their knees. The boys looked about this spaceship of an arena and located their families, who, like stars affixed to celestial spots, had found seats that corresponded to those they occupied in the Wildcat Den, the

Burbanks at midcourt, the Toms a little off to the side, Curtis's father and mother, too, Elijah's father in that distant, perspective-giving northwest corner. Ben, the canyon guide and friend of Cecil Henry's, waved. There were two Junction Diner waitresses and teachers who had called in sick to watch their students play. Shaun Martin was there, too, and he allowed himself to wonder if this finally might be Chinle's year.

The Wildcats came out strong, and after a nervous hiccup they grabbed the lead. Angelo hit a spinning bank shot and then rifled a pass to Elijah, whose jump shot looked butter smooth. Josiah faked and his defender went flying and he hit an up-and-under shot. The boys came to the bench during the first time-out and heaved their chests and shook their arms as if to say, Okay, we are okay, right? Cooper hit free throws and Dewayne hit a three-point shot to ignite a 7–2 run and the Wildcats finished the first quarter ahead 23–16.

Chance allowed himself a small smile as he jogged back to the bench. A championship round was thirty-two minutes of play away.

At the far end of the sideline, where the Bulldogs gathered, Darius James, a five-nine, 140-pound Navajo welterweight of a senior guard with Winslow, rallied his team, which had appeared no less rattled by the size of this arena and the fact that in this sea of howling, clapping fans at least three-quarters rooted for Chinle. C'mon, he told his teammates, we've been here before. "Let's stay calm and together. We can take them. C'mon. We can do this."

The buzzer sounded and the second quarter began and Darius took charge with stop-start dribbles, probing the defense, passing to cutters, launching a hybrid of a jump and set shot. He was deadly. He scored sixteen points in the first half, and with 4:03 left in the half, the Bulldogs went ahead for the first time. Winslow had found a gear for which Chinle had no quick match.

The Wildcats became tentative, passive, their guards picking up their dribbles too far from the basket, Elijah had begun the game by unfurling two elegant jumpers, and after that it was as if he disappeared behind a curtain. In the second quarter a ponytailed Winslow boy stripped him of a rebound and scored. Angelo pounded his foot and pointed to his temple. "C'mon, Elijah!"

Cooper, most often so unflappable, was strangely uncertain. He would unpack one of his many moves, spin, fake—and pass outside rather than shoot. Toward the end of the half he cut to the hoop, a scooping, dipsy-doo layup, and the ball rolled round and out. Save for a three-point shot, his scoring would be limited this game to eight free throws.

Darius of the Bulldogs ended the first half with another herky-jerky move, a ball spun high off the backboard, and a basket. Winslow led by three points.

Mendoza was calm at halftime, an emergency room medic who laid out how the Wildcats could repair themselves and get back into the game: Wake up. We just need to move, to cut, to roll on the floor and play like ourselves. The first minutes of the second half, he said, will tell our story. We will win.

Inside, he would tell me later, he felt the gnaw of worry.

Winslow's players came out in the second half passing and driving to the basket like wild-eyed riders. So much about the Bulldogs was familiar—their lack of height, their endurance, the pleasure taken in a pass, and their quiet intensity. It was as if Chinle had met its doppelgänger. The Wildcats were not easily run to ground, and they cut Winslow's lead to seven points with six minutes left in the game. They followed the lead of Angelo, who wrestled rebounds and waited for the weight of a defender on his hip before tossing down his spin moves. But his comrades struggled, watched as loose balls rolled across the floor, double-clutched on passes, stumbled. Chance, his hands most often deft as those of a pickpocket, got not a single steal.

"You're playing like it's over," Mendoza told the boys during a time-out, trying to breathe life into his team's lungs. "It's not over."

It was over. Wildcat fans chanted and pounded their hands and feet, and the Wildcats again closed the margin to single digits, but they had fallen into a gorge too deep.

The Bulldog guards played keep-away for the last minute or so, the Winslow fans on their feet whistling and cheering, and the margin was eleven points when the buzzer sounded at game's end. Chance and Angelo and Cooper and Curtis and Josiah and all the rest wandered toward their bench, gutted, faces slack, shoulders slumped, and exchanged handshakes with Winslow, players whose minds already were turning to the championship game in two days.

Mendoza stood a final time before his teenagers, the locker room silent. "You are a very good team and you simply lost to boys who played better. There's no shame to this. We wanted to make it here and we did. I want to thank all of you. Josiah, Angelo, you became leaders."

He turned to the side. "Elijah, you never said much, but I'm going to miss you."

Elijah peered at the carpeting and smiled despite himself.

Josiah, towel draped over his head, slumped on the floor, eyes dead, as though he'd seen this outcome long ago. Chance and Dewayne had arms draped over each other's shoulders, eyes red-rimmed. Shaun Martin stood and thanked them for this season and their run into the playoffs. He noted that their eyes were watering and nodded in approval. "It is good to feel what you are feeling. It is good to let yourselves as men cry. I guarantee you that the whole Chinle Valley is proud of you. Now apply this experience to life—this is your beginning, not the end."

Angelo remained silent long after Mendoza and Martin had stopped talking. He looked at the seniors, his childhood friends who would graduate and leave him behind in their desert town, and said, "I love you guys."

Then he walked out to the bus.

The boys straggled back to the reservation over the next few days, driving with their families through the cactus forests and pine-woods and across the plains into the land where morning mist rose like smoke around buttes and ice-cracked mesas and a turquoise sky stretched to the limit of vision. Oh, how they had yearned to return home with a state championship trophy, to hold that trophy high and kiss it. The depth of their ache surprised the boys. That Monday, Winslow won the state championship and Josiah took to Facebook and typed words of longing. *"Today would've been the day we made history! Things aren't just meant to be! But one day Chinle will win a state championship . . ."*

The coming weeks and months saw teenage boys seeking different answers and moving in different directions. Dewayne and Chance made plans to attend an evangelical native college in Phoenix where the coach promised they could play in the same backcourt. The college did not offer an engineering major, so Dewayne decided to put his dreams of that degree on hold for a year or two. Angelo, the playoff warrior, the man-child who appeared to mature in those final games, disappeared for days and even weeks at a time from Chinle High School. He did not answer his cell phone, texts went unanswered. Friends joked of 'Shlow's taste for Colt 45 malt liquor and other rumors were not encouraging. There were so many ways to get lost in the high desert; Mendoza would spend many weeks trying to find Angelo and make him sit and talk and listen.

He could not yet discern the shape and curve of his life.

Josiah learned he had gotten a scholarship to Arizona State University, a fine four-year university. It was a lightning strike. How could this be? He spent weeks suspended between elation and the fear that he was a fake and did not deserve this good fortune. If he could stay disciplined with grades and avoid distractions, if he could master big classes and stanch homesickness, he could earn the four-year degree that would open so many doors. "I've got one job," he said, "and that is to be successful and take care of the people who took care of me."

Not long after the season ended, after the news came of his scholarship and friends and cousins slapped his back and aunties wrapped him in hugs, his father started sending Josiah text messages. He wanted to meet his son.

Josiah sat down one night in his trailer and tapped out a public Facebook message to this father of his.

"How about you come by and pick me up and take me to eat or take me somewhere where we can enjoy, talk and catch up on stuff! And plz come by sober. I really want you in my life but not when all I'm going to be is your trophy when I succeed! I learned so little from you. My mom was a better dad. I'm ready to forgive you but you have to prove to me that you can still be the father I always wanted."

The April winds blew unrelenting that year.

Keanu, the Chinle valedictorian, felt himself grow antsy, anxious, restless, unable to sit still. He had sent off his applications to all those eastern colleges in distant cities that existed for him only on

maps. The Ivy Leagues and the top private colleges posted accep-
tances and rejections on March 26, a great cyber exhalation of
news good or bad. As Keanu's trailer lacked anything like an internet connection, he lugged his laptop to the Burger King in Chinle,
where he worked as a cashier. This boy who was born *Tó dích'íi'nii*
(Bitter Water Clan) and born for *Tótsohnii* (Big Water Clan) walked
to a back table and opened his laptop and logged on and closed his
eyes and asked God and the Holy People for help.

His test scores and grades had been top-notch. But he was a shy
rez kid from a trailer in the shadow of Balakai Mesa and he was
competing against kids who had spent a lifetime prepping. He
was knocking at a door to an unknown world. "I could feel my
stomach flipping."

He moved systematically from one college site to another. He
got into Swarthmore. And Dartmouth. And Brown, Columbia,
Case Western, and Harvard. Tears formed in the corners of his
eyes and he could not stop grinning. In the weeks to come, he
would visit Swarthmore and experience a reality that did not quite
match his dreams. It was the Harvard campus and professors who
captivated him.

Five months later Keanu would hug his mother and grandmother goodbye and hold them so long and whisper words of
Navajo love. And he would board a plane and land in Boston and
matriculate at Harvard.

Nachae's knee was slow healing. He had put on too much
weight during his convalescence, he developed a paunch, and as an
athlete, a good-looking young man, that pierced his ego. He
missed a semester of classes and returned in the summer to Tsaile
and his parents' home, to crops and harvests and horse rides with
Marcus and Julian deep into the Ponderosa forests in search of
recalcitrant cattle. He traveled north to his mother's people on the

Blackfeet reservation in Montana, and he walked with his cousins through a green forest to a grand river, its currents rippling like a vein of diamonds in the sunlight. He was a desert Indian; what to make of such wetness?

A coach at a community college there spoke bewitching words and expressed interest in perhaps having Nachae play on his team. He would return to Albuquerque captivated by hoop dreams. "I struggle, I know that," he said. "I'm coming to understand that God has a plan for each of us. I'm looking for mine."

A few days later he posted on Facebook a portrait photo of Mendoza holding a basketball and staring steadily at the camera. He typed one word to accompany it: *Shicheii.* That is the Navajo word for a maternal grandfather.

On the morning I was to leave Chinle to drive home, my car packed tight as a vagabond's wagon, I met Mendoza for a breakfast of blue corn pancakes and bacon at the Junction Diner. Our talk turned to that last game. He saw boys who looked emotionally played out, not sure if they could believe in their own possibilities. A playoff run, Mendoza said, exposed worries and anxieties as a ghost slips into your soul. He sounded tired. His wife, Marjorie, might retire from teaching, and if she did, they would have to surrender their school district apartment. That would leave them with few options in Chinle.

Mendoza let slip he had heard from the athletic director in Monument Valley, who asked if the coaching legend wanted to move there and coach. I squinted at Mendoza, who now had more than 740 wins.

Are you serious?

He answered with an ambiguous smile.

He was a child of the southern desert with nothing to pack in his satchel, he had moved from town to town, team to team, coaching native sons for thirty-nine years. Moving on, traveling through the desert to a new home, felt natural enough. We sat with that a minute or two and he ended his internal argument with a shake of his head. No. If he could still keep their school apartment, if he could stay closer to his grandchildren . . . "Personally, I want to stay here. I look at it this way: Window Rock has lost a few kids, Page loses two kids. I look at all the roster we have, and if I can keep Angelo in school, we'll be tough next year.

"I like it here. I think I'm comfortable."

He shrugged again. There was an ineffable mystery to this man, a well perhaps too deep for him to plumb. For now this wanderer would remain in this homely town at the mouth of a great canyon. We shook hands and slapped each other's back and exchanged vows to remain in touch, and I got in my Subaru and nosed north up the Chinle Valley, and he got in his pickup truck and headed back to the Wildcat Den to begin preparations for another season of tending to the restless teenagers of Dinétah.

ACKNOWLEDGMENTS

I wandered into Chinle and so into this book almost by accident. Exhausted by the idiocy of a Super Bowl week, I headed to Window Rock, the capital of that nation, to write a quick column for the *New York Times* on the whirling dervish sport of rez ball. This was the corner of the Navajo world in which I had lived with my wife, Evelyn, and our sons a quarter century earlier.

That night I met a remarkable coach and man, Raul Mendoza, and we hit it off. I mentioned that I would like to write a book on him and his team and the larger world of the Navajo. Not long after that—in the nature of the perpetually restless life of coaches here—Raul called to tell me that he had left Window Rock and taken up residence as coach of the Chinle Wildcats. I recalled Chinle as a dusty town sitting on the lip of a stunning canyon.

"Why don't you come out and watch us?" Raul said.

I took him up on his offer and wrote two longer pieces for the *New York Times*, and the seed was sown. I wanted to better understand this land, this people, this man. And I wanted to render it in vibrant and complex colors, as too many accounts of Native American life fall into reductively depressed tones.

To embark on a book such as this was to be aware of how much I did not know. So I sought out teachers, none finer than the Navajo journalist and professor Sunnie Clahchischiligi. She was a passionate and knowledgeable wunderkind and from the day we met in Window Rock she took me in hand, helping me understand the world of rez ball and of the Navajo. Shaun Martin, the athletic director, Ravis Henry, a federal park ranger, and Julian Parish, the assistant coach, stood out for their knowledge and the subtlety of their love for their land and people, and their patience in explaining that to me. Valentino Domingo, a medicine man and railway worker and scholar, was invaluable too, a man of nuanced understanding and good humor.

Without them, I would have been lost.

There are so many others who helped me understand. There was the courageous activist Rita Bilagody; strong women such as her are found across the reservation. Dee Steinem was indispensable as well. Quincy Natay, the Chinle school superintendent, took a leap of faith and allowed me to spend five months documenting life there, and he helped arrange rental housing for me, no small matter. Abraham Bitok, the housing director for the schools, was a sounding board and friend.

For the young men who played on that team—Elijah, Angelo, Cooper, Josiah, Chance, Dewayne, Curtis, Will, Payton, Jarious, and Cael—I have nothing but thanks and admiration. They were perceptive interpreters of their lives and world. Several players from the previous season—Nachae Nez and Marcus Litson and Ziggy Yeahquo and Nicholas Begay—were a great help as well, as was team manager Josie Tsosie. These young men and women are canyon dreamers and I trust they will find their way in the broader world without losing what is precious about Dinétah.

Nachae, in particular, has an intelligence and wisdom beyond his years. I hope only that he lets these serve as his north star.

To assistant coaches Julian Parrish, Lenny Jones, Ned Curley and Beau Natay, and the families of these players, who let me into their homes and lives and put up with my endless questions, an eternal thank you. Joni and Darrick Burbank and Virginia became like treasured family. Nathaniel and Jerilene Tom, Vernon and Jodonna Begay, and Rosalyn Tsosie showed me hospitality and warmth, and I hope I can someday repay them in kind.

Keanu Gorman, class valedictorian and now Harvard University student, is a wonder, and I remain in awe. I am eager to see where the rivers of life carry him. His teacher at Chinle High School, Parsifal Smith, is no less impressive, a guide for generations of students, and for me. I'm lucky to have met and come to know this student and his mentor.

The history, culture, and archaeology of Navajo holds many mysteries, and I leaned heavily on academic papers, readings, and conversations. Robert S. McPherson, a history professor at Utah State University Eastern in Blanding Stephen Lekson, an archaeologist at the University of Colorado Boulder, and Professor Donna M. Glowacki, an archaeologist at the University of Notre Dame, and Peter Iverson, an emeritus historian with Arizona State University, gave of their time and considerable insight. The work of Professor Janet Nez Denetdale of the University of New Mexico, and Deni J. Seymour was essential, as was that of Hampton Sides and his *Blood and Thunder: The Epic Story of Kit Carson and the Conquest of the American West*.

To the extent that I have written clearly about the history and anthropology of this world, I owe it to them. I own my errors.

ACKNOWLEDGMENTS

This story would have been impossible to tell without the humanity and quiet intelligence of Raul Mendoza, counselor, mentor and yes, a hell of a coach. It's a writer's great luck to find a man willing to peer inside himself and try to make sense of his own mysteries. My debt to him is great.

My editor, John Parsley, offered patience and a fine-grained intelligence, and righted me when I listed to starboard. I appreciate his mind and editing hand and his enthusiasm for this project. I owe a debt as well to editor David Rosenthal, without whom this book would not have taken wobbly flight, and who offered wise counsel and advice on a mid-course correction. Flip Brophy, my agent, was all that I could have hoped for, and she helped me navigate many shoals. After a quarter century of nudging and encouragement from her, I hope I've produced a book worthy of her representation.

I owe much to my friends and they never failed me. My lifelong buddies, Fred Cooper and Peter Kurz, offered unstinting encouragement. Nick Fox read my chapter drafts and gave me the benefit of his thoughtful editor's mind. Jesse Eisinger advised me on the precarious world of book writing, as did Jesse Drucker and Nell Casey. My *New York Times* colleagues Ken Belson, Joe Drape, John Branch, and Karen Crouse were true friends. Jason Stallman, my sports editor at the *Times,* understood my passion for this story and quickly arranged for the leave that made this book possible. I owe thanks as well to executive editor Dean Baquet, who allowed this book to happen.

My sons, Aidan and Nick, read chapters and talked through the characters and history and the many realities of that world. They understood what drew me to that place and I felt their presence always. It is a great gift for a father to watch his sons grow into incisive, thoughtful adults and friends. Thank you.

Finally, there was the incomparable Evelyn Intondi, my wife, my partner, my lover, who encouraged my wanderings and provided a hand always sure. It was her work as a superb and caring midwife that first took us to Navajo a quarter century ago. She read each chapter more than once, and her sense for words and pacing and story-telling allowed me to land this book in one piece. Her humane touch helped me to arrive in one piece as well. I owe her more than I could put into words in this life and in the next.

ABOUT THE AUTHOR

Michael Powell is a New Yorker born and raised, a product of its public schools and basketball courts. He is the "Sports of the *Times*" columnist for the *New York Times* after earlier incarnations as a *Gotham* columnist writing on New York City and a writer on national economics, poverty, and national politics, including a stint on the Obama campaign. He won a Polk Award for an investigation that freed wrongly accused men, and shared in the Pulitzer Prize for his writing on the fall of Governor Eliot Spitzer.

He spent ten years at the *Washington Post* as New York bureau chief during the 9/11 attacks and as a national political feature writer. At *New York Newsday,* he documented a month in a heroin shooting gallery and three years covering Rudy Giuliani.

He lives in Flatbush, Brooklyn, with his wife, Evelyn Intondi, and Monk, a golden lab mutt. They have two sons, Nick and Aidan.